OVER
WATER

Jonathan Glancey is a journalist, author and broadcaster who has written extensively about architecture, engineering, design and aviation. His books include *The Journey Matters, Concorde: The Rise and Fall of the Supersonic Airliner, Harrier, Giants of Steam*, the bestselling *Spitfire: The Biography, Nagaland: A Journey to India's Forgotten Frontier, Tornado: 21st Century Steam, The Story of Architecture, Dymaxion Car: Buckminster Fuller* (with Norman Foster), *John Betjeman on Churches* and *Lost Buildings*.

Praise for *Spitfire: The Biography*

'Hugely entertaining'
James Holland

'An authoritative and comprehensive tribute to
a unique aircraft.'
Adrian Swire, *Spectator*

'A drama that cannot help take wing. The elements still
excite the imagination and raise the heart.'
Tom Fort, *Sunday Telegraph*

'Eclectic and entertaining'
Patrick Bishop, *Literary Review*

By the same author

The Journey Matters
Concorde
Harrier
Giants of Steam
Spitfire: The Biography
Nagaland: A Journey to India's Forgotten Frontier
Tornado: 21st Century Steam
The Story of Architecture
London: Bread and Circuses
Architecture: A Visual History
Lost Buildings

WINGS OVER WATER

The Story of the World's Greatest
Air Race and the Birth of the Spitfire

JONATHAN GLANCEY

Atlantic Books
London

First published in hardback in Great Britain in 2020 by Atlantic Books,
an imprint of Atlantic Books Ltd.

This paperback edition first published in Great Britain in 2021
by Atlantic Books.

123456789

A CIP catalogue record for this book is available from the British Library.

E-book ISBN: 978-1-78649-420-7
Paperback ISBN: 978-1-78649-421-4

Printed in Demark by Nørhaven

Atlantic Books
An Imprint of Atlantic Books Ltd
Ormond House
26–27 Boswell Street
London
WC1N 3JZ

www.atlantic-books.co.uk

Contents

WINGS OVER WATER

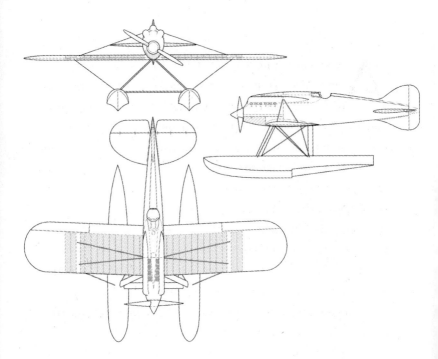

Prologue

At lunchtime on 13 September 1931, a beautiful blue and silver seaplane blazed backwards and forwards over the Solent, a tidal channel between Southampton and the Isle of Wight. From esplanades, from the decks of ocean liners and warships, an audience a million strong watched the aircraft's unprecedented progress as its RAF pilot, 30-year-old Flight Lieutenant John Boothman, accelerated the Supermarine S.6B monoplane to a mercurial 380 mph. Averaging 340.08 mph over the triangular 217-mile course while pulling G-force turns that brought him close to blackout, Boothman was both the fastest human in history and the winner for Britain of the coveted Schneider Trophy.

To cap Boothman's triumph, Reginald Mitchell, the aircraft's designer, installed a more powerful 'sprint' version of the Rolls-Royce R ('R' for Racing) engine into the wind-cheating S.6B seaplane. Thirty-one-year-old Flight Lieutenant George Stainforth flew this puissant machine on four straight runs over Southampton Water at an average speed of 407.5 mph, hitting an absolute maximum of a shade over 415 mph. No one had flown above 400 mph before. Britain's latest airliner at the time, the four-engine Handley Page H.P.42, cruised at 100 mph.

Neither Boothman nor Stainforth, nor their colleagues in Britain's official High Speed Flight (for a spell, T. E. Lawrence – Lawrence of Arabia – in the guise of RAF Aircraftman Shaw, was a part of the team), were flying to win the racy – if slightly vulgar – Art Nouveau sculpture that was the Schneider Trophy itself, along with the generous cash prizes. No. What they were competing for was what this trophy meant: international recognition for the world's fastest, finest and most advanced aircraft, engines, designers, manufacturers, pilots and mechanics.

Announced in 1912 by Jacques Schneider, a wealthy young French steel and armaments magnate – and passionate balloonist and pilot – the trophy stole the imaginations of pioneering aircraft manufacturers on both sides of the Atlantic. Of all the air races initiated in France from as early as 1909, the Schneider Trophy was to be the most coveted. It attracted a glamorous and hugely popular following, whether the contests were held in Monaco, the Venice Lido, the Solent or Chesapeake Bay.

Schneider's aim had been to encourage a new generation of high-speed civil seaplanes and flying boats that, to him, made more sense than airliners flying over land and cities. In the event, his competition became a driver and celebration of speed and engineering prowess. Because the trophy would be awarded to a national team only when it had won three contests within a five-year span, its rules encouraged long-term thinking about the future of aircraft design and, as it proved, of aviation.

While, ultimately, the British team succeeded – winning the Schneider air races in 1927, 1929 and 1931 – the trophy ignited an enduring passion for sheer technological prowess that saw developments in aircraft design leap forwards.

Because it was so compelling, the Schneider Trophy became a focus not just of remarkable aircraft, daring pilots and swooning public attention, but also of fierce national rivalries. The last three races saw Italy and Britain pitted against one another. Two of the world's finest aircraft designers – Reginald Mitchell and Mario Castoldi – worked feverishly hard to outdo one another with their exquisite Supermarine and Macchi aircraft. Rolls-Royce and Fiat aimed to produce more powerful and more reliable engines than the other. And, more than these ambitious struggles, two very different political and social systems were set against one another: democratic Britain and Fascist Italy.

Perhaps inevitably, the dynamism of rival engineering led not so much to the advanced commercial flying boats of Schneider's imagination, but to the most potent military fighters of the Second World War. Mitchell's record-breaking Supermarine seaplanes morphed, one way or another, into the Spitfire, while Castoldi's seaplanes led to Italy's highly effective Macchi C.202 and C.205 fighters.

The Schneider Trophy story is a tale of raw adventure, public excitement and engineering genius, told in a waft of petrol and oil. It is a story, too, of the ambitions of the United States, France, Britain and Italy, and of how France and the US dropped out of the race while Germany – its aircraft industry reined in by the 1919 Treaty of Versailles – was unable to compete, although Dornier made tantalizing designs for Schneider competitors for both the 1929 and 1931 races.

It is a story of mighty engines and larger-than-life characters, from James Doolittle, the barnstorming young American pilot who won the 1925 race and went on to become one of the most daring pilots and distinguished air commanders of the Second World War, to the extraordinary Lady Lucy Houston, a working-class chorus girl who (through advantageous marriages to much older men) became Britain's richest woman, and without whom Flight Lieutenant Boothman would not have made his victorious flight in September 1931.

Benito Mussolini, the Italian dictator, was one of the Schneider Trophy's most ardent fans, watching the races as he jutted his jaw from the balconies and beaches of the exotic Hotel Excelsior on the Venice Lido. Ardent Fascist Tranquillo Zerbi, a racing car and aircraft engineer, was the brains behind the mighty Fiat AS.6 engine that, though developed too late for the 1931 race, powered the stunning, blood-red Macchi MC.72 with Warrant Officer Francesco Agello at the controls to 440.68 mph in October 1934, setting a piston-engine seaplane record yet to be broken.

Intriguingly, a problem Zerbi had with the carburetion of his AS.6 engine in 1931 was solved the following year by Francis Rodwell Banks, a British high-octane fuel specialist who worked, independently, for Rolls-Royce and Supermarine – a reminder of how, in the face of contrary politics, engineers spoke an international language of development and design, even as Fascism morphed into something very dark and dangerous indeed.

The story of the Schneider Trophy is also one of particular places – not just the contest venues themselves, but also workshops and factories including the spectacular Fiat factory at Lingotto, Turin. An expression of Futurism, a driving intellectual and cultural force behind Italian Fascism, it was here that Zerbi nurtured his prodigiously powerful engines, and cars raced around the remarkable building's roof as if threatening to launch themselves into the Piedmont skies.

At the heart of the story, of course, are the air races themselves. How these took off. How popular they were. How publicity, the media and art promoted and embellished them. And what happened to air racing – the quest for aerial speed – to seaplanes and flying boats, and to military and civil aircraft design after Britain won the Schneider Trophy for keeps in 1931.

And, inevitably, the story is one of politics. How Ramsay MacDonald's Labour government did its best to scupper Britain's chances in 1931, and what this meant for the development of the Spitfire; how America's governments lost interest in the races, helping to delay the development of effective US fighter aircraft; and how Rolls-Royce engine technology, advanced during the Schneider races, came to Uncle Sam's rescue in the 1940s.

The last Schneider Trophy race took place nearly 90 years ago, so we can only ever see the contests with our own eyes through black-and-white images: largely grainy photographs taken by cameras too slow to catch racing aircraft, or else scratchy newsreels unable to catch the sound of what would become in the course of the races the world's fastest and most potent single-seat aircraft. But the races were, in fact, conducted in blazes of colour, not least those of contending machines – pale blue, royal blue, Cambridge blue, gold, white, silver-grey, blood red. One aim of this book is to bring a black-and-white story, which may seem far distant to those brought up in a world of supersonic military stealth jets and jet airliners omnipresent in 30,000-foot skies, into full, high-flying colour.

*

NB: Strictly speaking, the Schneider Trophy events were contests rather than races. They were, though, called races from early on by both the press and the public. In this book, I have used the words where they feel right in context. The same applies to measurements, imperial and metric.

Officially recognized attempts at world airspeed records were made over three-kilometre courses under the direction of time-keepers representing the FAI (Fédération Aéronautique Internationale), the world governing body for air sports founded in Paris in 1905.

In all the books, archives and websites I have consulted, figures and statistics relating to individual aircraft and events – from horsepower to average speeds – tend to vary, as do dates. I have aimed at consistency, but would be interested and grateful to hear from readers citing sources on this subject.

The Wright Stuff

O n 17 December 1903, the Wright brothers made the first successful powered flight in a heavier-than-air machine. John Thomas Daniels, a member of the US Life-Saving Station in Kill Devil Hills, North Carolina, was there to capture the scene with the Wrights' Gundlach Korona V glass-plate camera. It was the first time Daniels had seen a camera. Orville Wright had positioned it on a tripod immediately before he climbed into the *Flyer* and made history.

Thankfully, the photograph is remarkably good. Along with the aircraft in the air, piloted by Orville Wright, it shows Wilbur Wright looking on. If he had wanted to, Wilbur could easily have jogged along with the *Flyer* throughout its 12-second, 120-foot flight. Its average speed was 6.8 mph. The Wrights had tried to engage the US press in the story before 17 December, but there was no interest beyond local newspapers.

The *Dayton Daily News* covered its bare bones, while the *Dayton Evening Herald* printed a colourful front-page column telling of a three-mile flight under the headline 'Dayton Boys Fly Airship', with the sub-heading 'Machine Makes High Speed in the Teeth of a Gale'. It was actually a fresh to strong breeze and the *Flyer* was as much like an airship as a stickleback is like a basking shark. At the offices of an insouciant *Dayton Journal*, Lorin Wright – Orville and Wilbur's elder brother – told the story to Frank Tunison of the Associated Press, who turned him away saying the event was 'not newsworthy'.

In any case, newspaper editors knew that a man could run at 15–20 mph, Henry Ford's new Model A had a top speed of 28 mph, and American quarter horses grabbing the attention of sports pages across the country at least weekly could gallop at up to 50 mph. And, according to their imaginative reporters, No. 999, a high-stepping 4-4-0 locomotive of the New York Central and Hudson River Railway, had run at 112.5 mph 10 years previously between Batavia and Buffalo at the head of the *Empire State Express*. While the true speed would have been no more than 86 mph, even that was something to tell the folks back home about in 1893.

The reception given by European newspapers and aviation clubs to reports of the Wrights' achievement – especially in France – was at best incredulous, at worst arrogantly dismissive. When a letter describing their achievement from the Wright brothers to Georges Besançon, editor of *L'Aérophile*, was published in the daily sports newspaper *L'Auto* at the end of November 1905, French sceptics reacted condescendingly and even aggressively. The Wrights were called *bluffeurs*. Ernest Archdeacon – lawyer, balloonist, glider pilot and co-founder in 1898 of the Aéro-Club de France – was particularly disdainful, even though he flew a Wright Brothers No. 3 glider. 'The French', he opined, 'would make the first public demonstration of powered flight.' On 10 February 1906, an editorial in the Paris edition of the *New York Herald*, a newspaper evidently detached from events in the United States, sneered, 'The Wrights have flown or they have not flown. They possess a machine or they do not possess one. They are in fact either fliers or liars. It is difficult to fly. It's easy to say, "We have flown."'

Within three years, newspapers would be caught up in the story of powered flight and speed, to the extent that their sponsorship inaugurated early air races and long-distance contests – which, of course, promised sensational and popular news. Rather like Thomas declaring to his fellow apostles that he would only believe in the risen Christ when he had seen his master's wounds and thrust his hand into his pierced side, the sceptical and proud French needed direct evidence of the Wright brothers' ability to fly.

Wilbur arrived in France in summer 1908 with a machine that, in his expert hands, flew figures of eight above the crowds thronging the Hunaudières horse racing circuit near Le Mans. Apologies in print followed immediately afterwards – notably from Ernest Archdeacon, a doubting Thomas for whom the Wrights were now nothing less than the high priests of powered flight.

Over the following year, Wilbur made some 200 demonstration flights in France and continued his conversion of unbelievers in Italy, where he trained a new breed of military pilot. On 31 December 1908, Wright won the first International Michelin Cup, as it was soon known, taking home a bronze trophy by the French sculptor Paul Roussel depicting what looks like a Wright machine climbing into the sky, a winged spirit of victory perched on its prow bearing aloft a laurel wreath. Wright also pocketed 20,000 French francs. To win, he had to make the longest flight possible before sunset, over a 2.2-kilometre course at Le Mans laid out in the form of an isosceles triangle. Taking off at 2 p.m. he completed 56 circuits and, having landed and won, took off again to fly a further 1.5 kilometres to set a new world distance record of 124.7 kilometres (77.5 miles).

The revved-up fascination with powered flight was such that France hosted the world's first air race, the Prix de Lagatinerie. This was held on 23 May 1909, the opening day of Port-Aviation near Juvisy-sur-Orge, 20 kilometres south of Paris. The world's first purpose-built airfield boasted sheltered public grandstands, paid for by Baron Charles de Lagatinerie, that proved their worth when 50,000 or so people turned up on this blazingly hot day to witness the race. Charles and Bernard de Lagatinerie put up a prize of 5,000 francs for the pilot who covered 10 laps of a 1.2-kilometre course in the shortest time. Stops would be allowed. In the event of all aircraft being unable to complete the course, the prize would be awarded to the pilot who flew the longest distance.

There were nine entries, although only four showed up: three French pilots flying French Voisins, and the Austrian engineer Alfred de Pischof with a Pischof et Koechlin machine featuring three pairs of wings in tandem. This intriguing aeroplane, which Pischof designed and built with the Alsatian engineer Paul Koechlin, needed – or so it was thought – no more than a horizontally opposed 20-hp two-cylinder air-cooled engine by Dutheil and Chalmers to compete with the Voisins and their 50-hp water-cooled eight-litre Antoinette V8s.

In the event, an increasingly fractious crowd had to wait until a quarter to six in the evening before the go-ahead was given for the start of the contest. By this time, inadequately stocked bars and food stalls had run dry and empty. Even before the flying had begun, people hoping to get back to Paris on the crowded roads and trains before it got dark started to drift away from the grandstands. The day, they made clear, had been a fiasco.

Pischof was first to start. His machine refused to lift from the ground. Next came Léon Delagrange in an early-model Voisin. As he made his run, the elevator controls snapped. Delagrange ground to a halt. Up went Henri Rougier in a new Voisin. It was all looking good until a pair of spectators who had been sunning themselves in the long grass suddenly stood up as Rougier approached close to the ground. Their appearance caused him to swerve and crash. No one was hurt, but his Voisin was out of the race.

An impromptu entry by Louis Lejeune in a 12-hp Pischof et Koechlin–powered biplane of his own design followed. Lejeune scythed through the tall grass to cries of '*la moissoneuse*' ('the harvester') from the crowd, his aeroplane resolutely refusing to take off. Now, Delagrange was allowed to try again in a Voisin borrowed from the airfield's flying school. Climbing to an impressive 50 feet, he managed five laps at an average speed of 33.75 km/h (21 mph) before the engine overheated, encouraging him to land. Getting on for eight in the evening and with the weather turning, the fourth contestant, 'F de Rue', a pseudonym for Captain Ferdinand Ferber, chose to stay on the ground. Delagrange was declared the winner, although because he had failed to last the course, he was presented with half the prize money.

If the Port-Aviation event proved to be a bit of a joke in terms of organization, and a disappointment because there was so little flying in the course of a long day, it did show how keen the public was to come to a flying show. Many had never seen an aeroplane before. They were not there just for an entertaining day out, but also to bear witness to a new technology at work in a realm that, until now, had been exclusively that of insects, birds and gods. True, vultures in Africa might soar as high as 37,000 feet, butterflies close to 20,000 feet, locusts 15,000 feet and bats 10,000 feet; and yes, a peregrine falcon can dive at 220 mph and a dragonfly – with its ability to move its four wings independently of one another, and to rotate them forwards and backwards – can fly straight up, straight down, backwards, and can hover and turn in an instant at 30 mph. Yet humans had only just learned to power themselves into the air; and, until very recently, it had been said that this was impossible.

What was to prove truly remarkable in the following decades was the sheer pace of development in the speed, ability and reliability of aircraft. Many people alive in 1969, the year Concorde first flew and Neil Armstrong and Buzz Aldrin set foot on the Moon, remembered news of the Wright brothers and their first powered flight.

These early days of trial and error, sheer derring-do and earnest competition gave opportunities for men – and women, too – from a wide variety of backgrounds to take part in events and to fly machines that were often as dangerous as their pilots were inexperienced. Orville and Wilbur Wright, though, were safe and experienced pilots. It was typhoid fever that was to kill Wilbur in 1912 at the age of 45. He had stopped flying only the year before to concentrate on building up the Wright aircraft business. Orville last piloted an aircraft in 1914, giving up flying altogether four years later. He held the controls of an aircraft again in 1944, when a brand-new Lockheed Constellation airliner – piloted by Howard Hughes, TWA's major shareholder, and the airline's president Jack Frye – touched down at Wright Field on the return leg of a high-speed test flight from Burbank, California, to Washington, DC and back. Speaking from the co-pilot's seat, Wright noted wryly that the wingspan of the 375-mph 'Connie' was greater than the distance of his first flight. He died the year after Chuck Yeager broke the sound barrier in level flight in a Bell X-1 rocket engine aircraft.

The pioneers of powered flight were excited first and foremost by the adventure of flight, and by the future possibilities it offered. Just how fast, how high and how far might an aeroplane fly? They wanted to find out, and were in a hurry to do so. Although science-fiction stories had depicted flying machines as potential instruments of death in future wars, such thoughts would have been very much at the back of the mind of young men like Léon Delagrange, Henry Farman and Gabriel Voisin.

Delagrange's life was to be as intense and significant as it was brief. A sculptor trained at the École des Beaux-Arts, in March 1907 – at the age of 35 – he bought the first Voisin aeroplane. He did this even before it had proved capable of sustained and controlled flight in a circuit, which it did in January 1908 near Paris, with Farman (who had bought the second Voisin the previous October) in the pilot's seat. With the help of Farman and Delagrange, Voisin – a contemporary of Delagrange's at the

École des Beaux-Arts and the creator of Europe's first successful heavier-than-air aircraft – was on his way to becoming a major manufacturer of military aircraft during the First World War.

Having originally trained as an architect, Gabriel Voisin was to abandon aircraft production at the end of the First World War. He rued the production of Voisin bombers and the destruction they brought, by night, to towns and cities – and to enemy positions, too. Turning to cars, at which he excelled, Voisin was a man of peace again, yet one with an eye to the future. He sponsored the radical young Swiss-French architect known as Le Corbusier, including the sensational project Plan Voisin (1925), a proposal for a new high-rise quarter of Paris for 3 million people. Its construction would have spelled the erasure of the old 3rd and 4th arrondissements of the city that, sordid perhaps in the 1920s, have since been renovated and are treasured today.

'I shall ask my readers', wrote Le Corbusier in his description of the project,

> to imagine they are walking in this new city, and have begun to acclimatise themselves to its untraditional advantages. You are under the shade of trees, vast lawns spread all round you. The air is clear and pure; there is hardly any noise. What, you cannot see where the buildings are? Look through the charmingly diapered arabesques of branches out into the sky towards those widely spaced crystal towers which soar higher than any pinnacle on earth. These translucent prisms that seem to float in the air without anchorage to the ground – flashing in summer sunshine, softly gleaming under grey winter skies, magically glittering

at nightfall – are huge blocks of offices. Beneath each is an underground station. Since this City has three or four times the density of our existing cities, the distances to be traversed in it (as also the resultant fatigue) are three or four times less. For only 5–10 per cent of the surface area of its business centre is built over. That is why you find yourselves walking among spacious parks remote from the busy hum of the autostrada.

Le Corbusier's drawings depict aircraft weaving their way above and across this sky-high, yet verdant and airy, Paris of the future. Two years earlier, in his iconoclastic polemic *Vers une Architecture*, Le Corbusier had shown photographs of aircraft – cars, too – juxtaposed with great buildings of the past. This was a new machine aesthetic positing new ways of building; new forms of architecture every bit as valid as those of the past. Aircraft were revolutionizing the way we saw our towns and cities, and even the world.

Le Corbusier took up this theme again in 1935 with his startling book, *Aircraft*. These machines were not just beautiful things liberating humanity from the mire of the earth; they allowed us to look down on the mess we had created in what Le Corbusier saw as the formlessness and squalor of cities. From this modern perspective, he opined, 'Cities with their misery must be torn down. They must be largely destroyed and fresh cities built.' All the while, Le Corbusier drove Voisin cars, and had his daring new white villas in and around Paris – designed for well-heeled avant-garde clients – photographed for publication with a Voisin in view.

Unintentionally, Le Corbusier appears to have been heralding a time when aircraft would rewrite the history of our cities – which, of course, is what happened when, in the Second World War, entire quarters of historic cities were destroyed, their places taken all too often by piecemeal and third-rate versions of Le Corbusier's Plan Voisin.

Aviation had seemed a far more innocent preoccupation when, towards the end of 1907, Léon Delagrange was elected president of the Aéro-Club de France. The following summer, on a tour of Italy with his ash-framed Voisin aeroplane, he taught his friend Thérèse Peltier, a fellow sculptor, to fly. Her solo flight in Turin's Military Square – 200 metres at an altitude of eight feet – made this Parisian artist the first woman pilot, though she had yet to learn how to make a turn. Peltier fully intended to pursue her new sideline career. Sportingly, Delagrange put up a prize of 1,000 francs that autumn for the first woman aviator to pilot an aeroplane for one kilometre. Peltier began training.

In January 1910, she abandoned both the contest and flying altogether. Early that month, Delagrange was killed at Croix d'Hins, Bordeaux. Newly fitted with a 50-hp seven-cylinder Gnome rotary engine, generating twice the power of its original Anzani engine, Delagrange's Blériot XI – one of three machines he had bought in 1909 to form a display team – dived vertically into the ground from between 60 and 70 feet. A headline in the *New York Press* on 5 January trumpeted, 'Delagrange's skull crushed by fall of monoplane flying in a gusty wind'. The story underneath, one of many carried in newspapers worldwide, told of how Delagrange was mangled under the wreckage of his machine:

He had been flying in a wind that had been gusty which frequently blew at the rate of 20 miles an hour. In spite of this disadvantage, Delagrange continued and had circled the aerodrome three times when suddenly as he was turning at high speed against the wind the left wing of the monoplane broke and the other wing collapsed. The machine toppled and plunged to the ground. Delagrange was caught under the weight of the motor, which crushed his skull. Delagrange's flight was merely preliminary to the attempt, which he was to make in the afternoon, to break Henry Farman's record. The aviator did not have time to disengage himself from his seat.

From that inauspicious start at Port-Aviation in May 1909, Delagrange had become world-famous. He reached the zenith of his fleeting flying career less than three months before his death – not in France, however, but at Doncaster Racecourse, Yorkshire. The event, though, was organized by a Frenchman: Frantz Reichel, sports editor of *Le Figaro*.

A dynamic industrial town, Doncaster was famous for both the graceful high-speed locomotives – built at its Great Northern Railway works – that had taken part in the legendary Railway Races to the North of 1888 and 1895, and for its horse races, including the St Leger Stakes first run in 1776.

This being Doncaster, prizes included the Great Northern Railway Cup and the Doncaster Tradesmen Cup. Aside from Delagrange, high-profile competitors in the nine-day event included Samuel Cody, an American and former Wild West showman who was the first man to fly a powered aircraft in

Britain. Cody's mount was the *Cody Flyer*, which he had built the previous year as British Army Aeroplane No. 1 at the Royal Balloon Factory, Farnborough, in the hope of winning a military contract. It was not to be. In February 1909, the Aerial Navigation Sub-Committee of the Committee of Imperial Defence recommended that all government funding for heavier-than-air machines should stop. Airships yes, aeroplanes no. Their development, should it be thought necessary, was best left to the private sector.

This being England, the opening day of the Doncaster event was a write-off. Down came the rain. Winds were strong enough to provoke the collapse of Captain Walter Windham's Windham No. 3 biplane. Despite the appalling weather, the 50,000-strong crowd was in high spirits. The pilots, meanwhile, learned to wrap up in much warmer clothes than they were used to wearing when flying in France. Collars and ties were still largely de rigueur, although some competitors adopted polo necks, but heavy overcoats and flying suits were the order of the day. Flying in the Yorkshire wind and rain proved to be a chilling and trying experience.

The next day, when 20,000 additional spectators were there in the afternoon – factory workers for the most part, on their half-day off with pay packets in their pockets – Delagrange stole the show. In the morning he flew to the rescue of Cody, who was thrown from his machine after hitting soft sand while trying to avoid a course-marker pylon. In the early afternoon, Delagrange won the Doncaster Town Cup with a five-lap flight of 5.75 miles in a fraction less than 11 minutes and 26 seconds. He also wowed the crowd by starting his Blériot single-handedly, leaping into the cockpit and taking off within 40 feet seconds later.

Sunday spelled church, chapel and rest. Monday was wet and windy again, with pilots compelled to land because the rain whipped their faces. Their heads were protected not by helmets but by cloth caps or woolly hats. Newly repaired, Captain Windham's plane collapsed again. For the 50,000-strong crowd, this would have been the live, full-colour version of the grainy, fast-motion black-and-white film we watched over and again as schoolchildren, showing one venerable aeroplane after another shaking itself apart as it attempted to fly. The Doncaster crowd must have laughed at the self-destructing Windham biplane, just as we did at the improbable Edwardian aircraft that seemed guaranteed to do pretty much anything other than take off and fly.

Captain Windham was, in fact, a serious figure in early British aviation. He flew the first passenger flight in Asia – India, December 1910 – and, among his many other achievements involving automobiles and aeroplanes, in 1911 he launched the world's first official airmail service with a 13-minute flight from the polo field at Allahabad to Naini station on the Calcutta to Bombay railway. The aeroplane, carrying 6,500 letters including one to King George V, was a Sommer machine, designed in France and built under licence by Humber in England. The French pilot, 23-year-old Henri Pequet, who had trained with Gabriel Voisin, had travelled to India by ship with a team and six aircraft from the Humber Motor Company to demonstrate the aeroplanes, at Captain Windham's behest, at the United Provinces Industrial and Agricultural Exhibition in

Allahabad. Here, as at Doncaster, Anglo-French collaboration was on adventurous and gentlemanly display.

There were at least two more notable events at Doncaster. On Wednesday, 20 October, Roger Sommer flew his Farman at night under the light of the Moon. The following Tuesday, the last day of the Yorkshire meet, Delagrange claimed an unofficial world speed record of 49.9 mph. Perhaps he would have managed that tantalizing last 0.1 mph, but after his third lap he was simply too cold to fly any further, let alone faster.

Despite the weather, the event was considered to have been a success by its organizers, by most of those who took part, and by many of the 170,000 people who had made their way to the Doncaster Racecourse to watch these newfangled aeroplanes fly. Unfortunately, internal politics left the story with a sour ending. Because the meeting had been held independently and without approval from the Aero Club of Great Britain (renamed the Royal Aero Club in 1910), which had organized its own simultaneous event at Blackpool, Delagrange and three other French pilots were banned from taking part in any contests held under FAI rules (founded in 1905, the Fédération Aéronautique Internationale remains the governing body for air sports) for the rest of the year. Powered flight was not quite six years old, yet international regulations were already closing in, if not exactly clipping its wings.

Because it had attracted the cream of Europe's racing pilots – French and British alike – the Doncaster meet trumped both the Aero Club's Blackpool event and the Grande Quinzaine de Paris meet held at Port-Aviation. The latter was a hugely ambitious event stretched out over a fortnight. To make up for the fiasco of the first Port-Aviation event, the Parisian organizers enlarged the grandstands, provided parking areas and amply supplied the restaurants, as well as establishing a post and telegraph office to relay news. As the crowd was expected to be enormous, the Compagnie du chemin de fer de Paris à Orléans (PO) announced special trains from Paris running every four minutes to Savigny-sur-Orge, the nearest railway station to the airfield. With the French president, Armand Fallières, due to visit on 14 October, gendarmes on horseback with the 27th Dragoons and the 31st Infantry Regiment were there to maintain order.

Forty-three aircraft were entered, although just six pilots completed a lap of the course and much of the flying was by greenhorns and so decidedly patchy. On Monday, 18 October, Guy Blanck, a novice pilot who bought a Blériot for the event even before he had learned to fly, crashed into one of the grandstands without any attempt to cut his engine as he swerved towards it. Standing by the fence, a woman named Madame Féraud was, as the illustrated sports magazine *La Vie au Grand Air* reported, 'literally stripped by the propeller and had her left thigh and calf cut to the bone'. When Mme Féraud sued Blanck and the event's organizers for 100,000 francs, her attempt backfired. The following June, a Parisian court decreed that as there were no rules for safety at airfields and that aviation was a dangerous activity, Blanck and his fellow defendants were not guilty of culpable negligence. Mme Féraud was ordered to pay the legal costs of the case.

The show's star pilot, although he was eager to get away as soon as possible to Blackpool to take part in the Aero Club of Great Britain event, was Hubert Latham. Wealthy, daring and studiously insouciant, Latham had set a European non-stop flight record – one hour and seven minutes – with an Antoinette IV monoplane in May. One of the very best of early flying machines, the Antoinette proved sufficiently stable in the air for Latham to take both hands off the 'steering wheel' as he opened a silver cigarette case, lit up and smoked through his ivory holder. This may well have been the first intentional hands-free flight.

Like many – but by no means all – early aviators, Latham was a young man of independent means. His mother's family were French bankers; his father's English merchant venturers who had settled in Le Havre in the 1820s. Educated, for a spell, at Balliol College, Oxford, in 1905 the multilingual Hubert went on to fly a balloon across the Channel by night with his cousin Jacques Faure, competed in power boat races with an Antoinette motor yacht at that year's Monaco Regatta, and led an expedition to Abyssinia the following year on behalf of the French National History Museum, to carry out surveys for the French Colonial Office. For this confident pioneer pilot, flying was, perhaps, little more than *une part de gâteau*.

In July 1909, Latham had attempted to cross the English Channel, both times ditching in the sea when his engine faltered – becoming, by default perhaps, the first pilot to land successfully on water. When asked on returning to Calais, by Harry Harper of the *Daily Mail*, if he was discouraged by his failure, Latham replied, 'Not in the very least... A little accident to a motor, what is that? Accidents happen to bicycles, to horses, even to bath-chairs... We have a machine that can go on land, in the air, and in the water. It runs. It flies. It swims. It is a triumph!'

In August, Latham set a world altitude record of 155 metres (509 feet), flying an Antoinette IV at Reims. October's Port-Aviation event, however, was not to be his finest hour. On Sunday, 10 October, the roads were jammed as an estimated 300,000 people attempted to travel down from Paris to Juvisy-sur-Orge. Latham felt forced to walk the last few miles. When he got to the airfield, the brand-new Antoinette VII he was posted to fly was unready. Three days later, strong winds and a misfiring engine prompted Latham to make an emergency landing, damaging his machine as he touched down on one wheel and buckling a wing. Back in the air again the following day and with President Fallières watching, Latham was forced to land prematurely again, after just half a lap.

Several more minor accidents interrupted the show. Nevertheless, despite a paucity of actual flying, as well as strong winds, crowded roads, a total failure on the part of the PO to run sufficient and adequate trains to anything like a realistic timetable, and a wildly overambitious programme, it was looked on as a popular event, if not a critical success.

The crowning glory of the meeting was something wholly unexpected. The gist of it is happily and urgently conveyed in a cable sent to the *New York Times* by the paper's reporter on the ground:

OVER EIFFEL TOWER IN WRIGHT BIPLANE; Count de Lambert Flies from Juvisy to Paris, 15 Miles, and Back Again. WRIGHT WITNESSES FEAT Calls It the Finest

Flight Yet – Lambert Says He Reached a Height of 1,300 Feet.

Charles de Lambert took off from Port-Aviation at 4.37 p.m. on Monday, 18 October, in his Wright machine. Wilbur Wright's first French student-pilot, Count de Lambert was a confident flyer who had confided his audacious plan that day to just two of his friends. At Juvisy there was concern that de Lambert had vanished. Had he crashed? Far from it. The count had flown on to Paris, where he circled the Eiffel Tower and, it seems, climbed 300 feet above it, before heading back to Port-Aviation where he landed to thunderous applause at 5.25 p.m.

But while the public was thrilled, aviation experts were unsure how to respond. Orville Wright considered de Lambert's exploit to be a dangerous stunt. The British weekly *The Aero* commented 'like the Channel flight, it will be done again and again, and unless stopped by legislation, someone will be killed at it, but de Lambert is and remains forever the first man to do it. Therefore, all honour and glory to his performance, though he deserves permanent disqualification from all future competitions for having done it.'

The 'Channel flight' had caught the public's imagination that summer. In October 1908, the *Daily Mail* announced a prize of £500 (at least £50,000 in 2020 money) for the pilot of the first powered flight across the English Channel before the end of the year. The French press said it was impossible, while *Punch* offered £10,000 for the first flight to Mars.

The British newspaper was surely asking too much of aircraft makers when it gave them two months to meet the challenge, but when the prize money was doubled for 1909, the race was on. For Lord Northcliffe, proprietor of the *Daily Mail*, aviation was the most exciting phenomenon of the era. It promised to sell not just thousands or even hundreds of thousands, but millions of newspapers.

Founded by Northcliffe, then Alfred Harmsworth, in 1896, the defiantly populist *Daily Mail* saw its circulation rise to over a million within six years. By the time the Wright brothers made their epochal flight in December 1903, it was the world's biggest-selling newspaper. Flight offered the *Mail*'s readers the kind of thrills and spills that would be superseded a century on by shopping, house prices and celebrity culture. And because by their very nature aeroplanes and air competitions were quick – 'here today, gone this afternoon' events, skimming through the public consciousness – they were a perfect fit for the fast-paced and youthful newspaper.

Lord Northcliffe let his editor, Thomas Marlowe, know exactly what he thought of the *Daily Mail*'s readers: 'No good printing long articles. People won't read them. They can't fix their attention for more than a short time. Unless there is some piece of news that grips them strongly. Then they will devour the same stuff over and over again.'

Get them hooked on flight. Sponsor headline-fodder competitions. Print racy articles. Repeat in ever more exciting ways. Sweep up readers. Please advertisers. Make a fortune.

Louis Blériot, the French aircraft maker and pilot who claimed the prize on 25 July 1909, became an instant celebrity when – after a hair-raising flight from Sangatte near Calais lasting 36½ minutes, made without a compass in strong wind and deteriorating weather – he arrived at Dover Castle. Charles Fontaine of *Le Matin* was the first to meet him, much to the chagrin of the *Daily Mail*'s correspondent who, assuming Blériot would land elsewhere, had to dash by car to reach Northfall Meadow by the castle. Blériot had not been to Dover before and had been unsure where to land. Fontaine had selected a favourable spot and waved a large Tricolour to mark it as his fellow Frenchman came into view.

The news spread very quickly indeed, not least because the Marconi Company had established a cross-Channel radio link with stations at Cap Blanc-Nez in Sangatte, and on the roof of Dover's Lord Warden Hotel. For Blériot, already a successful engineer and businessman – he had patented the first practical automobile headlamps, selling them from a Paris showroom – came fame followed by considerable wealth. By the end of the year, he had taken orders for a hundred aeroplanes, establishing himself as a major manufacturer. Buyers were inevitably impressed with the Blériot XI monoplane's ability to cross a body of particularly demanding water from one country to another. And they were equally attracted to the arrangement of Blériot's aircraft. These were monoplanes that, starting with the Blériot VIII of 1908, featured hand-operated joysticks and foot-operated rudder controls. This meant that they were easier and more natural to handle in the air than rival machines. The Blériot XI was also fitted with a strong and aerodynamic laminated-walnut propeller made by Lucien Chauvière, together with an equally sophisticated and reliable three-cylinder, 25-hp, three-litre engine by Alessandro Anzani, an Italian engineer settled in France.

The following month, in August 1909, Blériot took part in the Grande Semaine d'Aviation de la Champagne. Held in Reims, this was the world's first international aviation meet. A grand and lavish event sponsored by champagne makers, featuring a 600-seat restaurant, a temporary railway station, 38 entries (23 of which flew) and a galaxy of cash prizes, the Grande Semaine received half a million visitors – among them David Lloyd George, the British Chancellor of the Exchequer.

Lloyd George was an early champion of powered flight. Eight years on from Reims, and by now wartime prime minister, he celebrated what he saw as the noble role played by the Royal Flying Corps (RFC). Its aircraft were helping to end slaughter in the trenches. 'The heavens are their battlefield', the lyrical Welsh politician proclaimed. 'They are the cavalry of the clouds. High above the squalor and the mud.' In 1918, Lloyd George was responsible for the formation of a Royal Air Force (RAF) independent of the British Army and Royal Navy. His first President of the Air Council, the RAF's governing body, was Harold Harmsworth, Lord Rothermere – younger brother of Alfred Harmsworth, Lord Northcliffe, and co-founder of the *Daily Mail*.

Although Blériot won the Prix du Tour de Piste at Reims for the fastest single lap in his Type XII monoplane, flying at 76.95 km/h (47.8 mph), the celebrated pilot crashed on the last day, his machine bursting into flames. Blériot walked away from the accident, as did most early pilots from theirs, because his and most other early aircraft were light, and the speed and the height at which they flew were low. The French pilot would have been more concerned at coming second in a new, American-sponsored, contest the day before.

This was the first Gordon Bennett Trophy, an eponymous prize donated by the newspaper tycoon. It was the event that aviators, aircraft makers, bookmakers, organizers and the crowd were to take most notice of at the time. James Gordon Bennett Jr was an adventurous New Yorker whose father had made him editor of the sensationalist *New York Herald* in 1866. It was Gordon Bennett who financed Henry Morton Stanley's presumptive and successful search for Dr Livingstone in Africa, and an ill-fated American expedition by ship to the North Pole. As the crew of the unfortunate USS *Jeannette* starved to death in and around the Bering Strait, circulation of the *New York Herald* soared.

Ever restless, Bennett, a Civil War Union Navy veteran, had competed in the first transatlantic yacht race in 1866, and won. His scandalous and racy behaviour in polite New York society – triggering the well-known British phrase 'Gordon Bennett' (another way of saying 'gor'blimey' or 'bloody hell') – caused Bennett's move to Paris, where he launched the forerunner of the *International Herald Tribune*. Back in the States, his enthusiasm for polo, tennis, ballooning and automobiles encouraged him to announce a plethora of Gordon Bennett Cups in different disciplines. By 1909, and resident in Paris again, he became caught up in the newfangled craze for flying. His new trophy was, however, different from those to date. Entry would be by national teams rather than individuals. It set the tone and pace of aviation competitions for several years to come.

For the first contest, Louis Blériot, flying one of his own aircraft, had teamed up with Eugène Lefebvre, flying a French-built Wright Model A, and Hubert Latham in an Antoinette

VII. George Cockburn, piloting a French Farman III, represented Great Britain. Glenn Curtiss was the one and only American pilot, his mount an aeroplane of his own design, the Curtiss No. 2, fitted with a 63-hp water-cooled V8 engine. Teams from Italy and Austria failed to materialize. The rules of the competition meant that the next contest would be flown in the winning team's country, and the trophy would go permanently to the team that won the contest three times in succession.

Glenn Curtiss won the first Gordon Bennett Trophy contest at an average speed of 75.3 km/h (46.8 mph). He was named 'Champion Air Racer of the World'. Blériot came second, only seconds behind the American whose 'Reims Racer' was a more manoeuvrable machine than the Blériot XII. Latham came in third and Lefebvre fourth. Cockburn was unplaced: on his first lap he flew into a haystack. After the event, Curtiss took off on a tour of Italy where, aside from winning prizes, he took Gabriele d'Annunzio for a brief spin in the air. Wilbur Wright had flown with the acclaimed poet the previous year. These fearless Americans and their aeroplanes were to have a powerful and lasting effect on D'Annunzio's psyche.

Signing up for the Italian Air Force in the First World War, and by this time in his early fifties, D'Annunzio proved to be a daring military pilot. In August 1918, commanding 87th Squadron 'La Serenissima', he led 11 fast and serenely competent Ansaldo SVA biplanes on a return flight of more than 1,100 kilometres (700 miles) from Due Carrare, near Venice, to Vienna, dropping tens of thousands of green, white and red propaganda leaflets on the enemy city. Written by D'Annunzio, these warnings to the citizens of Vienna were in the form of orotund and provocative prose:

> On this August morning, while the fourth year of your desperate convulsion comes to an end and luminously begins the year of our full power, suddenly there appears the three-colour wing as an indication of the destiny that is turning...
>
> On the wind of victory that rises from freedom's rivers, we didn't come except for the joy of the daring, we didn't come except to prove what we could venture and do whenever we want, in an hour of our choice.

As no one had translated the maestro's lines into German, these may well have been ineffectual. Not so the leaflets dropped together with D'Annunzio's and written by Ugo Ojetti, the respected journalist and wartime Royal Commissioner for Propaganda on the Enemy. This text was translated into German. In English, it reads:

> VIENNESE!
>
> Learn to know the Italians.
>
> We are flying over Vienna; we could drop tons of bombs. All we are dropping on you is a greeting of three colours: the three colours of liberty...
>
> VIENNESE!
>
> You are famous for being intelligent. But why have you put on the Prussian uniform? By now, you see, the whole world has turned against you.

You want to continue the war? Continue it; it's your suicide. What do you hope for? The decisive victory promised to you by the Prussian generals? Their decisive victory is like the bread of Ukraine: You die waiting for it.

D'Annunzio was to become an inspiration for Benito Mussolini and his Italian Fascist movement, for whom high-speed powered flight and the urgent pulse of new technology were as important to Italy's twentieth-century renaissance as the revival of Roman architecture and city-making. Back in 1909–10, however, daring young pilots would not have known how the often awkward and dangerous aircraft they flew would shape political movements and war over the next 10 momentous years.

When Glenn Curtiss took part in the first US air meet, held at Dominguez Field, Los Angeles, in January 1910 – where he raised the world airspeed record to 55 mph – one of its main sponsors, Henry Huntington, the railroad and streetcar magnate, looked on unaware that within a few short decades the trains of the long-distance US railroads his family had built would be trounced by airliners capable of crossing the continent in a matter of hours rather than days.

Although hazardous and often frustrating for competitors, early air meets could be high-spirited events. On 4 November 1909, John Moore-Brabazon, the first English pilot to fly a powered aircraft in England, took a piglet dubbed Icarus the Second into the air with him to prove that pigs could fly. The following summer, Moore-Brabazon's wife persuaded him to give up flying after his close friend Charles Rolls, of Rolls-Royce fame, was killed when the tailplane of his Wright machine broke off during an aerial display at Hengistbury Airfield, near Bournemouth.

Moore-Brabazon was to fly again, however, as a decorated pilot during the First World War. Appointed Minister of Aircraft Production by Winston Churchill in 1941, he resigned the following year after publicly expressing his hope that Germany and Russia would destroy one another. He went on to chair the Brabazon Committee focused on the development of the post-war British aircraft industry, and was closely involved in the development of the giant Bristol Brabazon airliner. In later life, he was president of the Royal Aero Club.

In the days of Edwardian flight, Moore-Brabazon had been one of those dashing and seemingly carefree young men whose exploits were to be recreated in *Those Magnificent Men in their Flying Machines; Or, How I Flew from London to Paris in 25 Hours 11 Minutes*, a 1965 film set in 1910. Directed by Ken Annakin, who had worked with the RAF Film Unit during the Second World War, it tells the story of a £10,000 prize offered by the fictional *Daily Post*, and starred a cornucopia of reliable British actors and comics, among them Sarah Miles, Terry-Thomas, James Fox, Robert Morley, Eric Sykes, Benny Hill, Tony Hancock, Flora Robson, Fred Emney, John Le Mesurier, Willie Rushton and Cicely Courtneidge. In 1910, Courtneidge had played lead role in *The Arcadians*, a hugely popular musical comedy, at London's Shaftesbury Theatre. Doubtless some of the real-life young flyers would have gone to see her in that entertaining piece.

Stuart Whitman, Red Skelton, Alberto Sordi, Gert Fröbe, Jean-Pierre Cassel and Yujiro Ishihara played the roles of fictional and archetypal American, Italian, German, French and Japanese pilots. Replicas of aircraft that took part in early air meets were realistic, six of them flying for Annakin's cameras. This made for a film that did much to capture the technology and spirit of the era of competitive Edwardian aviation. It was also silly and fun. 'The trouble with these international affairs', says Lord Rawnsley (Robert Morley), the English press baron, 'is that they attract foreigners.' Which, of course, they did, although in reality these troublesome foreigners shared engines and components and flew machines from countries other than their own. Although highly competitive, the early air races and contests proved to be truly international in name, spirit and shared technology.

A little uncertainly, perhaps, but by 1910 aeroplanes were flying fairly well. Control and manoeuvrability were improving in quick, progressive steps; what was lacking was speed, reliability and endurance. Early engines required continual fettling. They could lose power almost without warning. Under duress, bits and pieces of early machines could break off, causing them to crash. In any event, pilots looking cheerful enough in their assortment of caps, ties and costumes were wholly exposed to the elements. If flying was thrilling, it was also a nail-biting and, for much of the year, intensely cold experience.

The Michelin tyre company had sponsored the first long-distance prizes as early as March 1908, and the International Michelin Cup was won that December by Wilbur Wright. While Wright's and subsequent records were broken with each International Michelin Cup event, the flights themselves involved long and complex sequences of taking off, landing – even after individual circuits – and refuelling. Rules became increasingly complex, and while Emmanuel Helen flew a total distance of just over 10,000 miles in a Nieuport monoplane to win the cup in 1913, it took him from 22 October to 29 November to do so. The event did not attract those pilots, already well known to the public, for whom speed was uppermost in their minds and who found the sheer complexity of the Michelin rules off-putting.

The British Empire Michelin Cup announced in 1909, however, was rooted in the simple equation of speed and distance. John Moore-Brabazon won the inaugural 1909 'Pegasus' event in March 1910, with a flight in the Short Biplane No. 2 of 18.75 miles around a circuit at Eastchurch on the Isle of Sheppey. That December, Samuel Cody raised the winning distance to 185.46 miles at Laffan's Plain, Farnborough.

For 1911, Michelin added a second prize – 'Winged Blacksmith' – for the fastest time on a 125-mile cross-country circuit. This aerial steeplechase was a prize truly worth winning, pushing the limits of aircraft and pilots. Samuel Cody took the first Winged Blacksmith Cup in September, completing a circuit flown from Farnborough and back again, via Andover, Hendon and Brooklands, in 3 hours, 6 minutes and 30 seconds. Cody won again in 1912, with the cross-country circuit now extended to 186 miles.

In terms of the future of civil aviation, perhaps the most significant challenge to pilots and aircraft makers in 1910 was the *Daily Mail*'s London to Manchester contest, for which as early as 1906 the newspaper, printed in both cities, had offered a prize of £10,000 (about £1 million in 2020). Intercity flight was an exciting idea that would surely revolutionize the young aviation industry and perhaps the press and business in general. No aircraft was up to the challenge in 1906, however. The 185-mile flight had to be made within 24 hours with no more than two stops along the way, and with take-off and landing made within five miles of the *Daily Mail* office in that city.

Four years later, two pilots – one British, the other French – were ready to have a go, both making the attempt in Farman III machines powered by seven-cylinder, 50-hp Gnome Omega rotary engines. The confident pilots were 30-year-old Claude Grahame-White, a Hampshire-born motor engineer and big-game hunter who had learned to fly the previous year with Louis Blériot at Reims, and 26-year-old Louis Paulhan, a balloonist and model-aircraft maker.

Paulhan's prize in an aircraft design competition in 1907 had been a full-scale Voisin airframe. Raising the money to buy an engine, he taught himself to fly the timber and canvas biplane. By 1910, Paulhan had flown displays in France, England and the United States. He had also flown one of the very first seaplanes. A future First World War pilot decorated with the Croix de Guerre, Paulhan was to become an important figure in aircraft engineering and manufacturing.

Grahame-White made the first attempt, taking off at 5.12 a.m. on 23 April from frosted grass close to the Plumes Hotel in West London. This was an Edwardian establishment built to serve the Royal Agricultural Society's showgrounds, Park Royal, opened in 1903. Developed into an industrial area, and then a business estate after the First World War, it is hard now to imagine a crowd of some 300 spectators turning up at Park Royal in the early hours of a particularly cold morning to watch a young man take to starlit air in the wholly exposed cockpit of a skeletal timber and canvas biplane.

As planned, and with his puppet mascot tied to a strut alongside him, Grahame-White turned to follow the tracks of the London and North Western Railway's main line heading north from Euston. The railway had painted its wooden sleepers white to help the pilots follow its tracks from London to Manchester in low light – and, as it turned out, in darkness, too. Although fascinated by the *Daily Mail*'s challenge, the railway, known as the Premier Line, saw aircraft as not much more than a novelty. After all, its own extremely comfort-able, warm and thoroughly equipped dining car trains, with powerful new George Whale–designed Precursor class 4-4-0s at their head, could steam from Euston to Manchester in under four hours.

Remarkably, a number of the mechanics travelling from London by automobile – normally a slow means of transport in Edwardian England – arrived in Rugby ahead of Grahame-White, who came down to land at 7.15 a.m. He had averaged 40 mph over these first 80 miles.

According to *The Times*, Grahame-White was 'blue with cold and walked rather painfully for a few moments. He tried to smile in answer to the cheers with which he was greeted. His hands were numbed and his teeth were chattering. He asked for food and a fire, saying "I am starving". Lady Denbigh, who was present with Lord Denbigh, lent him her muff, and another lady put some furs around his neck.'

Thawed in front of a fire at nearby Gellings Farm and fuelled with coffee and biscuits while Boy Scouts guarded his machine, Grahame-White took to the air again at 8.25 a.m., aiming to reach Crewe. The inlet valves of his engine gave up the ghost after just 30 miles. His mother arrived to look after him, but after lunch and a snooze, it was clear that there was no point in Grahame-White carrying on. He had damaged the Farman on landing. Overnight, the wind blew the machine over. Pilot and battered aircraft were taken back to London.

By now, Louis Paulhan had arrived in Dover from California. His crated Farman III was assembled at Hendon Aerodrome in less than 11 hours, and at 5.21 p.m. on the evening of 27 April, he flew the short distance from there to his curious starting point, Hampstead Cemetery. Picking up the LNWR main line, he headed north as Madame Paulhan and Henry Farman overtook him in a train laid on for the occasion.

News of Paulhan's attempt was relayed at 6.10 p.m. to Grahame-White, who was asleep in bed at a hotel near the *Daily Mail*'s hangar at Wormwood Scrubs, where his Farman had been repaired. Within 20 minutes, the Englishman had 'scrambled' and was in the air. With the sky darkening, Grahame-White landed in a field beside the railway at Roade, Northamptonshire. Ahead of him, but running out of fuel, Paulhan had touched down for the night near Lichfield. He, too, must have felt the cold, but put on a brave face. As he told a *Daily Mail* reporter:

I shouted and I sang. I do not think my voice is particularly fascinating, but nobody seems to mind that in the upper air.

A pelting rainstorm lashed me for 20 minutes when I was in the neighbourhood of Rugby. Fortunately I am not unused to flying in the rain; therefore, although it was uncomfortable, it had no effect upon my flight. I kept on flying at a steady pace, although my altitude varied remarkably.

In other words, his flimsy machine was buffeted about in the uninviting folds of a cold and wet English sky.

Grahame-White, meanwhile, made the decision to take off very early the following morning in order to overtake the slumbering Frenchman. This meant flying in the dark. With the aid of car headlamps, he took off at 2.50 a.m., and after accidentally shutting off the engine and very nearly crashing found his way to the LNWR main line, where he followed the line of lamp-lit stations north. Forced to land at Polesworth – weighed down with fuel, his aeroplane was flying too close to the ground to be able to tackle the hills ahead – Grahame-White was just 10 miles behind Paulhan.

Not knowing where Grahame-White was, Paulhan took to the air just minutes later, and at 5.32 a.m. he touched down at Barcicroft Fields near Didsbury on the outskirts of Manchester – within the necessary five miles of the *Daily Mail* office. Grahame-White proved to be a sporting loser, and Paulhan a gracious winner. The pair toasted one another at a luncheon held soon afterwards at London's Savoy Hotel. Paulhan was presented with a cheque for £10,000 in a golden casket. Grahame-White received a white-silver bowl filled with red and white roses.

In April 1950, Louis Paulhan was flown from London to Manchester in a two-seat Gloster Meteor T7 jet trainer at 10 times the speed of his epoch-making flight 40 years earlier. 'It was all I had ever dreamed of,' he said. 'No propellers, no vibration.' Back in London he was wined and dined by the *Daily Mail* at the Royal Aero Club, where he was sat next to Claude Grahame-White, by this time a prosperous property developer resident in warm, dry and sunny Nice. Ten years later, Paulhan was one of the passengers invited on board Air France's inaugural non-stop flight, by Boeing 707, from Paris to Los Angeles.

As for the *Daily Mail*, it set even more ambitious challenges to excite its readers and further the rapid development of aircraft. Its next aerial adventure was the Circuit of Britain air race. Scheduled to take place on 22 July 1911, the race required entrants to fly a 1,010-mile circuit to and from Brooklands in Surrey, with 11 stops – as far north as Stirling – on the way.

Thirty aircraft were entered. A Handley Page Type D and a Bristol Prier monoplane crashed before the start. Graham Gilmour in a Bristol Type T was unable to start because his licence had been suspended. Marcel Brindejonc des Moulinais was in hospital in France, having crashed on the way to England. Five aircraft failed to take off. Two crashed as they attempted to do so. Falling ill, H. J. D. Astley had to land at Irthlingborough in Northamptonshire. Others ditched on various legs of the flight as fog and engine problems took their toll.

Just four aircraft completed the course, and once again the French led the way. The first aircraft to return to Brooklands was a Blériot XI flown by 'André Beaumont', the nom de plume of Lieutenant Jean Louis Conneau of the French Navy. Second place went to Jules Védrines, a famously foul-mouthed and popular French socialite who was to become the first pilot to fly at over 100 mph and would place first in the Gordon Bennett Trophy race of 1912. In third was James Valentine, a future RFC officer who died on active duty in Russia in 1917; and fourth was Samuel Cody, the American showman, in an aircraft of his own design.

The *Daily Mail*, meanwhile, kept up the pace. In 1913 it offered a £10,000 prize for the first transatlantic flight. While not a race, this epic journey was a thrilling challenge, and one not to be won for another six years. That same year the *Mail* also put up a £5,000 prize for a Circuit of Britain for 'waterplanes'. This was certainly something different, not least the development of what became known as seaplanes (aircraft with floats instead of wheels) and flying boats (aircraft with hulls) had only recently followed in the wake of the first generation of land-based heavier-than-air machines.

The 1,540-mile contest held in August 1913 was a disaster. On a test flight over Hampshire with his first seaplane on 7 August, Samuel Cody and his passenger, the cricketer William Evans, were killed when Cody's machine broke up at 200 feet. In the event, there was just one entry: Harry Hawker, with fellow Australian and Sopwith colleague Harry Kauper, in a Sopwith seaplane. To comply with the rules of the contest, each 'waterplane' had to carry a passenger.

Although flying a decidedly more modern machine than Cody's, albeit with the same 100-hp Green E.6 six-cylinder inline engine, Hawker was beset by bad weather, illness, engine problems and exhaustion. Two-thirds of the way around the circuit that had taken him and Kauper as far north as Cromarty on the east coast of Scotland and Oban on the west, Hawker crash-landed into the water near Dublin. Kauper broke an arm; Hawker was unhurt. In London shortly afterwards, Hawker was much praised for his attempt by Winston Churchill, First Lord of the Admiralty, and was presented with a consolation prize of £1,000 by Thomas Marlowe, editor of the *Daily Mail*.

Four months earlier, a contest for 'hydroplanes' had been held in Monaco. This was the first Schneider Trophy air race – or, more properly, contest. In this first incarnation it seemed almost insignificant compared to the great, carnival-like French air meets or the aerial dramas sponsored by the *Daily Mail*. And yet the Schneider Trophy, born of a noble and civil ideal, was to spur on the development of (largely military) aircraft to unprecedented heights of speed, power, efficacy and international fame, within two intense decades.

But if the Schneider Trophy was to introduce the world to a new generation of high-speed aircraft and daring pilots, it did so on the back of the pioneers of aviation who, from flying 120 feet at jogging speed in 1903, had attempted to circuit the British Isles just 10 years later.

Among the up-and-coming stars of Schneider races was the American pilot Jimmy Doolittle, who saw his first aeroplane at that very first US air race held at Dominguez Field, Los Angeles, in January 1910. I met General Doolittle 80 years later, shortly after he became involved in fundraising for the American Air Force Museum at Duxford – a brilliant design by Norman

Foster, conceived in the mid-1980s, engineered with Chris Wise of Arup, and completed and opened in 1997.

While Doolittle, a fabled airman, lived very nearly into the twenty-first century, other pilots of those early racing years vanished as if into the realms of pure myth. Harry Harper, appointed the *Daily Mail*'s first air correspondent in 1906, recalled the exploits of Hubert Latham in his last book, *My Fifty Years in Flying*, published in 1956. When Latham crashed into a roof at Brooklands in 1911, it seemed certain that the cucumber-cool pilot had been killed. As Harper described it:

> The impact had appeared so tremendous – the crash so complete. But suddenly, amid the drifting dust clouds, a slight, dapper figure could be seen disengaging itself from the battered fuselage, and lowering itself deftly to an undamaged part of the roof. Then out came that inevitable cigarette case, and Latham sat there smoking till someone arrived with a ladder.

At the end of that year, Latham undertook an expedition, wreathed in mystery, for the French government to the heart of the Congo. He was killed perhaps by his porters – or was it a raging buffalo, as some reports claimed? It seemed such an earthy, if exotic, end for a pilot who looked death in the eye virtually every time he flew. 'Slight, dapper, pale of face,' wrote Harry Harper, 'Latham always seemed languid and fatigued until he took his place at the controls of his beloved aeroplane. Then he seemed to become a different man. His eyes sparkled. He appeared in a flash to become intensely alive.'

Rooted in those early aerial contests and flying on the shoulders of undaunted pilots – with or without silver cigarette cases to hand – the story of the Schneider Trophy and what it led to deserves to be told as if intensely alive.

PART ONE

The Race

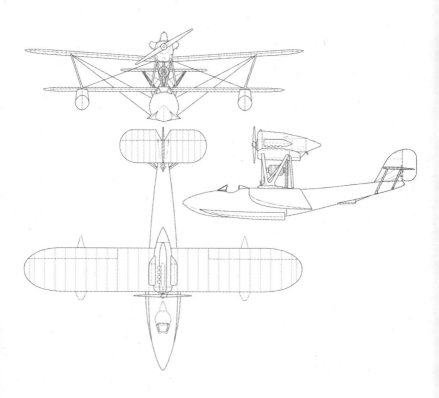

ONE

The French Connection:
1913–22

O wned by the Royal Aero Club, the Coupe d'Aviation Maritime Jacques Schneider can be seen today in London's Science Museum. A florid sculpture, it takes the form of a silver-plated bronze casting mounted on a dark-veined marble base and depicts a winged and naked Spirit of Flight kissing one of four cherubic faces – Neptune and his sons – emerging from the crest of a wave. Its sculptor, Ernest Gabard, was an early aviation enthusiast, although it is clear from the design of this trophy that artists had yet to respond in kind to the true thrill and excitement of flight. They would come to do so, especially in Italy some 20 years later. By then the aircraft themselves were becoming not just highly potent machines, but sleekly streamlined kinetic sculptures, too.

Gabard's trophy, known by competition pilots as the 'flying flirt', was commissioned by Jacques Schneider, son of the owner of a mighty iron foundry, engineering and armaments works founded by Schneider's grandfather and great-uncle at Le Creusôt in eastern France in the mid-1830s. By the twentieth century this works was a volcanic realm of iron and steel mills, steam hammers, steam locomotives, submarines, armoured vehicles, machine guns and artillery pieces.

Born in 1879, Schneider was trained as a mining engineer, an occupation that might have kept his thoughts earthbound. This wealthy young man, however, was as excited as his contemporaries by the newfound freedoms and sheer excitement offered by novel ways of moving through the world at speed. Motorcycles. Motor cars. Powerboats.

In 1908, Schneider witnessed Wilbur Wright in the air above Le Mans. He learned to fly both heavier- and lighter-than-air machines, setting a French altitude record of 10,081 metres (33,074 feet, the height airliners cruise today) in his balloon *Icare* – named, of course, after the mythical Icarus, who, fleeing Crete and the threat of the Minotaur with his inventor father, Daedalus, flew too close to the sun with fatal results, his waxed wings melting over the sea. While pushing himself hard in a competition held in 1910 at Monte Carlo with his racing *hydroglisseur* – a shallow punt powered by an air propeller – Schneider suffered multiple arm fractures and, handicapped for life, was no longer able to fly. Not that this dimmed his enthusiasm for sea, speed and powered flight. Far from it.

At an Aéro-Club de France dinner held in Chicago on 5 December 1912, to celebrate the French team's first and second places in that year's Gordon Bennett contest held in Clearing, Ohio, Schneider announced his competition. It would be unlike any other that had gone before. His vision was not one of small aircraft taking off and landing from inland airfields, with just a pilot on board, but of commercially viable seaplanes or flying boats that would carry useful payloads and passengers from port to port around the world. His was a big picture of what aviation might be, and his logic was sound. Given that most of the world's surface is water and that most key trading cities are by the sea, seaplanes made good sense. And from a twenty-first-century perspective, the idea is certainly appealing. Imagine being able to travel from city centres by fast trains to seaports free of all the encumbrances and frustrations of sprawling modern airports, as free as a seabird.

Schneider's vision was exciting, not least because of the challenges it offered aircraft designers and pilots. Seaplanes were new and largely untried and untested. Early manufacturers had concentrated on land-based machines. The most potent of these at the time of the Chicago dinner was, significantly, the Deperdussin Monocoque, flown by Jules Védrines and winner of the 1912 Gordon Bennett Trophy event. Where no American aeroplane had been able to better 78 mph, Védrines had flown the Deperdussin at over 100 mph. And it was the Deperdussin that was to rise to the occasion in the first Schneider Trophy contest the following year.

Schneider explained that the trophy would be awarded to the first national aero club to win the annual event three times within five years. The victorious nation would get to keep the trophy in perpetuity. There would also be a cash prize of 25,000 gold francs (£1,000, or about £100,000 in 2020) for the winning pilot of the deciding event. The rules were clear. The contest was to be held over the sea, the distance to be flown not less than 150 nautical miles. Aircraft must be seaworthy. Each country could enter a maximum of three aircraft in the annual competition. Each team had to be sponsored by the governing body for aviation sports in that country, which in turn had to be affiliated to the Fédération Aéronautique Internationale. The winning team would be responsible for hosting the next annual contest.

While the national rivalries would encourage the development of the fast and reliable commercial seaplanes Jacques Schneider had imagined flying from seaport to seaport around the world, it also led to the rise of the supremely powerful, fast and deadly fighter aircraft of the late 1930s. To win the Schneider Trophy, aircraft would have to develop the ability to take off from and land on water. But because seaplanes needed more power to lift off from water than aircraft running on wheels along airfields, competitive aircraft of this type demanded increasingly powerful engines. And while these were to equip steady, comfortable and sensibly quick payload-carrying seaplanes and flying boats, they also paved the way for puissant British, American, Italian and, to an extent, German military designs.

This was not foreseen at that Chicago dinner in 1912. Aircraft competing in the early Schneider events were for the most part, and to their detriment, converted landplanes; while hydro-aeroplanes – as they were known in Britain until Winston Churchill insisted on calling them seaplanes in 1913 – were truly in their infancy.

In March 1910, Henri Fabre, the Jesuit-educated and scientifically minded son of a wealthy ship-owning family who lived to be 101, made the first successful take-off from water in a heavier-than-air machine. This was achieved in the Hydravion, powered by a 50-hp Gnome engine, at the Étang de Berre, a Mediterranean lagoon near Marseilles. Never having flown before, not even as a passenger, Fabre lifted the machine – which looked like an illustration from a fairy tale – to six feet above the ripples for a distance of 1,500 feet in four consecutive flights. Happily, the Fabre Hydravion is on display today at the Musée de l'Air in Paris.

The following January, Glenn Curtiss – winner of the first international air race, the Gordon Bennett Trophy at Reims in 1909 – made a sustained flight at 50–55 mph from San Diego Bay, California, in a biplane powered by a water-cooled engine of his own design. Curtiss had been in touch with Fabre beforehand.

That same month, Eugene Ely, a private pilot, landed a Curtiss biplane on a platform mounted on the stern deck of the four-funnelled armoured cruiser USS *Pennsylvania* in San Francisco Bay; and, in doing so, initiated the era of aeroplanes that could fly around the world without needing to take off from or land on water. Eugene Ely was killed aged 24 in October 1911, when, unable to pull out of a dive, he crashed into the ground while performing at an air display at Macon, Georgia. He climbed out of his machine, but his neck was broken. He died seconds later.

By then, Glenn Curtiss had sold the US Navy its first aircraft: the amphibious A-1 *Triad*, fitted with floats and retractable wheels. Today, this elegant, insect-like machine hangs from a roof in the National Naval Aviation Museum, Florida. On the much colder and damper Cumbrian coast, at Barrow-in-Furness, in January 1911 Commander Oliver Schwann RN (later, and with a less German-sounding surname, Air Vice Marshal Sir Oliver Swann) experimented with a modified Avro Type D machine. Like Henri Fabre, Schwann had never flown before. While he entered the aviation book of fame as the first person in Britain to take off from salt water, he crashed the Avro on that very same flight. Under considerable strain, the aeroplane's 35-hp Green inline engine overheated and lost power. The Avro had begun life as a landplane weighing just 500 lbs; shipped by train from Brooklands to Barrow and fitted with floats by a Royal Navy team, it weighed a full 1,000 lbs by the time Schwann coaxed it up from the water to 40 mph.

Clearly, there was much to learn. It was found, for example, that hydroplanes were unable to take off from a smooth surface; they needed some chop to the water for their floats or hulls to break adhesion, especially because early floats were rudimentary, boxy devices and barely aerodynamic. To push through the weight and resistance of choppy water, hydroplanes needed more power than landplanes, yet while existing inline water-cooled engines fitted to contemporary racing cars and aeroplanes could be powerful enough for the job, they were also very heavy. Beyond these challenging constraints, the stresses on the timber frames of early aircraft were immense as they battled through seawater.

Solutions to these problems came quickly, making the Schneider Trophy contest a valid proposition by 1913. In France, Laurent Seguin, the inventor and industrialist, had developed his Gnome rotary air-cooled engine, first shown at the Paris Aero Salon in December 1908. Cylinders arranged in a star pattern rotated around a central crankshaft. Although heavy on the castor oil that spattered pilots' goggles and gave Gnome-powered aircraft their distinctive smell, Seguin's motor was small and powerful. The seven-cylinder model exerted 50 hp from 75 kg, or twice the power-to-weight ratio of contemporary water-cooled engines. With air flowing freely around its finned cylinder blocks as the aircraft took flight, it was not prone to overheating. Compared with rival motors, the Gnome rotary was also reliable.

The oldest-known airworthy British aircraft – a 1912 Blackburn Monoplane currently in the care of the Shuttleworth Collection, Bedfordshire – still flies today courtesy of its Gnome Omega engine, while the prototype of the revolutionary Gnome Omega is on display at the National Air and Space Museum in Washington, DC. By 1912, the year of the first hydroplane meeting at Monaco, the Gnome et Rhône company offered a choice of six engines of up to 160 hp.

One particular advantage seaplanes and flying boats had over landplanes was – although at first this sounds counterintuitive – the pronounced length of their take-off runs. As was commonly understood by 1913, landplanes needed long wings to lift them as quickly as possible above trees, buildings and power lines. A seaplane, with plenty of space to manoeuvre, could make do with shorter wings, and because of this it promised tighter turns and less drag in flight than many landplanes. As the military began to take a close interest in the Schneider contests, the event developed into an increasingly nationalistic race for sheer speed and power that, when backed by governments, led to the design of a new generation of competing military aircraft very unlike the timber and canvas 'stringbags' of 1913.

The first outing for the Coupe d'Aviation Maritime Jacques Schneider was on 16 April 1913 during the Grand Prix de Monaco. This two-week-long meet was a gala affair with as many as a quarter of a million people attending from across Europe. South Eastern and Chatham Railway adverts posted in Victoria and Charing Cross stations promised 'Frequent Daily Express services from London to the Riviera'.

For the Schneider event, a triangular 10-kilometre course was superimposed on the Baie de Roquebrune between Monte Carlo and Cap Martin. There were entries from Belgium, France, Britain, Italy, Spain, Switzerland and the United States, although just four aircraft were turned out on the day, all French landplanes equipped with temporary floats and powered by Gnome engines.

Luckily the weather was good. The day before, the cold mistral had scythed through Monte Carlo and across the bay. A French Artois flying boat piloted by François Louis Gaudart was upended by the fierce wind and vanished into the sea. Three weeks after the crash, local fishermen found his body near the harbour entrance.

On the morning of the Schneider contest, the mistral had given way to a gentle breeze. The sea was calm, the sky clear blue and the temperature comfortably warm. The pilots drew lots to see who would go first. This was not an out-and-out race, but a contest with aircraft setting off at different times and aiming to fly the circuit in the fastest time. The winner was

25-year-old Maurice Prévost, pilot of a deep blue and beautiful Deperdussin monoplane.

Designed by 32-year-old Louis Béchereau for Armand Deperdussin, a wealthy silk trader turned aircraft maker, this new type – flying at over 100 mph – had taken first and second place in the 1912 Gordon Bennett Trophy held in Chicago. With its revolutionary monocoque fuselage inspired by contemporary racing yachts and formed from hickory, ash, pine and tulipwood ply, its streamlined nose cone, aerodynamic floats by Alphonse Tellier (an expert in hydroplaning hulls), small wings and batwing tail, the Deperdussin monoplane was – certainly in terms of aesthetics – a nod to the future. It marked the end of wholly exposed airframes, looking like cat's cradles or big and complicated kites. Powered by a double-row Gnome Lambda-Lambda 14-cylinder rotary engine of 160 hp, the Deperdussin was as fast as it looked. Black-and-white photographs of the time are unable to do full justice to the appearance of this bright blue mechanical insect.

The temptation to paint too rosy a picture of even this – the best racer of its short-lived day – must, however, be tempered by the fact that no aeroplane of the time was particularly easy to fly, and mechanically they left much to be desired. During trials for the first Schneider contest, two Deperdussin machines were wrecked and a third was declared uncompetitive. One of the wrecked machines was a single-seater designed specially for the race, leaving Prévost with a heavier two-seater.

On 16 April, Prévost set off at 8 a.m., powering along the water as demanded by the contest rules as a test of seaworthiness, and then taking to the air for what seemed an all-but-effortless 28 laps flown at a height of around 50 feet and an average speed of 61 mph. But because after flying those 28 laps he chose to taxi across the finishing line rather than pass over it, Prévost was initially disqualified.

Prévost was followed by Roland Garros, a bantamweight 24-year-old pilot born in Réunion and with several aviation records to his credit. Much was expected of the dashing young aviator, but in his bumpy attempt to get his 80-hp Gnome-powered Morane-Saulnier monoplane off the water and into the air, he soaked the engine. It stopped, and Garros was towed back to port.

Gabriel Espanet, a doctor and aviation enthusiast, was next, in a 100-hp Gnome-powered French Nieuport monoplane. Espanet made a good start, but on the eighth lap a fuel-line fracture took him out of the running. In a second Nieuport – a 100-hp Gnome engine again – Charles Weymann, the fourth contender, lapped the circuit at 70 mph, faster than Prévost. After 20 laps, Weymann was in the lead by three minutes with a best lap average so far of 71 mph. On lap 25, an oil pipe burst and the Haitian-born Franco-American pilot was forced to land.

With his Morane-Saulnier dried and firing anew on all cylinders, Garros set out again, prompting Prévost to take off, fly an extra lap and cross the finishing line in the air. His average speed was now down to just 45.75 mph, but he had won the contest after all. There is a delightful photograph of Prévost at the end of the race and back on terra firma, dapper in a polo-neck jumper, a leather jacket with silk handkerchief, and lace-up leather shoes, standing alongside his mother, a fur over her arm, and Louis Béchereau in flat cap, tweed plus fours and leather boots. Soon enough, flying suits would be de rigueur, yet in these early days of competitive flying, collars, ties, tweeds and caps were in vogue among the young pilots who, judging from photographs, appeared keen to cut a dash.

From a modest background, Maurice Prévost had studied at the Practical School of Commerce and Industry of Reims before joining the Betheny Deperdussin Aviation School in 1910, rising to become chief instructor. In September 1913, Prévost came first in a 1-2-3 win for France in the Gordon Bennett Cup at Reims, flying his Deperdussin at an average speed of 200.4 km/h (124.5 mph). This triumphant moment for Prévost, France and Deperdussin came a month after the arrest of Armand Deperdussin for a £1-million fraud. Louis Blériot took over the company, reconstituting it as Société Pour l'Aviation et ses Dérivés (SPAD), which, like Nieuport – and in the hands and with the brain of chief engineer Louis Béchereau – was to design and produce some of the most effective fighter aircraft of the First World War, including the superb SPAD S.XIII. With its manoeuvrability, its light and precise controls, and its Hispano-Suiza water-cooled V8 engine designed by the Swiss engineer Marc Birkigt, the S.XIII was the choice of French, British and American aces, and was flown by 20 air forces around the world.

If slightly chaotic, the 1913 Schneider Trophy contest had been a glorious moment for France – and perhaps deservedly so, as its manufacturers, pilots, sponsors and event organizers had done much to further aviation since Wilbur Wright's momentous visit to the country in 1908. The French aircraft industry had developed at breakneck speed. The Schneider was put proudly on display in the Paris headquarters of the Aéro-Club de France.

This happened to be on Rue de Galilée, named after the lake on which Jesus walked in the gospels of Matthew, Mark and John. As for the trophy, this was to be the first and last time the French held it.

Aviation had become a thrilling and fast-paced new venture, drawing in some of the best young engineering talent from across Europe and the United States. Everything was new. Aviation was the future. Sponsorship was readily forthcoming. There were no set ways of doing things: anything might happen, any nation might win. What seems so very remarkable from a twenty-first-century perspective is just how quickly aircraft manufacturers set up in business, and how they had machines ready for international contests within a year of opening their doors. Morane-Saulnier, for example, was formed in 1911 by Léon and Robert Morane, sons of a wealthy industrialist, and Raymond Saulnier, a childhood friend who had worked as an engineer for Louis Blériot.

By 1913, the joint founders of the Nieuport company – Édouard de Nieuport and his brother Charles – had both been killed in flying accidents, a sign of just how mercurial the aeroplane industry was at the time Jacques Schneider was dreaming of long-distance commercial flying boats that could only ever exist when aircraft manufacturers and their machines were altogether more reliable propositions.

As for the heady optimism and fearlessness of early pilots – most of them young and devil-may-care by nature – this was all the more impressive given their largely untried and untested, handmade and far-from-perfect machines. Their ranks swelled in April 1914 when Schneider competitors included Howard Pixton and Lord John Carbery, representing Great Britain, Ernest Burri from Switzerland, William Thaw from the United States, and the German pilot Ernst Stöffler. Charles Weymann was competing, too, but this year, as was his birthright, for the United States rather than France.

Twenty-one-year-old John Evans-Freke, Lord Carbery, was a past master at looking the part but would have little luck at the Schneider event. After abandoning his Morane-Saulnier, he took to the air in a spare Deperdussin that packed up after two laps with engine trouble. What Carbery did have was fashion sense and panache, and this counted for something in these massively popular *belle époque* carnivals.

Brought up at Castle Freke, a battlemented mid-eighteenth-century house in County Cork, Carbery bought a Morane-Saulnier in France when he was just 20, learned to fly it there and winged it safely home. He delighted and frightened his family and the locals with daredevil flying stunts at the Bandon and Clonakilty agricultural shows, and was dubbed 'Lord of the Skies'. When he packed the Morane-Saulnier off to Monaco for the Schneider event in April 1914, he drove ahead of it from Ireland in his 1911 60-hp 10.6-litre Cottin et Desgouttes racing car fitted with a touring body by Cann & Co. in London. Chain-driven, this mechanical beast could cruise at 60 mph with the tachometer showing just 1,000 rpm, and could also top 100 mph.

When war broke out in July, Carbery signed up with the Royal Naval Air Service (RNAS), bringing his aeroplane with him into action as a light bomber over German lines. At the time of the Irish War of Independence, he sided with the IRA, dropped his title and sold the 1,100-acre Castle Freke estate for a fraction of its worth. Before he left, he blasted the portraits of his ancestors that hung from its walls with a shotgun. Mr John Evans Carbery, as he was now known, took to bootlegging in the United States, adopted an American accent, then moved on to the White Highlands of Kenya, where he farmed and served a year in jail for currency offences – while, it seems, attempting to sponsor a transatlantic air race. His second wife, Maia, an aviatrix, died in a flying accident in 1928.

With Prévost's victory in the first Schneider Trophy contest and the team's 1-2-3 win at Reims, the French were feeling cocky. Unconcerned with the German, Swiss and US entries, they felt confident of beating Lord Carbery's Morane-Saulnier, which was, of course, a French aeroplane, and one the French competitors – Prévost with the Deperdussin; Gabriel Espanet and Pierre Levasseur in Nieuports; and Roland Garros, also with a Morane-Saulnier machine – knew inside out.

The German Aviatik Arrow flown by Stöffler – an interesting biplane balanced on a large central float, counterbalanced by wingtip floats and powered by a 150-hp inline water-cooled Benz engine – was said to be heavy and slow with a maximum speed of 75 mph, or 50 mph slower than the race-proven Deperdussin. The FBA flying boat built by Louis Schreck's Franco-British Aviation company – intended as a production machine to sell to the Royal Navy, and entered by the Swiss pilot Ernest Burri – might be half the weight of the Aviatik Arrow, but what chance did it have with a reputed top speed of 68 mph? In any case, this untried aircraft had yet to be flown by Burri or anyone else. Weymann's Nieuport was a known quantity, while Thaw had jumped at the opportunity of flying a Deperdussin instead of a tired Curtiss flying boat.

There was, though, one complete unknown. This was the second British entry: a Sopwith Tabloid to be flown by 28-year-old Mr C. Howard Pixton. When the pale golden-yellow, polished aluminium and varnished wood Sopwith arrived at Monaco, the French team looked at it with more than a degree of disdain. The tiny biplane – its name taken from a well-known patent pill made from compressed powder by Burroughs, Wellcome & Co. – was just two-thirds of the length of the all-conquering Deperdussin. Its wingspan measured 25 feet, 6 inches, compared to the French aeroplane's 44 feet, 3 inches. Its motor, a Gnome Monosoupape (meaning 'single-valve') nine-cylinder rotary, was rated at 100 hp – considerably less than the engine of the Deperdussin.

If the French had known the full story of the Tabloid's development, they would have laughed and shrugged their shoulders all the more. On April Fool's Day 1914, less than three weeks before the Schneider contest, Howard Pixton had taxied out from a jetty on the River Hamble on floats made by Syd Burgoyne, a former boatbuilder now working for Sopwith. The Tabloid promptly performed a cartwheel and Pixton was thrown into the water. Upside down, the biplane drifted midstream. Clearly, the set-up with a single central float and small auxiliary floats under the wings was flawed.

Pulled by ropes from the Hamble the following day, the Tabloid was hastily repaired. With the aircraft now fitted with twin floats, Pixton attempted to take off from the River

Thames at Kingston, but was halted by officials from the Thames Conservancy. Granted permission by the Port of London Authority to fly below Teddington Lock, a few days later Pixton finally got the Tabloid off the water. In the three miles before the engine began to splutter as it misfired, Pixton worked the Tabloid up to 85 mph.

When the biplane was unpacked and reassembled in the British team tent at Monaco, the engine showed unmistakable signs of rust. Perhaps it was just as well that the polished aluminium casing with vents for cooling hid it from sight. The engine itself had been something of a last-minute purchase by Tommy Sopwith, who had taken the train to Paris to see the Seguin brothers and brought the Gnome rotary back to Surrey with him. It is hard to imagine stowing an aero-engine in the baggage compartment of one of today's Eurostar trains.

When, on Monday, 20 April, Pixton took off behind the two French-entry Nieuports and the FBA flying boat – shockingly, the Deperdussins had failed to qualify – the French were in for a surprise as big as the Sopwith was small. The team had made some urgent modifications to help Pixton's machine around the Monaco circuit, including an extra six-gallon petrol tank and a change to the length of its propeller to keep the Gnome engine from over-revving.

Competition from the German team, meanwhile, failed to rise to the occasion. The Aviatik turned over on one wing on a practice take-off run. It was a sorry end to Ernst Stöffler's brave attempt, as he had flown 963 kilometres from Gotha to Marseille on the way to Monaco, surviving a crash landing in a vineyard near Orange en route.

A new rule requiring Schneider entrants to land and take off from water twice during the first lap proved to be in Pixton's favour. He met the rule by having the Tabloid merely kiss the water while barely losing speed. The Sopwith was lithe and nimble, and much faster than pretty much anyone had expected. Pixton's first lap was twice as fast as the Nieuports. Pushing their machines as hard as possible, Espanet and Levasseur were forced to drop out on the 16th and 17th laps as the rear cylinder banks of their engines overheated and the pistons seized.

For several laps, Pixton's engine lost power in one of its nine cylinders. But he flew to applause from the Monte Carlo crowd each time he passed. How many laps had he flown? To be sure, Pixton had pulled out one of the 28 drawing pins stuck in the dashboard every time he lapped the circuit. The method was crude, but it worked. The Sopwith completed the course at an average speed of 86.78 mph. Rather than land, Pixton flew an extra two laps to claim a world record of 300 kilometres for a floatplane in a closed circuit. Thinking in both metric and imperial measures was not a difficulty for pilots of the era of the Entente Cordiale between Britain and France.

The son of a stockbroker from West Didsbury, Howard Pixton had attended Manchester Grammar School and was a competitive swimmer as a young man. Apprenticed to a local engineering firm, by 1910 he was working as a mechanic and driver at a garage at Leek, where he learned of Claude Grahame-White and Louis Paulhan's *Daily Mail* race from London to Manchester. Rushing to Lichfield to see Louis Paulhan's Farman, he decided he had to learn to fly. Employed as a mechanic with

A. V. Roe at Brooklands, he gained his pilot's licence and began teaching pupils of Avro's flying school.

In 1911, Pixton moved to what became the Bristol Aeroplane Company, teaching army officers to fly near Salisbury. His oldest pupil, 49-year-old Brigadier General David Henderson, went on to command the Royal Flying Corps in the field in the early stages of the First World War – and, in 1918, to play an important part in the formation of the RAF. Pixton also taught German officers to fly at the Deutsche Bristol Werke in Halberstadt. He taught Spanish and Romanian princes to fly, too, became a friend of Samuel Cody, and then joined Tommy Sopwith, an excellent pilot who had made the decision to concentrate on building aircraft.

Like other pioneers of aviation, Pixton packed an enormous amount of experience into a very few years. At Monaco in April 1914 he became the first pilot to win an international event for Britain in a British aeroplane; although, of course, the engine Tommy Sopwith had brought back with his luggage by train from Paris was French. Rowed to shore after his victory, Pixton was congratulated in person by Jacques Schneider. At the grand dinner that evening at Monaco's Sporting Club, known to have one of the finest wine cellars in Europe, the wholly unpretentious 'Picky' Pixton turned down a celebratory glass of vintage champagne. 'Thanks very much,' he said, 'but mine's a small Bass.'

For the record, the one other pilot who completed the Schneider course in 1914 was Ernest Burri, with the steadfast FBA Type A – a flying boat made of marine plywood and resembling a winged fairy-tale canoe sporting a scorpion tail – at an average speed of a shade over 51 mph. The FBA might have been slow, yet its qualities were recognized by the French, British and Russian militaries. The Royal Navy bought 40 examples.

The Tabloid, though, offered the military something else: the basis of fast and agile reconnaissance and, ultimately, fighter planes. It was also the making of Tommy Sopwith, whose later companies – H. G. Hawker Engineering, Hawker Aircraft and Hawker Siddeley – were, especially under the design direction of Sydney Camm, to design and manufacture some of the very best and most innovative fighters and interceptors of the twentieth century, including the Fury, Hurricane, Tempest, Sea Fury, Hunter and the VTOL (vertical take-off and landing) P.1127, precursor of the Harrier jump jet. When Hawker Siddeley was nationalized in 1977, Sopwith, by then in his late eighties, carried on as consultant.

Sir Thomas Sopwith was to come a very long way indeed from the 10-year-old boy who accidentally killed his father in a gun accident on the Isle of Lismore in 1898; the former ice hockey champion who, while teaching himself to fly at Brooklands in a Howard Wright Avis monoplane, crashed on his first attempt at taking off; and the 24-year-old who, in 1912, set up an aircraft factory with Harry Hawker and Fred Sigrist in a former roller-skating rink in Kingston upon Thames. When, nearly 85 years later, I sat and talked with Sopwith at his Hampshire home – he lived to be 101 – he told me, with the sky in his eyes and a playful smile, that everything he did from the Tabloid onwards had been a matter of pure luck. As if. *Pure Luck*, though, was to be the title of his authorized biography.

It must have been very hard, and seemed much more than bad luck, for those taking part in the 1914 Schneider contest to understand the speed with which Europe erupted into apocalyptic war within three months of that champagne and small Bass dinner in Monte Carlo. On 8 October 1914, a pair of RNAS Sopwith Tabloids flown by Commander Spenser Grey and Flight Lieutenant Reginald Marix took off from besieged Antwerp on a raid on Germany. In heavy mist, Grey dropped two bombs on Cologne's central railway station, while Marix dive-bombed the Zeppelin shed at Düsseldorf in the teeth of enemy machine-gun and rifle fire, successfully destroying the LZ-25 airship which had been used to bomb Antwerp. Damage to his Tabloid caused Marix to land some 20 miles from Antwerp, which he reached by train and bicycle. Grey was there to greet him. They left by lorry with a group of Royal Marines, and none too soon. Antwerp fell the following day.

The Tabloid led on to – among other highly effective designs – the Sopwith Snipe, Strutter, Triplane, Dolphin, Pup and Camel fighters. Sopwith was to build more than 18,000 First World War military aircraft. While the Schneider contests were also to have a considerable and indeed vital impact on the development of fighter aircraft in the 1930s, his experience with the winning Tabloid in 1914 first focused the minds of Tommy Sopwith and his team on the development of aircraft for the imminent fight against Germany, Austria, Turkey and Bulgaria.

During the ensuing four years of conflict, aircraft design and engineering developed at an increasingly furious pace. Lightweight monoplanes gave way to sturdy biplanes and even triplanes. Power and speed rose as if exponentially, driven by increasingly reliable aero-engines. Where pilots shot at one another with pistols and rifles in the earliest dogfights, by mid-war they swooped down on or turned tightly towards enemy aircraft, machine guns blazing through the spinning propellers of their fighters.

Whether fervent patriots, licensed killers or bloody-minded aerial conscripts, by November 1918 it might have been thought that young men had flown quite enough for anyone's good. Who, in the light – and the mind-splintering darkness – of the First World War could even begin to think of reviving competitive air events within months of the Armistice?

On 11 November 1918, the fledgling RAF numbered 27,333 officers, more than half of whom were pilots, and 263,842 other ranks. Its 133 squadrons were equipped with 3,300 front-line machines. And, yet, as Harry Harper observed in *The Aeroplane in War* (1941), 'Having... given ourselves air power, we now proceeded to strip ourselves of it.' In next to no time, these figures were reduced to 3,280 officers, 25,000 other ranks, 33 squadrons and 500 aeroplanes.

Flight, though, had an ever-stronger hold on young people and the public imagination. It was aircraft that had risen above the mud and barbed-wire carnage of the trenches; aeroplanes that promised a somehow cleaner form of warfare. And there were many pilots in November 1918 who, despite all they had experienced during combat, still revelled in the sheer exultation of flight. Those who read poetry – and quite a few did – would have understood these lines from 'An Irish Airman foresees his Death', written in 1918 by W. B. Yeats:

Nor law, nor duty bade me fight,
Nor public men, nor cheering crowds,
A lonely impulse of delight
Drove to this tumult in the clouds

Held on 10 September 1919, the first post-war Schneider contest, however, proved to be what pretty much everyone involved said it was at the time: a fiasco. A shambles. A shower. Given just four months' notice ahead of the event, teams from Belgium, Spain and the United States pulled out. And, when the big day came, there was little for either crowd or competitors to see. When not cloaked in fog, Bournemouth Pier, Hengistbury Head, and Swanage and Studland bays were wreathed in sea mist – as were HMS *Barham* and HMS *Malaya*, a brace of great grey Royal Navy dreadnoughts anchored in Swanage Bay.

Communication, let alone flying, was tricky: the British organizing committee was huddled on board *Ombra*, a remote motor yacht in the Solent belonging to the Royal Aero Club; the starting area was situated on the shallow beach at Bournemouth, with no facilities laid on for either the French or the Italian teams, who were surrounded by sightseers; and the aircraft had to be prepared and serviced in sheds at East Cowes on the Isle of Wight. Even then, this was only possible because of the remarkable generosity of Sam Saunders, maker of S. E. Saunders flying boats and rescue launches. Saunders happily helped all teams, providing repairs, technical backup, food, drink and even gangplanks at Bournemouth Beach.

Public catering at Bournemouth was inadequate – although, well out of sight, members of the Royal Aero Club tucked in to a splendid lunch on board *Ombra* – and by mid-afternoon the crowd was not in the best of moods. Even so, while waiting for the event to start, some plucky bystanders took foggy jaunts around the bays on pleasure boats as others went bathing. Aircraft making their way to and from Cowes and Bournemouth Beach had to negotiate their way between swimmers and steamers. In a letter to *Flight* magazine, Squadron Leader James Bird observed, 'Of organisation, as we know it, there was, as must have been seen, absolutely nil.'

There were seven entrants to the competition: three French, three British and one Italian. Harry Hawker was to fly the blue and white Sopwith Schneider. This was an updated and uprated 170-mph version of the Tabloid – which, of course, had won the 1914 Schneider contest with Howard Pixton at the controls. Hawker had been in Australia at the time, demonstrating the lively biplane.

In its post-war guise, the Tabloid was powered by a 450-hp Cosmos Jupiter nine-cylinder radial engine. This had been designed by Roy Fedden and Leonard Butler for Brazil Straker, a London firm taken over by Cosmos Engineering during the war. While the increase in power over the aero-engines of 1914 was marked, improvements in materials, machining and general engineering refinement were very significant indeed. With four valves per cylinder, as with the most advanced contemporary racing cars, three carburettors and the use of aluminium as well as steel, the Jupiter was not just powerful but also very reliable.

Although Cosmos went bankrupt and was taken over by Bristol in 1920, the Jupiter went from strength to strength. Many thousands were manufactured in Britain and under licence in 14 countries – including France, which had taken the lead in aero-engine design in the first decade of powered flight. The Jupiter would be the engine of choice for the RAF's Bristol Bulldog fighter of 1927, Imperial Airways' dependable Handley Page H.P.42 airliner from 1930, and – a dozen of them working in tandem – Claude Dornier's hugely ambitious Do X flying boat, first flown in 1929.

Sopwith's 30-year-old Australian-born test pilot Harry Hawker knew the Tabloid inside out. He had been involved in its design with Herbert Smith and George Carter, and had flown it extensively. The son of a blacksmith from Moorabbin, Victoria, Hawker started work when he was just 11 years old helping to build engines for Hall and Warden in Melbourne. A mechanic and a chauffeur, in 1910 he witnessed the first flight by a powered aircraft in Australia, and made his way to England to be a part of the nascent aviation industry.

After brief spells with the engineering workshops of Commer and the London branches of Mercedes and Austro-Daimler, Hawker was taken on by Tommy Sopwith. He flew solo after just three hours, proved that it was possible to recover from a spin, and quickly became one of the best and most daring of all pioneering pilots. With the fastest aircraft entered in the 1919 Schneider contest and one of the world's top pilots, where could Sopwith go wrong?

Hawker would be flying with – and against – his British teammate Lieutenant Colonel Vincent Nicholl, whose white and blue Fairey IIIA was an altogether bigger machine. Its significance was twofold: its engine, the 450-hp Napier Lion; and its future life as a reconnaissance aircraft with the Royal Navy.

First flown in 1917, 964 Fairey IIIs of various marks were built. They served in front-line duties until at least 1935 and were still serving in subsidiary roles as late as 1941, when Fairey Swordfish biplane torpedo bombers of 825 Naval Air Squadron, flying from the decks of HMS *Ark Royal*, played a key role in the sinking of the formidable German battleship *Bismarck*.

Fairey specialized in seaplanes. Established in 1915 in Hayes, Middlesex, by Charles Fairey and the Belgian engineer Ernest Tips, its Campania patrol seaplane was the very first designed to fly from an aircraft carrier. The ship in question was HMS *Campania*, the former Cunard liner that had once held the Blue Riband for the fastest sea crossing of the Atlantic. While not as fast as the Sopwith, the Fairey was expected to last the Schneider course without difficulty. Its engine, the Napier Lion, was to become legendary in racing circles on land, sea and air.

The Lion was a very different type of engine to the Sopwith's Jupiter. Designed by Arthur Rowledge, it was a water-cooled 24-litre W12 comprising three banks of four cylinders sharing a common crankshaft with roller bearings. With four valves per cylinder and twin overhead camshafts, the Lion had a notably high power-to-weight ratio; and with its short crankshaft it could rev more freely than inline engines or those with cylinders arranged in a V formation. Long crankshafts could be distorted and otherwise damaged when subject to sudden bursts, as they were in combat and in races. Another advantage of engines with short crankshafts was that, because they were compact, they were marginally less vulnerable to attacks by enemy aircraft.

Napier's pedigree was impeccable. The company dated back to 1808, when David Napier, a blacksmith's son, came to

For the 1919 contest the French put up a pair of 340-hp Nieuport seaplanes developed from wartime variants and piloted by Lieutenant Jean Casale, a renowned Corsican fighter pilot, and Henri Mallard. Choosing to fly to Bournemouth, both suffered mishaps along the way. Casale hit a buoy while seeking shelter on the Medina estuary as he flew low over the Isle of Wight in poor weather. Sam Saunders rebuilt Casale's Nieuport – new wings, new undercarriage, new tail, and repairs to its fuselage – and the French factory sent a new engine and floats. It was ready for action within 48 hours. Meanwhile Mallard had ditched in the Channel on the way over from France. He clung to the wreckage of his Nieuport for 24 hours before help arrived.

The third French entry was the SPAD-Herbemont, a late-wartime model modified for competitive events by its designer André Herbemont. Its pilot was Joseph Sadi-Lecointe; he chose to travel to Bournemouth by boat and train. An experienced test pilot, Sadi-Lecointe went on to win the Gordon Bennett Trophy for France the following year. A military pilot in the 1920s, as he had been during the 1914–18 war, in 1936 he was appointed Inspector General of Aviation by the French Air Ministry and was the Inspector of Flying Schools when war broke out with Germany in 1939. A member of the French Resistance, Sadi-Lecointe was to be arrested and severely tortured by the Gestapo. He died shortly after his release from interrogation, in July 1944.

The water-cooled Hispano-Suiza V8 of 300–340 hp, developed from his automobile engines by the Swiss engineer Marc Birkigt, powered all three French machines. This highly respected engine had been fitted to huge numbers of Allied aircraft. Developed throughout the First World War, total production ran to 49,400 units across Spanish, French, British, American and Italian factories.

Here, then, at Bournemouth on 10 September 1919, were a number of fine, powerful and well-engineered French and British aircraft with well-qualified pilots, ready to push the Schneider into new realms of speed and endurance. But because of the fog, poor communication and general mismanagement, the 2.30 p.m. start was pushed back in stages to late teatime. In breaks in what was proving to be very uncertain weather, Supermarine offered joyrides on its flying boats to more intrepid spectators.

Finally, at 4.50 p.m., Nicholl was first away in the Fairey, followed by Squadron Leader Hobbs in the Supermarine and then Harry Hawker's Sopwith. Visibility was close to zero. Hawker and Nicholl gave up on their first lap. After narrowly avoiding a collision with Nicholl, Hobbs upended the dark blue Sea Lion. It began filling with water. Hobbs managed to return to Bournemouth and, undeterred, had the Supermarine bailed out in preparation for a fresh start. He managed to do so, but hit an unidentified object floating in the water, holed the hull and began to sink. Hobbs, who had been thrown from the aircraft, was rescued by a launch while the wreck of his aircraft was tied to Boscombe Pier awaiting recovery at low tide.

The French decided not to take their chances, and withdrew. This left one competitor in the running – Sergeant Guido Janello, flying the slowest of the entrants, a rather pretty and aerodynamic 140-mph Savoia S.13 flying boat. This was a light, stable and aerobatic biplane, fitted with a sweet-running 250-hp inline, water-cooled, six-cylinder, 16.6-litre Isotta Fraschini engine.

The red and white S.13 was the work of Raffaele Conflenti, chosen as chief designer of Savoia by Laurent-Dominique Santoni, a Swiss-born entrepreneur who had built Deperdussin aeroplanes in Britain. Savoia itself had begun life in August 1915 as Società Idrovolanti Alta Italia (SIAI) to manufacture FBA machines under licence for the Italian military. Merged later that year with the Società Anonima Costruzioni Aeronautiche, the company, based at Sant'Anna on the shores of Lake Maggiore, was to make some of the most effective and exquisite of all flying boats.

In Bournemouth and despite the weather, Janello soldiered on gamely, although his lap times were beginning to seem rather too quick for the speed of his machine. Misjudging course markers – perhaps understandably so, given the weather – Janello had turned too soon on what appeared to be 11 of his laps. The Swanage marker boat said it had not once caught sight of the Italian aircraft.

When Janello landed, Lorenzo Santoni, president of SIAI, set out on a motorboat to encourage the pilot to fly another lap, but as he tried his fuel ran out. By now, it was all but dark. Janello needed to be rescued, but the rescue launches appeared to have called it a day. The crew of the salubrious *Ombra* were too busy in their dash to reach Cowes before darkness and fog ensnared them to help. Sam Saunders sent out a fast boat from East Cowes, towed the stricken Savoia to Bournemouth, and overtook the *Ombra* on his way back to the Isle of Wight.

Janello was disqualified, but after negative press coverage, the Royal Aero Club met on 22 September and decided that the Italian pilot had won after all. A month later, a meeting of the FAI in Brussels turned this decision on its head. To declare Janello the winner was unfair on the other pilots who had tried to fly the correct course. It was, though, agreed that the Royal Aero Club of Italy should organize the 1920 event.

Venice was the venue in 1920. With a course running the length of the Lido and out into the Adriatic, the contest would surely be fast – and glamorous to boot. The Lido itself had become one of the chicest of all European resorts, a playground for the international elite and a place of long sandy beaches and safe bathing for day-trippers from Venice. In 1846, the city became connected to the mainland via a railway bridge, and the number of visitors had risen considerably since then. More than this, Venice had begun to modernize, with industrial concerns around its venerable hem.

In 1910, from the top of the Renaissance clock tower in St Mark's Square, Filippo Tommaso Marinetti – poet, editor and founder of the Futurist movement – had thrown handbills at the crowds and pigeons below. 'We repudiate the old Venice', he declared:

We want to cure and heal this putrefying city, this magnificent sore from the past... Let us hasten to fill in its little reeking canals with the ruins from its leprous and crumbling palaces. Let us burn the gondolas, rocking chairs for cretins, and raise to the heavens the imposing geometry of metal bridges and factories plumed with smoke, to abolish the cascading curves of the old architecture.

It was time for old Italian cities and the weight of age-old Italian culture to go.

For Marinetti, one of the best ways to do this was by aerial bombardment. The aeroplane heralded a new form of warfare, cleansing a fetid and unhygienic past. The aeroplane offered something else attractive to the Futurists, too: unmitigated speed. In February 1909, the Paris newspaper *Le Figaro* had published the *Manifesto of Futurism* on its front page. Promising to free Italy 'from her innumerable museums which cover her like countless cemeteries', Marinetti wrote:

> We intend to sing the love of danger, the habit of energy and fearlessness... We affirm that the world's magnificence has been enriched by a new beauty: the beauty of speed. A racing car whose hood is adorned with great pipes, like serpents of explosive breath – a roaring car that seems to ride on grapeshot is more beautiful than the Victory of Samothrace. We will glorify war – the world's only hygiene – militarism, patriotism, the destructive gesture of freedom-bringers, beautiful ideas worth dying for, and scorn for woman.

'Scorn for woman'? For Marinetti, Futurism was a masculine tonic to an effeminate country. Very soon, Futurism would march arm in arm and at a pace with Italian Fascism.

Self-declared Futurist artists attempted to capture the sensation of speed on canvas, as Giacomo Balla did with paintings like his truly dynamic abstraction *Speeding Automobile* (1912). In 1928, painter Tullio Crali learned to fly. Thrilled, he sought out Marinetti, and the following year the *aeropittura* ('aeropainting') movement was announced in the manifesto *Perspectives of Flight*: 'The changing perspectives of flight constitute an absolutely new reality that has nothing in common with the reality traditionally constituted by a terrestrial perspective... Painting from this new reality requires a profound contempt for detail and a need to synthesise and transfigure everything.' Crali's most dramatic work was unveiled, perhaps significantly, in 1939. Named *Nose Dive on the City*, the painting depicts a pilot's vertiginous view of a city as he powers down into it, ready to release the bombs that will destroy what he sees.

And yet, few of those involved in the 1920 event would have made the connection between Futurism, the speed and fury of the Schneider contest aircraft in flight, and destructive warfare, not least because the latest Schneider rules were loaded more heavily than before in favour of the practicalities of civil aviation. Competing aircraft would have to carry a 300-kg load of ballast, simulating a commercial payload. This new rule favoured flying boats like those built by the Italian companies SIAI and Macchi. Unsurprisingly, the countries whose teams had been fielding largely lightweight seaplanes based on fighters felt resistant to the change, so much so that none entered the 1920 competition.

In any case, Venice and its Lido seemed a long way away geographically to potential British and American contestants. Faced with draconian taxation on the profits it had made from the production of so many thousands of warplanes, Sopwith had gone into liquidation and was yet to be reborn as Hawker. At Supermarine, Reginald Mitchell was thinking perhaps two years ahead, to a much faster flying boat. The British government was unclear on the future of military aviation. Enthusiasm for the event dropped away until Italy was left to go it alone. Lieutenant Luigi Bologna of the Italian Navy flew the course in a bright red Savoia S.12 fitted with a 550-hp V12 Ansaldo 4E engine, at an average speed of 107.22 mph.

A week after the Schneider competition in Venice, Joseph Sadi-Lecointe won the Gordon Bennett in perpetuity for France, flying a Nieuport landplane at an average speed of 168.5 mph. What this meant, in effect, was that the only international speed championship was the Schneider Cup contest. The 300-kg ballast rule was repealed and a new rule introduced to test competing aircraft for watertightness. While things seemed set for an exciting competition, the 1921 event proved to be yet another damp squib. Any critic examining the state of the Schneider Trophy at this time could be excused if they found the whole enterprise something of an embarrassment, and perhaps even pointless. Just look at Luigi Bologna's winning Savoia S.12 of 1920. The Italian Navy showed no interest in it and no orders were taken.

While there were plenty of potential Italian entries, the 1921 event flown at the Lido on 7 August 1921 attracted just a solitary foreign competitor. This was Sadi-Lecointe, with a specially built and state-subsidized Nieuport 29 equipped with a 300-hp Hispano-Suiza V8. But the aircraft was damaged when an attempt was made to refit the floats to the fuselage on arrival at Venice, and the Nieuport was withdrawn. This left the Italians on their own again. Giovanni de Briganti took first place at 117.9 mph with a green and silver, 250-hp Isotta Fraschini–powered Macchi M.7bis, a lightened version of the M.7 – an attractive single-seat fighter flying boat with slightly swept-back wings, designed by Alessandro Tonini.

His teammate Piero Corgnolino, in another M.7bis, had been lapping faster than de Briganti, but had run out of fuel on lap 16 of 20. Arturo Zanetti's one-off Macchi M.19 was out of the contest when its 650-hp Fiat V12 caught fire. A fractured crankshaft caused either by over-revving or a manufacturing fault had ruptured a fuel line. By default, the Italians had won the Schneider contest a second time. If they were to win in 1922, they would keep the trophy – and that, in a very disappointing manner, would be that.

The winning M.7, however, had done itself proud. This was not in terms of speed – Schneider aircraft were by this time slow compared to the feats of contemporary landplanes – but in that of commercial success. Fitted with folding wings, the svelte little seaplane fighter served, along with its younger and bigger M.18 sibling, with the Italian Navy's *Giuseppe Miraglia*, and equipped six Italian naval squadrons along with the naval air forces of Argentina, Brazil, Paraguay and Sweden. It was last in service as a civil rescue trainer in 1940.

The last M.7 can be seen today in the Flygvapenmuseum at the Malmen Airbase in Malmslätt, Sweden. The team that restored the Macchi, built at the end of the First World War, discovered a contemporary inscription inside the aircraft's cockpit. It reads '*Pace e non più Guerra*' ('Peace and no more War').

The 1922 contest was held in Naples in mid-August, with aircraft flying 13 laps of 28.5 kilometres around the bay of that beautiful and chaotic city against a backdrop of Mount Vesuvius and, more explosively, Mussolini's threat of a Fascist march on Rome. The organization this year was in the more than capable hands of aviation enthusiast Italo Balbo.

August witnessed nationwide strikes and savage fights between Communists and Fascists in Ancona, Genoa and Milan. Many thought a civil war was inevitable. In this political turmoil, the Schneider Trophy lost its innocence. The Italian and French teams were state-sponsored now that Italy could see its hands clasping the cup, and France was determined to stop them doing so. And Britain? The resistance to Italy would be in private hands, with Supermarine's Reginald Mitchell–designed Sea Lion II sponsored by Napier, Shell Petroleum, the General Steam Navigation Company and Wakefield Oil.

Intriguingly, 1922 was the year that saw the British Empire at its zenith. It ruled a quarter of the world in terms of both land mass and population. But it had got to this extraordinary position more through trade than military ambition. For Great Britain, free trade and free enterprise were the rules of the imperial game. Britain, though, was a country and an empire that wanted both freedom and a degree of order. It was all but wholly antithetical to the dictates of rising Italian Fascism – and, of course, to the French and German love of codified rules and laws. And while Mussolini did march on Rome to seize power that October, the British media and public were far more interested in Howard Carter's exploration of Tutankhamun's wondrous tomb in the Valley of the Kings.

Britain sent a single Supermarine Sea Lion II flying boat to Naples. The French entered a pair of CAMS (Chantiers Aéro-Maritimes de la Seine) 36 military flying boats, and the Italians a Savoia S.50 seaplane, a Savoia S.51 flying boat, and a Macchi M.17 and a Macchi M.7bis flying boat. The French team pulled out after one of the CAMS machines capsized during trials. Meanwhile, Henri Biard, Supermarine's chief test pilot – Anglo-French, he called himself both Henry and Henri – flew his Sea Lion II slowly and with a deliberate insouciance, as if he had little chance of competing against his Italian rivals.

Despite its slightly cumbersome lines, the Supermarine aircraft could be looped and rolled. Biard was to be glad of Mitchell's burgeoning sorcery when he flew over Vesuvius on a test flight and was lifted high on a thermal. The Sea Lion II took this comfortably in its stride. It was a very forgiving aircraft.

Biard himself was an assured long-distance pilot. Born in Godalming, Surrey, to a French father who taught at Charterhouse School and an English mother, at the outbreak of the First World War he was staying at his paternal grand-father's farm in northern France. Here he witnessed streams of refugees struggling west, pursued by German cavalry who set fire to the farm. Back in England, he flew anti-submarine patrols during the war in a Wright seaplane and, soon after the Armistice, piloted British Marine Air Navigation's pioneering cross-Channel flights from Woolston to Le Havre. Stormy weather meant that such flights were as prolonged as they must have been unsettling. One of Biard's cross-Channel trips took five hours.

The day of the race was very hot. Biard, flying in shirtsleeves and flannels, gunned the Sea Lion II, climbing up and over the Italians who, bunching in the turns, tried to block his progress. The S.51s should have been faster, but Biard crossed the finishing line in 1 hour, 34 minutes and 51.6 seconds, at an average speed of 145.7 mph – two minutes ahead of Alessandro Passaleva's S.51, with Arturo Zanetti (Macchi M.17) and Piero Corgnolino (Macchi M.7bis) not so very far behind. Italy had not won the Schneider Trophy after all. And yet, on 28 December that year, 27-year-old Passaleva recorded a new world record for seaplanes, taking an S.51 to 174.08 mph.

By the skin of its mechanical teeth, a technically much slower Supermarine flying boat had won the 1922 contest. The Schneider Trophy was open to all comers. And, in 1923, the Yanks came.

TWO

The Yanks are Coming:
1923–26

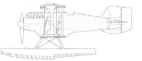

Over there, over there
Send the word, send the word over there
That the Yanks are coming, the Yanks are coming
The drums rum-tumming everywhere

George M. Cohan, 'Over There'

When the American Schneider competition pilots arrived at East Cowes in August 1923, a month ahead of that year's Schneider contest, one of the first things anyone noticed about them was their height. All four US Navy lieutenants from the Anacostia Naval Station, Port Washington, were six feet tall. Fit, well-nourished and smartly turned out in crisp uniforms, they had arrived in style on board the United States Lines flagship, the 60,000-ton liner SS *Leviathan*.

This was the era of Prohibition, so *Leviathan*'s brand-new Art Deco bar was dry, although in most every other way this mighty ship – the world's biggest and fastest, boasted the Americans, even though Cunard's RMS *Mauretania* held the official east- and westbound Blue Ribands for the fastest transatlantic crossings – was as opulent as any voyager could expect.

At Cowes, the Americans offered lavish hospitality and warm entertainment – complete with a ritzy saxophone band – on board USS *Pittsburgh*, a four-funnel armoured Pennsylvania-class cruiser launched in 1903 and the flagship of United States Naval Forces Europe. Aviators partying on *Pittsburgh* would have known, or would have been told by her crew, that it was on her afterdeck 12 years ago that Eugene Ely made the first successful landing of an aircraft on a ship.

And then there were the American aeroplanes: a pair of Curtiss CR-3s and a Navy Wright NW-2, with a 350-hp Naval Aircraft Factory TR-3A seaplane in reserve. These purposeful and determinedly modern Curtiss and Wright seaplanes made their rivals seem old-fashioned.

The Americans practised day in, day out. They were every bit as professional as the British and other rival teams had, up to this point, seemed amateur. And yet, when the Armistice was signed in November 1918, there had been just 200 US-built aircraft at the front, all of them British designs manufactured under licence. In between the Armistice and the 1923 Schneider contest, however, there had been a revolution in the design of and the demand for fast military aircraft in the US. This was triggered by the announcement of the Pulitzer Speed Classic Trophy, sponsored by the owners of the *New York World*. The first race – held at Roosevelt Field, New York, on 25 November 1920 – was won by US Army captain Corliss Champion Moseley with a 638-hp Verville-Packard R-1 biplane, at 156.5 mph.

Moseley's one-off racer had been commissioned by the US Army Air Service and designed by Alfred Verville, a civilian engineer working with the military. During the war, Verville had supervised the production of US-built British de Havilland DH.4 light bombers. His Pulitzer racer, a very different kind of aircraft, owed its existence to Brigadier General William 'Billy' Mitchell, Assistant Chief of the Army Air Service, a fearless pilot and famous wartime leader who by 1918 was in command of all US air combat units in France.

Mitchell believed the Great War might be the first of a series of global conflicts. 'If a nation ambitious for universal conquest', he said, 'gets off to a "flying start" in a war of the future, it may be able to control the whole world more easily than a nation has controlled a continent in the past.' The United States, he believed, needed an independent and dynamic air force. And what better to stimulate and nurture the best in contemporary military aviation than competition?

A healthy rivalry developed between Mitchell, after whom the Second World War North American B-25 Mitchell bomber of *Catch-22* fame was to be named, and Rear Admiral William Moffett, in charge of the newly founded Bureau of Aeronautics. Early in 1921, the US Navy commissioned a pair of 'pursuit-type' biplanes from the Curtiss Aeroplane and Motor Company of Garden City, Long Island. With its strong wooden monocoque fuselage – made in two halves and joined lengthwise like an Airfix kit – powerful, water-cooled Curtiss CD-12 V12 engine designed by Arthur Nutt, and wing radiators to assist cooling, the CR-1 was a potent machine. Flown by Curtiss chief test pilot Bert Acosta, one of the pair, A-6081, won the second Pulitzer Speed Classic contest at an average of 176.75 mph.

Not to be outdone, Mitchell ordered two improved Curtiss CR-2 racers, designated R-6, to compete in the 1922 Pulitzer event. These boasted Arthur Nutt's latest 18.8-litre aluminium block V12, the D-12 – a hugely influential engine in the making. Weighing 671 lbs (dry), it produced 430 hp at 2,250 rpm. In other words, it produced a powerful punch for its weight. Mitchell's pilots, first and second in the 1922 contest, beat the navy team who came third and fourth flying Curtiss CR-2s.

It was the US Navy, though, that sailed its pilots and planes to East Cowes in August 1923. They had three machines newly fitted with floats: their two original 1921 CR-1 racers upgraded to CR-3 specifications, and the NW-2, a mighty biplane powered by the daunting Wright T-3 ('T' for Tornado) 31.9-litre water-cooled V12. Wright was aiming for 700 hp with the Tornado series, but the 1,000-lb T-3 offered 575 hp, its power-to-weight ratio considerably inferior to Nutt's Curtiss D-12.

All up, with its welded steel tube fuselage, the NW-2 tipped the balance at 4,447 lbs. At the other end of the scale, the CR-3 weighed in at 2,746 lbs. Its designer Rex Beisel – the son of a coal miner, he had driven mules and washed coals at mines before winning a place to study engineering at Washington University – went on to shape the Vought F4U Corsair. This fast, powerful and supremely effective long-distance Second World War fighter weighed about twice as much as a late-model RAF Spitfire. A heavyweight, perhaps, but it remains – along with the Spitfire, of course – one of the greatest of all military aircraft.

1. Portrait of a pre-Schneider Trophy competition pilot. This is nattily dressed Claude Grahame-White at the helm of his wholly exposed French-built Farman III biplane, complete with puppet mascot tied to a timber strut. Immediately after learning to fly, Grahame-White competed in the 1910 *Daily Mail* challenge to fly from London to Manchester within 24 hours. He was never so cold again.

2. Twenty-five-year-old Maurice Prévost at Monaco in April 1913 with the Deperdussin monoplane that took him took him to victory in the first Schneider Trophy contest. Designed by Louis Béchereau, the lithe Deperdussin was a graceful and fast machine for its day, its slim wings braced – and warped for turning – with a fine cat's cradle of wires.

3. Howard Pixton (*centre*) in conversation with Jacques Schneider after his victory in the 1914 contest. Pixton was the first British pilot to fly a British aircraft in an international competition and win, although the engine of his Sopwith Tabloid – seen on the right – was French. The Tabloid led on to successful fighters like the Sopwith Pup and Camel.

4. The organisation of the 1919 contest held at Bournemouth left much to be desired. Spectators got in the way of flight preparations and then fog descended making flight all but impossible. Harry Hawker managed just one lap before giving up, although he and his puissant blue-and-white 450hp, 170mph Sopwith Schneider were the favourites to win. The event was a washout.

5. Henri Biard, in waders, looks on as his Supermarine Sea Lion III – with sea lion faces on its nose and floats – is checked over before competing in the 1923 Trophy. Supermarine had been a reluctant entrant, finally tweaking the Sea Lion II to race against the formidable American Curtiss machines that took first and second places at Cowes.

6. US Army Lieutenant James 'Jimmy' Doolittle, his flying jacket soaked with sea spray, at Chesapeake Bay with his Curtiss R3C-2 having just taken first place in the 1925 contest. Doolittle's average speed had been way higher than his British, Italian and fellow American pilots. Beaten by Italy the following year, the US Army and Navy withdrew from the Schneider contests.

7. The most adventurous and striking machine to compete in 1925, with its unbraced wings and floats, was Reginald Mitchell's Supermarine S.4. Formidably fast on test in England, its Schneider pilot, Henri Biard, found it tricky to see out of and hard to control. Wing flutter, though, was one cause of his smashing into Chesapeake Bay during trials, destroying the plane.

8. For the 1927 Venice Lido contest, Mitchell produced the S.5, seen here undergoing an engine test at Cowes soon after completion. The pilot sat much further forward than in the S.4 with an improved view. The wings and floats were braced. With this compact, sleek and reliable machine, Flight Lieutenants Sidney Webster and Oswald Worsley took first and second places.

9. Impeccably dressed, as always, Macchi's chief designer Mario Castoldi leads a procession of engineers and mechanics attending one of the Italian engineer's blood-red M.67 monoplanes at Calshot. Pilots of both machines, powered by mighty Isotta Fraschini W-12 inline engines, were forced to retire from the 1929 race itself, one choked by fumes, the other scalded after a water pipe burst.

10. Mouths agape, the impeccably turned out Italian M.67 pilots, Lieutenants Remo Cadringher and Giovanni Monti, appear to be suitably impressed by the sheer beauty of *Golden Arrow*, one of Harry Folland's two pencil-thin Gloster Napier VI aircraft built for the 1929 contest. Teething problems with their Napier Lion VIID engines, however, led to both machines being scratched from the race.

11. Alessandro Marchetti's twin-engine Savoia Marchetti S.65 was unprepared to compete at Calshot in 1929, yet one of these intriguing machines was shipped to the Solent where it was wheeled out of the sheds for the press and newsreels. Its test pilot, Tomasso dal Molin, who came second at Calshot in a Macchi M.52R, was killed in 1930 flying the S.65.

12. The youngest member of the 1929 British Schneider team was most probably fifteen-year-old mechanic Raymond Lane, posing in the cockpit of a Gloster Napier VI. This charming image is a reminder of how flight was very much a young person's game and of how young school leavers could find apprenticeships in dynamic manufacturing concerns promising high levels of achievement.

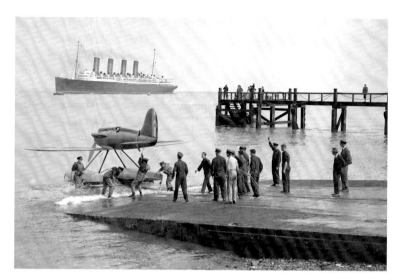

13. Supermarine S.6 N248 launched on the Solent at Cowes in August 1929 with a backdrop of the record-breaking Cunard liner RMS *Mauretania*. The S.6 was raced by Flight Lieutenant Dick Atcherley who was disqualified after turning inside a pylon. His goggles were splattered with oil on take off and, against the slipstream, he was unable to don a spare pair.

14. Framed by the wing, nose, propeller, struts, bracing and floats of his 1931 Supermarine S.6B, Reginald Mitchell discusses some points about the aircraft at Calshot with Flight Lieutenant (later Air Vice Marshall) Francis Long, adjutant to the RAF's High Speed Flight. In the event, Flight Lieutenant John Boothman flew the Solent circuit alone. Truly, the impressive S.6B had no competition.

15. Ten days ahead of winning the Schneider Trophy, members of the RAF High Speed Flight line up for the camera at Calshot. From left to right, Flight Lieutenant George Stainforth, Flight Lieutenant John Boothman, Squadron Leader Augustus Orlebar, Flight Lieutenant Francis Long and Flying Officer Leonard Snaith. Stainforth was killed in action over the Gulf of Suez in September 1942.

16. The convergence of nationalist politics and record-breaking flight. The Italian Duce, Benito Mussolini, decorates Lieutenant Francesco Agello at a ceremony in Rome in 1935. In October 1934, Agello flew a Mario Castoldi-designed MC.72 at 440mph, an absolute world air speed record. The complex MC.72 was to have competed in the 1931 Schneider contest, but was held back by technical problems.

Both 1923 US Schneider competitor types were clearly very fast aircraft, as anyone observing the Yanks roaring over the Solent could tell. The Curtiss machines flew confidently at 180 mph, the Wright at a full-blown 200 mph. Their pilots, meanwhile, had something of an idea of the competition they should expect to meet on 28 September. In December 1921, Brigadier General Mitchell had sailed to Europe on a fact-finding mission with his aide, Lieutenant Clayton Bissell, and Alfred Verville. They visited factories and airfields in England, France, Germany, Holland and Italy, and wrote up their findings in a government report. The London *Times* might sniff, as it did in 1923, 'British habits do not support the idea of entering a team organised by the State for a sporting event', but the Americans were clearly well prepared; and if the Schneider Trophy was a sporting event, it was also an opportunity to pursue and test designs for the next generation of military aircraft, and in particular land- and sea-based fighters.

Not that everything went according to the US Navy's plan. As Lieutenant Frank Wead, the team's leader, scythed over the Solent at considerable speed, the three-bladed propeller of the NW-2 disintegrated and slashed the aircraft's floats apart. The Wright racer sank; Wead was rescued. He could have broken his neck.

Years later, in late April 1926, the *San Diego Union* reported:

Lieut. Frank Wead, one of the best known aviators in the naval service, was operated on for a fractured neck at the naval hospital... Wead sustained the injury which came near costing his life when he slipped and fell from the top of the stairway of his home in Coronado late Wednesday night. The aviator had just moved into the home and was unfamiliar with the staircase. Physicians, following the operation yesterday, said that Wead will recover but it is doubtful if he will be able to fly again. Wead's outstanding exploit since entering the naval flying corps was his flight against British pilots in the international seaplane races off the Isle of Wight in 1923...

Wead had heard his daughter crying and fell on his way to find her in the family's new home in San Diego County. His story is a reminder of how these young men who held near god-like status as they soared at unprecedented speeds through the heavens were in fact quite human. They might be expected to die in the air, but equally they might fall down a stair at home as Wead did, or tumble fatally from a roof while fixing an aerial, as the British wartime Sopwith Tabloid pilot Commander Spenser Grey did in the late 1930s.

The French had their fair share of accidents, too. The Société Latham of Caudebec-en-Caux on the Seine in Normandy had built a pair of twin-engine Latham L.1 flying boats for the contest. They were advanced in some ways, with Duralumin hulls and 830 hp on tap from push-pull configured Lorraine-Dietrich V12s, but with a top speed of 160 mph, they had little chance of beating the Americans. One of the pair flown from Normandy to the Isle of Wight in dismal weather by a pilot named Benoit made an emergency landing on a shingle beach at Littlehampton, and was damaged both by the impact and by the helping hands of local people. The L.1 was out of the race.

On test in France, the big, though not unduly heavy, C.1 high-wing monoplane built for the contest by the Société Aéronautique Blanchard at Les Coteaux de St-Cloud near Paris was, at 136 mph, disappointingly slow. A Captain Teste is said to have taken off for East Cowes, but, held up by bad weather in the English Channel, returned to base. A second C.1 fitted with a 540-hp Bristol Jupiter engine, instead of its sibling's 380-hp Gnome et Rhône nine-cylinder radial motor, was unready for the competition and was, in any event, written off in a collision soon afterwards.

In the event, the CAMS 36bis piloted by Lieutenant Georges Pelletier d'Oisy hit a steam yacht at anchor on the Solent before the contest and was written off, while Maurice Hurel, the company's chief test pilot, lost power on the second lap when the 380-hp Hispano-Suiza V12 of his CAMS 38 refused to play ball. The engine of the second Latham backfired as it started up and, as it did so, sheared its magneto drive. No pilot of a piston-engine plane would ever dare to take off without knowing the engine's magnetos – providing electrical power to the spark plugs – were working. The Latham was out of the race.

While Italy was, in theory, keen on the contest, the political situation after Mussolini's March on Rome meant that, for now at least, the Schneider Trophy would have to take a back seat. This left the British team to fly the five laps of 42.8 miles (68.9 kilometres) around the Solent as fast as technically and humanly possible. For them, there was no government funding. Supermarine entered its Sea Lion III. This was the Sea Lion II, winner of the 1922 contest, with improvements made by Mitchell to the streamlining of its hull, and with its Napier Lion engine uprated to 550 hp. Its pilot, as in the previous year, was Henri Biard. The only other British competitor was Reginald Kenworthy, chief test pilot for the Blackburn Aeroplane and Motor Company of Leeds, with the brand-new Blackburn Pellet.

At first sight, the Pellet looked promising. It was a rather beautifully streamlined wooden sesquiplane – a biplane with the lower wing shorter and thinner than the upper wing – fitted with a 525-hp Napier Lion mounted on top of the centre section of the wings. The pilot sat in a cockpit with a raked windscreen, his head resting on a streamlined faring. The nose of the Pellet looked ahead of its time – like that of a Hawker Hunter jet of the 1950s. But where Hunters could very nearly break the sound barrier in level flight, the elegant Pellet promised a maximum speed of just 122 mph.

Launched on the Humber in the first week of September, the Pellet was caught by strong cross-winds and promptly capsized. Packed off to Fairey's workshop on the River Hamble by Southampton Water and reassembled there, the Pellet took to the air for the first time two days before the Schneider contest. Kenworthy found the Blackburn nose-heavy; he needed all his strength to maintain level flight. And then the engine overheated. He landed near Calshot Spit and waited for a tender to tow him to S. E. Saunders at East Cowes. Overnight, the Pellet was fitted with an enlarged radiator and a three-bladed metal propeller in place of its broken twin-blade wooden airscrew.

The morning before the contest, Kenworthy opened the Pellet up along the River Medina. As he gathered speed, a pair of rowing boats threatened to cross his path. He applied a lot of rudder to avoid them. The Pellet porpoised, and tipped over. Trapped underwater for more than a minute, Kenworthy had passed out by the time Lord Montagu of Beaulieu came to the rescue in a motor launch with the pilot's wife on board. Artificial respiration got Kenworthy breathing again. The aircraft, dubbed the 'Plummet', was withdrawn from the contest. The following day, Biard would fly alone for Britain.

Was the result a foregone conclusion? The answer has to be a qualified 'yes'. Although any aero-engine of the time might overheat, or a pilot make a mistake, the Curtiss machines had the look and sound of winners.

Around they went from 11 a.m. onwards on 28 September, in fine weather above the Solent and a crowd estimated to be a quarter of a million strong – a pair of grey, yellow-finned and white-ruddered CR-3s, their pilots in collars, ties and smart flying jackets. Lieutenant David Rittenhouse came in first at 177.38 mph; Lieutenant Rutledge Irvine second at 173.46 mph. Henri Biard plugged away with the blue, white and silver Sea Lion III – a sea lion's face complete with whiskers painted on its nose – coming in third at 157.17 mph.

The Americans had revolutionized the Schneider contest. As for 1924, unless rival teams got a grip, the US team looked set to win again. Eight days after their victory at Cowes, the US Navy took the top two places in the 1923 Pulitzer Trophy at St Louis, flying a pair of improved CR-3 landplanes. The Curtiss R2C-1 was a smaller aircraft with its top wings flush with the fuselage. Lieutenant Alford Williams completed the course at 243.67 mph. His Curtiss was 35 times faster than the Wright brothers' *Flyer* that had taken to the air just 20 years earlier. By now, aeroplanes were very much faster than land-speed record cars or express trains. The strange cracking sound the Curtiss machines made as they roared overhead was caused by the tips of their metal propellers breaking the sound barrier.

The American advance was so forward that no other country could keep up. Planned for October at Baltimore, the 1924 Schneider contest was called off. This was a very generous move by the Americans, who could have entered, if they had wanted to do so, a single Curtiss aircraft. Unopposed, all it had to do was complete the circuit and so notch up a second Schneider win for the US.

Rival teams had a long way to go to catch up with the Americans – and, of course, Baltimore was a long way from Europe. The logistics of the event would have been extremely demanding. The French had nothing to offer. In Italy, Lieutenant General Alessandro Guidoni – Director in Chief of Aeronautical Engineering and Construction with the newly independent Italian Air Force, Regia Aeronautica – bought a pair of second-hand Curtiss D-12 engines for two possible Schneider competitors. These were a pair of flying boats, one by the newly formed Cantieri Aeronautici e Navali Triestini and the other by Piaggio, an engineering and shipbuilding company with no previous experience in aircraft design. The Piaggio failed to materialize, while the Triestini machine sank before it took off.

Although unable to compete in 1924, the Italians had not wasted their time. The Curtiss D-12s shipped from the States proved to be invaluable to Italian engine designers and makers.

As the Italian aeronautical attaché to Washington from 1920 to 1923, Guidoni, a much-liked military engineer, had been on particularly good terms with the Americans. An early seaplane pilot, he was to die in 1928 while testing a new type of parachute at Montecelio, just outside Rome.

At Supermarine, Reginald Mitchell had been working on the design of the Sea Urchin. A single-seat biplane flying boat, its engine, a 675-hp Rolls-Royce Condor V12, was to have hidden in the fuselage and driven a pusher propeller mounted on the upper wing by geared shafts. The transmission was a mechanical stumbling point and the Sea Urchin would not be ready to fly in 1924. It was to remain a 'what if?' project.

This left Henry Folland's Gloster II, a smoothly lined if chunky biplane equipped with a 585-hp Napier Lion and an estimated top speed of 225 mph. Folland had form. The son of a Cambridge stonemason, he rose from an automobile apprenticeship with Lanchester of Birmingham to become co-designer of the superb Royal Aircraft Factory S.E.5/S.E.5a fighter first flown in November 1916. He moved, eventually, to the Gloucestershire Aircraft Company, Cheltenham, in 1921 (the company was renamed Gloster five years later, as foreign buyers found 'Gloucester' hard to pronounce). The prototype Gloster II proved to be tail-heavy. When Captain Hubert Broad, de Havilland's chief test pilot who was on loan to Gloster, attempted to land on choppy water at Felixstowe five weeks before the planned 1924 Schneider competition, one of his aircraft's forward struts collapsed. The Gloster sank. Unharmed – and unhampered, as he said, by a seat belt – Captain Broad got a ducking. He was, though, to be in action in the 1925 Schneider contest, this time in the cockpit of a more fully resolved Gloster IIIA.

All eyes at Chesapeake Bay in October 1925 were on a radical new design. This was the strikingly clean-lined Supermarine S.4 monoplane designed by Reginald Mitchell, its cantilever wing free of struts, wires or any other form of bracing. No monoplane had won an important international race, or indeed any key race, since the Deperdussin in 1913. Fast on test at Calshot, on 13 September 1925 the beautiful S.4, piloted by Henri Biard, set a new world speed record for seaplanes of 226.75 mph. Mitchell had worked closely on the design of the S.4's wing with the Royal Aircraft Establishment (RAE), Farnborough, where it was tested to destruction. When the British team set sail for Baltimore on board the Atlantic Transport Line's SS *Minnewaska*, with the Supermarine S.4 and a pair of Gloster IIIAs on their way, their hopes ran understandably high.

The Supermarine team included a Mr Powell (erector), a Mr Pickett (engine mechanic), a Mr Broome (rigger) and a Mr Grimes (launchman). What did these working-class men from Hampshire make of travelling across the Atlantic in a deluxe liner? Perhaps they went steerage. Whatever the case, bad luck struck in the middle of the Atlantic. Biard broke a wrist playing deck tennis, but although he healed quickly, he went down with flu for the first time in his life. On arrival at Baltimore in foul weather, he holed up in the city's Southern Hotel, a 14-storey affair opened in 1918 and with a bathroom for every bedroom. Rain lashed down and strong winds whipped up across Chesapeake Bay – so strong that, two days before the contest, seven Glenn Martin SC-1 floatplanes out of the 17 waiting to perform at a naval air pageant were wrecked.

The wind had also blown down some of the team tents provided by the organizers. One of these was Supermarine's, damaging the S.4's tail. The management of the event was far from perfect, and the teams had expected more than makeshift tents. The venue, Bay Shore Park, was a generously provided for weekend leisure centre complete with a funfair, 15 miles south-east of Baltimore. Owned by the United Railways and Electric Company, it was linked to the city by electric trams. It seemed as if the public was being looked after far better than the teams that had braved the Atlantic to be there.

The spirits of the British team were to be sorely dampened on Friday, 23 October. On a trial run and careering down from 200 feet, Biard side-slipped the S.4 into the water, narrowly missing the White Star liner RMS *Majestic* and wrecking his machine. Mitchell, watching from a speedboat owned by Lieutenant Commander Louis Mountbatten, was wearing swimming trunks under his trousers just in case he had to swim to Biard's rescue. The speedboat broke down and Biard was in the water for the best part of an hour before he was picked up. All Mitchell could think of saying when he reached his pilot was, 'Warm enough?' Not quite. Cold, shocked, with two broken ribs and an injured wrist, Biard was taken to the Southern Hotel to recuperate.

On tests with Mitchell's racer, Biard had complained of 'perfectly dreadful' visibility – it would have been hard to see beyond the engine – and of being afraid of the aircraft. Biard put his crash down to wing flutter rather than not being able to see where he was going, however. In *Wings*, his colourful 1934 autobiography, he wrote:

> I worked feverishly at my controls – got the machine almost round – tried to relieve that awful pressure that was making the wings flutter almost like a moth's wings – felt the air tearing at them like a living, vicious thing superhumanly bent on smashing and twisting and wrenching this mechanical intruder and hurling it to destruction – spinning down like a leaf before a gale – and then with an effort that tore at every muscle in my body, I got her righted again and on an even keel, only to find that we had lost flying speed and that it was too late…

Wind tunnel tests conducted on models of the S.4 after the event suggested that airflow, or wash, over the wing had interfered with the aircraft's elevators and tailplanes. In Leslie Howard's film *The First of the Few*, the blame was to be placed on a high-G turn that caused Biard to black out. This was pure fiction, yet whatever the cause of the accident, it was a sorry end for the supremely sleek Mitchell monoplane that had promised so much.

The French had not entered the 1925 contest. If they had, they might have done well with their Bernard-Ferbois V.2 racing monoplane, should it have been fitted with floats. Designed by Jean Hubert, one of Wilbur Wright's first French passengers in 1908, for the Société des Avions Bernard of La Courneuve, Paris, the mid-wing V.2 may well have influenced Mitchell's S.4. The two aircraft shared many similarities, and – all importantly in the context of the Schneider Trophy – the V.2 was very fast. On 11 November 1924, Chief Warrant Officer Florentin Bonnet, a First World War fighter pilot, recaptured the world airspeed record for France from the United States, his speed 448.17 km/h (278.28 mph). Bonnet was to have taken part in the 1929 Schneider contest, but he was killed in training that summer flying a Nieuport-Delage NiD.62 sesquiplane fighter.

The day the British had set sail for the States on SS *Minnewaska*, the Italians left Genoa on board SS *Conte Verde*, a Scottish-built liner of the Lloyd Sabaudo Line. Without government support, the Italian entry consisted of a pair of Macchi M.33 strutless shoulder-wing monoplane flying boats. Their well-worn Curtiss D-12 engines were mounted on struts above the centre of the fuselage. Although graceful and streamlined, the Mario Castoldi–designed M.33s lacked the power to win the competition. Like the Supermarine S.4, they suffered from wing flutter.

The contest went ahead, now that the winds had dropped, on Monday, 26 October, with many of those who had attended over the weekend back at work in Baltimore and beyond. Riccardo Morselli had ignition problems with his M.33 and withdrew. Giovanni de Briganti flew steadily, afraid to apply full throttle in case his engine lost power, while wing flutter was a concern throughout his flight.

Hubert Broad chased the Americans hard, but found his Cambridge-blue Gloster a little too slow and prone to turning wide 'like the back wheels of a car on an icy road'. The brand-new Curtiss R3C-2 ahead of him drew further and further away, sweeping around corners at a sensational speed, its 22.9-litre

Curtiss V-1400 engine providing more than ample power. Its pilot was Lieutenant James Doolittle, a modest and unassuming former bantamweight boxing champion with a scientific and engineering turn of mind. This was the same 'Jimmy' Doolittle, a pilot veteran of the First World War, who was to lead the first – and much celebrated – carrier-based bomber attack on mainland Japan in 1942.

This highly disciplined pilot completed his seventh and final 30-mile lap in his blue-black and chrome-yellow R3C-2 having averaged 232.57 mph. The Curtiss machines, however, were not invincible. Flying the same type of aircraft, Doolittle's teammates, Lieutenant Ralph Ofstie and Lieutenant George Cuddihy, had given up on the sixth lap (engine failure) and final lap (oil loss and fire) respectively. Hubert Broad took second place, at 199.17 mph, with the Gloster IIIA. After due pause – and 21 minutes after Doolittle – Giovanni de Briganti cruised in third at 168.44 mph. His had been a well-judged race, yet his white Macchi M.33, sporting fasces on its sides, was to be the very last Schneider competition flying boat. It might have been the kind of aeroplane Jacques Schneider approved of, but it was far too slow – and especially so given it was the product of a country hooked, from the very top down, on speed.

The Americans seemed unassailable, and so Italy and Britain asked the FAI for a delay. If the next contest were to be held in 1927, their teams would have a sporting chance. Having been more than generous once, the Americans were not inclined to do so again. They planned to take the Schneider Trophy home for good in 1926; the focus in the future would be on commercial flight. President Calvin Coolidge made this clear in September 1925, when his Aircraft Board called for a boost in federal funding for civil aviation. The state would not fund teams entering sponsored races, and this included the Schneider contest.

In late February 1926, Air Vice Marshal Sir Sefton Brancker, chairman of the Royal Aero Club's Racing Committee, set sail for America for a meeting with Orville Wright, chairman of the US National Aeronautic Association – a founding member of the FAI. A Boer War veteran who had learned to fly in India in 1910 and had served in both the army and the RFC in the Great War, Sir Sefton was a man of charm, energy and diplomatic skill. Impeccably dressed and sporting a monocle, he was every inch the British imperial soldier, although one who went on to play significant roles in the development of civil aviation in the United Kingdom. He was on board the state-sponsored British airship R101 when it crashed near Beauvais on its maiden flight in October 1930. There were no survivors.

Sir Sefton's trip to the States was to no avail. The Americans wanted the Schneider done and dusted. But if Britain had to take on the Americans in 1926, then perhaps the RAF could help in persuading the British government to sponsor Schneider entrants. Air Chief Marshal Hugh 'Boom' Trenchard, Chief of the Air Staff, had previously looked down on air racing and contests, but he changed his mind after reading a report written in light of the 1925 Schneider event by Air Vice Marshal Geoffrey Salmond, Air Member for Supply and Research at the Air Ministry. A hugely experienced army and RFC officer, who had been in the thick of action in the Boer

War and First World War, Salmond made a case for the RAF taking charge of the next British Schneider team, although the year he had in mind was 1927.

Trenchard spoke with the Secretary of State for Air, Sir Samuel Hoare, who had helped Boom form the RAF as an independent force in 1918. Hoare was keen. He understood the value of propaganda. He also knew quite a bit about Italian ambitions – working for MI6, he had been posted to Rome in March 1917. His key duty there was to persuade Italy from dropping out of the war. Hoare had recruited the former socialist firebrand Benito Mussolini, then editor of the right-wing *Il Popolo d'Italia*, paying him £100 a week (£6,000 in 2020 money) to keep up a flow of pro-war propaganda. By the time of the 1925 Schneider contest, Mussolini had become dictator of Italy, styling himself 'Il Duce' that year. Hoare was keen to support Trenchard, agreeing that 1927 was the year to aim for. The Air Ministry would place orders for new racers from Supermarine, Gloster and Short Brothers, and for 12 purpose-built engines.

In giving his backing to Salmond, Trenchard must surely have recalled his own flying days. He had been persuaded to take up flying by Captain Eustace Loraine, who had served with Boom's 1907 Nigerian expedition to make contact with the Munshi tribe. 'You've no idea what you're missing', wrote Loraine. 'Come and see men crawling like ants.' Trenchard arrived in London from Ireland on 6 July 1912, on his way to Tommy Sopwith's Flying School at Brooklands. He was told that Loraine had been killed the previous day in a flying accident near Stonehenge. Loraine and his passenger, Staff Sergeant R. H. V. Wilson, were the first RFC airmen to be killed in an air crash. The Larkhill aerodrome issued an order: 'Flying will continue this evening as usual.'

Trenchard went solo after just 64 minutes. His tutor, 21-year-old Evelyn Copland Perry, said that this had been 'no easy performance', although given that Boom was 39 – the upper age limit for pilot training was 40 – had lost a lung in the Boer War and had limited vision in one eye, he had done well to get his licence so quickly. The 'founder of the RAF' lived to be 83 years old. Perry was dead at 23. Killed in a flying accident near Amiens on 16 August 1914, he was reputed to be the first British Army officer to die in France in the First World War.

Given the Americans' refusal to postpone the 1926 Schneider contest, the FAI proposed that, in future competitions, aircraft should carry payloads. The French suggested 250 kg, the Italians 400 kg. This, they said, would cut freak machines – one-offs designed for pure speed – from the contest, as these were not in the intended spirit of Jacques Schneider's competition.

The Americans and the British rejected the idea, the former seeing it aimed at undermining Curtiss, and both understanding that it would favour flying boats – which were better able to carry such payloads – thus saving the French and Italians from investment in high-speed seaplanes that might compete with Curtiss, Gloster and Supermarine. Given, however, the lack of funding, there would be no British aeroplanes competing at Hampton Roads, Virginia, in the fall of 1926. As the French said no, too, this left the Italians to challenge the Americans on their own.

And this time, the Italians were prepared. Mussolini had stabilized his new regime. While the time was tight to take on the Americans, the Royal Aero Club was told that all necessary funds would be provided. It must ensure an Italian win, ordered Il Duce, 'at all costs'. Italian manufacturers needed to switch from flying boats to out-and-out competition racers in a matter of months. Generous to a fault and confident in their own aircraft and pilots, the Americans agreed to push the date of the contest back from 24 October to 11 November.

This time around, the Italians concentrated their energy on the design of a single aircraft type, of which five would be built and four shipped to Virginia. This was the Macchi M.39, a firmly braced yet clean-lined monoplane designed by Mario Castoldi that drew its inspiration from both the Supermarine S.4 and the 1925 Curtiss racers. The airframe was shaped around a new engine by Fiat, the 800-hp AS.2 engineered by Tranquillo Zerbi using the Curtiss D-12 as its starting point.

Castoldi's blood-red M.39 was a hunched and powerful-looking machine. It was also tricky to fly, and this was largely due to the haste with which its design had been pursued. The designer had been ill at the start of the project, dragging himself from sick bed to workshop. There was no time to rest. There were, however, rewards for the engineering teams' hard work. On 17 September, Major Mario de Bernardi flew a three-kilometre test course over Lake Varese at an encouraging 414 km/h (257 mph). However, four days later, one of the Italian team – 26-year-old Captain Vittorio Centurione Scotto, a decorated wartime seaplane pilot – stalled on his first turn after take-off. The M.39 crashed and Centurione Scotto was killed. Mussolini himself had selected the young aristocrat after he broke the world altitude record for seaplanes.

With little time for the extensive testing this new type of aircraft needed, the Italian team nevertheless set sail for the States on board SS *Conte Rosso*, a Scottish-built liner that, converted into a troop carrier in the Second World War, would be sunk by the U-class submarine HMS *Upholder* off the coast of Sicily in May 1941, with the loss of 1,300 lives. As the *Conte Rosso* scythed across the Atlantic in 1926, the Italian team enjoyed fine food and wine. Concerned about what lay ahead from a gastronomic and vinicultural perspective, they had filled the floats of the Macchis with Chianti. The States at this time was still dry. Prohibition would finally be lifted in 1933.

On his first flight from Norfolk on 3 November, a week before the contest, Mario de Bernardi heard his Fiat engine backfiring. By the time he landed the Macchi, it was on fire. Major de Bernardi tried smothering the flames with his leather flying jacket, and then, successfully, with a fire extinguisher handed to him by a US seaplane pilot who, spotting the fire, had raced to help. The Chianti in the fuel tank floats, since decanted, was not the cause, although with the AS.2 pushed to an exacting 850 hp at 2,500 rpm in racing trim, the engine was highly strung. Before the contest, there had been problems with carburetion and oil-cooling, while a combination of the immense torque generated by their engines and propellers and the weight of their floats caused the Macchis to lean disturbingly on take-off. Might they flip over?

The Americans were having problems of their own. Without financial help from the US government, Curtiss had stretched the design of the winning machines it built for the 1923 and 1925 Schneider contests that bit further. Two of the three R3C-2 racers entered for the contest were fitted with new engines, one a geared 650-hp Packard 2A-1500 V12 (on what became the R3C-3), the other a direct-drive 685-hp Curtiss V-1550 (on the R3C-4). And then tragedy struck. One of the team, Lieutenant Harmon J. Norton, was killed when the reserve Curtiss CR-3 he was flying over the Potomac stalled and plunged into the water.

A veteran of 35 different types of aircraft, Lieutenant Frank 'Hershey' Hersey Conant died when flying a training plane low over Winter Harbor, 30 miles south of Norfolk, on his way to join his teammates. He had hit a pole in the water. Then, the day before the race, Lieutenant William 'Red' Tomlinson misjudged his height on approach, crash-landed and wrecked the Packard engine of his R3C-3. This particular aircraft had proved especially tricky on take-off; at full throttle, its right float would submerge. In the last of the team's series of misfortunes, reserve pilot Lieutenant C. Champion fell ill and took to his bed.

The contest took place on Saturday, 13 November. The weather was fine. Major Mario de Bernardi set the pace in the Macchi, although he had to climb higher than planned to keep his engine from overheating. He flew the seven-lap 217-mile course in record time, averaging 246.5 mph. Lieutenant George Cuddihy was heading for second place in the R3C-4 when his fuel pump packed up. He was forced to land within sight of the finishing line. Lieutenant Christian Frank Schilt took Cuddihy's place, completing the course at 231.36 mph. Third place went to Lieutenant Adriano Bacula at 218.01 mph with his M.39. Trailing well behind these three was Lieutenant Red Tomlinson, who took fourth place in the reserve Curtiss F6C-I Hawk biplane fighter at 136.95 mph.

At the soonest opportunity, Major de Bernardi wired a telegram to Mussolini: 'Your orders to win at all costs have been carried out.' The Americans were magnanimous in defeat. The Italians were swept off to a banquet at the Monticello Hotel in Norfolk, followed by a reception at the White House with President Coolidge and a grand party in New York hosted by the flamboyant Mayor 'Beau James' Walker. It was at this point, though, that the Americans pulled out of future involvement in the Schneider Trophy. This was not a case of sour grapes; it was more because further investment in racing machines at an international level seemed irrelevant. As President Coolidge himself put it, 'The chief business of the American people is business', and within the next few years the US would steal a march in the design and performance of what were to become known as airliners.

The 1926 contest was the last that Jacques Schneider saw in person. His family business had been driven into bankruptcy after the First World War and he was to die stony broke in 1928 at Beaulieu-sur-Mer on the French Riviera – not far from Monaco, where the first competition in his name had been held 15 years earlier. In any case, the trophy had not gone the way he had intended. A blood-red Italian monoplane designed to win what effectively had become a race between rival nations, and which was unable to carry a single passenger, was not the type of seaplane Jacques Schneider had dreamed of. It was, though, a seaplane that the British were determined to beat.

THREE

Interim

One seaplane design for the 1924 non-event cannot fail to intrigue. It exists perhaps only in rare photographs of a wind tunnel model. And yet, the Dornier S.4 Greif (Griffon) has the look of a winner. Beautifully streamlined from the tip of its pointed nose cone to the tail of its oval fuselage, this cantilever monoplane preceded Reginald Mitchell's striking Supermarine S.4. The Dornier, though, was a thoroughbred in the making, unable to reach the starting line of a contest that never happened; a dream machine from a brilliant designer representing a country that, in any case, was an unwelcome guest in any major aviation event of the era.

That country, of course, was Germany. Having lost the war in 1918, Germany was subject to the conditions of the punitive Treaty of Versailles. This demanded reparation payments from the new Weimar Republic on a scale that, one way or another, all but guaranteed bankruptcy, hyperinflation and the rise of an angry nationalism that, 15 years later, would bring Adolf Hitler and the Nazi Party to power through the ballot box.

Germany and Bavaria, a kingdom within the Prussian-led Deutsches Reich, had been prosperous industrial powerhouses

up to and through the First World War. Their technical univer-
sities and science laboratories were second to none. Many of
the most advanced military aircraft of the Great War were
German. Under the auspices of the Treaty of Versailles, however,
the Military Inter-Allied Commission of Control clipped the
wings of Germany's aviation industry in draconian fashion.
Until October 1919, the Commission would allow Germany
a maximum of 100 seaplanes for temporary mine-sweeping
operations, and no more than 145 military aircraft converted to
civilian use. There would be no German air force.

A further agreement of 1922 permitted limited production
of commercial aircraft, with the size of airframes and engines
severely limited. What the Germans did have, though, was
ingenuity and a scientific approach to engineering, research
and development. There was little or nothing the Allies could
do about these qualities and factors which spurred German
designers to great heights in the 1920s, even while the country's
manufacturers were kept away from the mainstream currents
of international aviation technology – and from the Schneider
Trophy, too, in the years when the contest began to push the
boundaries of potential civil and military design.

To get around the strictures imposed by Versailles, Claude
Dornier built aircraft in Denmark and Italy, while Hugo Junkers
opened a factory in a converted automobile plant at Fili, a
suburb of Moscow. Like the Germans, the Russians had been
isolated by the Allies – who feared the spread of communism –
at the end of the Great War. The two countries signed a treaty
in 1922 absolving one another for the roles they played during
the conflict.

The Germans wanted to build military aircraft; the Russians wanted to learn from them. And who better to learn from than Junkers, who as early as 1915 had built the first practical all-metal aircraft, the J 1, an experimental cantilever-wing monoplane that, despite its limited performance, heralded a new era in aircraft construction.

From 1925, for the following eight years, German military pilots were trained at a secret air combat school at Lipetsk. In the guise of the 'Scientific Research and Test Institute for Aircraft', the school produced a core of pilots who went on to train recruits to the new Luftwaffe. Given the constraints of the Treaty of Versailles, a significant number of these had first learned to fly on gliders. The Germans took the lead with glider design and established gliding as an officially recognized sport. A national gliding organization formed in 1924, the Rhön-Rossitten Gesellschaft played an invaluable role in the scientific research of both sailplanes and powered aircraft. One of its leading lights was Theodore von Kármán, the Hungarian-born scientist, mathematician and aerospace engineer who left Germany for the United States in 1930 to take up the directorship of the Guggenheim Aeronautical Laboratory at the California Institute of Technology. Looking back later in his stellar career, von Kármán observed of this time:

I have always thought that the Allies were short-sighted when they banned motor flying in Germany. They stimulated the very development they wanted to stop: the growth of German aviation. Experiments with gliders in sport sharpened German thinking in aerodynamics, structural design and meteorology... In structural design, gliders showed us in Germany how to distribute weight in a light structure and revealed new facts about vibration... we uncovered the dangers of hidden turbulence in the air, and in general opened up the study of meteorological influences on aviation.

While studying aircraft design and aerodynamics at the Institute of Technology, Hanover, with his twin brother Walter, Siegfried Günter took part in the design of a high-performance glider. One way or another, this led to a job with Ernst Heinkel's company at Rostock, where Siegfried developed low- and high-speed wind tunnels. Walter joined him there in 1931, and the two worked closely on the design of the He 70, a low-wing mono-plane for fast mail services that captured eight long-distance speed records.

When Reginald Mitchell saw the He 70 on test with a Rolls-Royce Kestrel engine, he wrote to Ernst Heinkel:

We, at Supermarine Aviation, were particularly impressed, since we have been unable to achieve such smooth lines in the aircraft that we entered for the Schneider Trophy Races... In addition to this, we recently investigated the effect that installing certain new British fighter engines would have on the He 70. We were dismayed to find that your new aircraft, despite its larger measurements, is appreciably faster than our fighters. It is indeed a triumph.

While the He 70's clean lines and elliptical wings were not, as has been suggested, a direct influence on the Spitfire, Mitchell's letter is evidence of the extent to which design engineers in different countries were aware of one another's projects and were in direct touch until the Second World War broke off contact between many of them. Did Mitchell see photographs of the wind tunnel model of Claude Dornier's S.4 Griffon as he worked on his S.4 seaplane?

The Günter twins also worked on the designs of the He 111 twin-engine bomber, which began life nominally as a fast passenger plane; the He 100, the very fast single-engine fighter that lost out to the Messerschmitt Bf 109 in terms of government contracts; the He 178, the world's first practical jet; and the He 176, the world's first operational rocket plane.

In the end, the Treaty of Versailles backfired spectacularly in terms of helping Adolf Hitler achieve absolute power over Germany, while the attempt to suppress German aviation prowess only encouraged the country's engineers to think differently. If engines had to be small, then aircraft would be light – and this meant the use of new materials and new forms of construction that were to prove invaluable in the design and manufacture of military aircraft, especially in wartime. If there was only so much power to be wrung reliably from a piston engine of a given size, then aerodynamics and wind tunnels were all-important. This 'more from less' way of thinking went hand in hand with the introduction of short-hop intercity flights by small, lightweight civil passenger planes. To enable reliable schedules in different weather conditions and at all times of the day, the German aviation industry ensured its pilots could fly safely relying on the information displayed on their instruments, even when they could see little or nothing through the windows of their cockpits, and airstrips that lit up at night.

Two months before the 1926 Schneider contest, Dornier's Do R Superwal took to the skies. This was a 19-seat monoplane flying boat airliner, seven of which were bought by the newly formed Deutsche Luft Hansa. Who was doing more to realize Jacques Schneider's dream – the Italians and the Americans with their furiously fast and dangerous single-seat V12 racers, or the Germans with their capacious and comfortable long-distance flying boats?

And surely, had he lived to hear about it, Jacques Schneider would have applauded the launch on 22 July 1929 of the solitary Heinkel HE 12, a low-wing strut-braced seaplane, with the assistance of a compressed-air catapult from a side deck of SS *Bremen*. At the time, this magnificent Norddeutscher Lloyd liner was on her maiden voyage from Bremen to New York. Mail was sent ahead to New York over the last 250 miles, in a compartment behind the pilot and radio operator of the Deutsche Luft Hansa seaplane. Passengers thrilled to the sight of the seaplane accelerating to 70 mph – and thus able to fly – in a distance of less than 70 feet. New Yorkers responded by turning out in large numbers to see Mayor Jimmy Walker naming the German aeroplane after their vertiginous city.

A second – larger and faster – seaplane, the He 58, was built for *Bremen*'s sister ship, SS *Europa*. The Heinkels were replaced in 1932 by Junkers Ju 46 seaplanes with an extended range of 750 miles, allowing mail to arrive in New York 24 hours ahead of the liners.

As early as 1928, Deutsche Luft Hansa was Europe's biggest airline, its motto 'Commerce follows the Flag'. By 1930 it was flying regularly to China, a country as yet bereft of airports, aerial maps, radio stations and workshops able to service aeroplanes. The service was dependent on the crews and in particular on highly competent pilots who had learned to fly, and so very well, against the grain of the Treaty of Versailles.

Even so, at least one German aircraft designer would have liked to compete in the Schneider contests. This was, of course, Claude Dornier. A graduate of Munich's Technical University, Dornier was the son of a French wine importer and a German mother. He worked for Count Ferdinand von Zeppelin on the structural design of dirigible airships and on the engineering of aeroplanes. The Zeppelin-Lindau D.1 all-metal monocoque biplane fighter of 1918 was very much his. Dornier saw the big picture of what aviation was capable of, especially in terms of long-distance commercial flight. He was particularly keen to produce an 'air liner' that could fly the Atlantic with a large payload and on a regular basis.

For the five years between 1924 and 1929 he worked on the design of the Do X, a massive triple-decker flying boat that on a test flight from Lake Constance in October 1929 set a new world record by carrying 150 ticket-holding passengers along with a 10-strong crew and 9 'stowaways' who had sneaked aboard in the crush. Very much an 'air liner', the state-sponsored Do X featured a bridge, radio room and engine room on the top deck – where orders to increase or reduce power were relayed by the captain to the flight engineer – and a bar, kitchen, dining salon and lavatories on the deck below. Reclining seats could be turned into beds. Typewriters were made available and internal telephones allowed passengers in separate cabins to speak to one another and to order drinks. All this just 10 years after Captain John Alcock and Lieutenant Arthur Brown, two former RFC pilots, had first flown non-stop across the Atlantic – as competitors in the *Daily Mail* contest – in atrocious conditions, in the open cockpit of a modified First World War Vickers Vimy twin-engine bomber, their only comfort soggy sandwiches, bars of chocolate and coffee laced with a dash of spirits.

The watertight lower deck of the Do X was for fuel, mail and luggage. To get this leviathan off the water – and, hopefully, well above the Atlantic waves to New York – Dornier installed no fewer than 12 Siemens Jupiter 525-hp nine-cylinder air-cooled radial engines, mounted in six pairs on top of the wing.

On 3 November 1930, and newly fitted with a dozen 610-hp Curtiss V-1570 water-cooled V12s, the Dornier left Friedrichshafen for New York with 60 passengers. It arrived 10 months later, via Holland, England, France, Spain, Portugal, Cape Verde off the west coast of Africa, Brazil, Puerto Rico and Florida. Various delays, including a fire that kept the flying boat in Lisbon for six weeks while repairs were made, had turned the journey into an aerial odyssey.

New York gave the Dornier – including, of course, its complement and crew – a hero's welcome. Newsreel cameras ran from boats on the Hudson. They recorded footage, so very moving today, of the great flying boat passing by the Statue of Liberty and making a pitch-perfect landing. Footage from the aircraft, shot through open portholes, shows Manhattan's skyline almost close enough to touch.

While the Do X made headlines in New York, Wall Street had crashed not long before its epic flight. There were to be no orders from America for the 50-ton aircraft, and just three were built. Yet this was the kind of aircraft and airline service that, tantalizingly at the time, came closest to realizing Jacques Schneider's vision of commercially operated long-distance flying boats.

What Dornier did not have to hand was an engine with sufficient power to produce flying boats that were fast, able to cruise above bad weather, and economical to run. The Schneider Trophy, however, was showing just how fast and powerful seaplanes, and perhaps even flying boats, could be. In 1928, Claude Dornier produced an enticing model of a racing seaplane, a theoretical Schneider contestant, featuring a pair of 800-hp BMW V12 engines mounted in a streamlined nacelle. The pilot sat between the engines – one in front of him, one behind – and high above elongated floats incorporating fins, rudder and tailplane. Displayed at the Berlin International Air Show in October 1928 and again at the London Olympia Air Show in July the following year, Dornier's model looked like no existing Schneider aeroplane, but as a fully working prototype and with 1,600 hp on tap it might have been very fast indeed.

For the 1931 contest, Dornier made drawings not of a seaplane, but of a twin-engine flying boat. The engines – of 2,000 hp apiece – concealed in the forward section of the fuselage were, through a gearbox, to drive a pusher propeller mounted on a pylon ahead of and above the wing. Looking at the drawings and scaling them up in the mind's eye, it is not hard to see what Dornier might have been getting at: a truly fast and powerful commercial flying boat, the nucleus of its design tested through the rigours of a Schneider contest.

But while German governments were keen to promote civil aviation, they were also interested in the design of light and fast aircraft that could be developed quickly into military machines. Despite degrees of political isolation, social turmoil and a precarious economy, German aviation developed apace in the 1920s, and accelerated hard the following decade.

Officially at least, the Americans gave up international racing after 1926 to focus on civil aviation. They appeared to slow the development of fast military aircraft, too. These moves were logical enough. In terms of national security, the US had little to worry about. No potential enemy aircraft could reach America. And, even if they could, the well-armed country that would be ahead of them was vast. What the American aviation industry was more interested in was developing commercial flight within the US, down to South America and across the Atlantic and Pacific oceans. While their success with the Curtiss machines in the Schneider contests had been a source of pride and satisfaction, the publicity generated by these shows paled into insignificance compared with the media coverage given to Charles Lindbergh's non-stop solo flight from New York to Paris in May 1927.

A 25-year-old US Air Mail pilot and officer in the US Army Air Corps Reserve, Lindbergh made his epic 3,600-mile flight in the *Spirit of St Louis*, a custom-built high-wing Ryan monoplane. Through weather fair and foul, from as high as 10,000 icy feet over storm clouds to as low as 10 feet above threatening waves, its single Wright Whirlwind radial engine droned away flawlessly for 33½ hours as he crossed the Atlantic. A crowd estimated at 150,000 met him when he landed at night in the glare of a phalanx of car headlamps at Le Bourget Aerodrome. Hero-worshipped and highly honoured back home in the States, Lindbergh's contribution to the development of long-distance commercial flight was incalculable.

As Elinor Smith, the record-breaking US pilot who took her first flying lesson when she was 10 years old and made a 26½-hour solo flight in 1929 at the age of 18, was to recall decades later:

> People seemed to think we were from outer space or something. But after Charles Lindbergh's flight, we could do no wrong. It's hard to describe the impact Lindbergh had on people. Even the first walk on the moon doesn't come close. The twenties was such an innocent time, and people were still so religious – I think they felt like this man was sent by God to do this. And it changed aviation forever because all of a sudden the Wall Streeters were banging on doors looking for airplanes to invest in. We'd been standing on our heads trying to get them to notice us but after Lindbergh, suddenly everyone wanted to fly, and there weren't enough planes to carry them.

Within a few short years a new generation of fast, comfortable and reliable 'airliners' would criss-cross the United States, although the first transatlantic and trans-Pacific aircraft worthy of that name was to be a flying boat.

Long-distance flying boats were to serve the vast British Empire, too. It would be some while, though, before Britain developed a thoroughly thought-through plan for civil aviation. As for the military, the very future of the RAF hung in the balance for some time after the First World War, and this had an effect on government attitudes towards the Schneider Trophy. Even though – or perhaps because – the RAF had emerged as a military force independent of the British Army and Royal Navy, old-guard military and many politicians viewed it with a degree of suspicion. In simple terms, the RFC had done its job in the Great War and there was no longer the need for an expensive full-time air force, and certainly not a new force with ambitions of its own.

What seems remarkable is the extent to which the press was involved – and, in particular, Lord Rothermere of the *Daily Mail*. Appointed air minister in 1917 by David Lloyd George, the press baron chose Major General Hugh Trenchard as the first Chief of the Air Staff. Rothermere wanted Britain to win the war, but he also wanted to sell newspapers. One of his pet initiatives was the 'air warfare scheme', through which British armies would be withdrawn from the Western Front and replaced by the RAF. This made interesting newspaper copy but, in practice, poor military sense. Another ruse was to supply the Royal Navy with 4,000 aircraft for the fight against German submarines, when there were precious few to spare for the fight over land. Frustrated and finally infuriated by Rothermere's imperious and rash meddling, Trenchard resigned his post. If the new RAF was to be an independent force, it needed to be free from interference.

Although Rothermere resigned in April 1918, Trenchard had to fight for his reputation at home. According to his biographer, Andrew Boyle, he was sat on a bench in Green Park the following month when he heard one uniformed Royal Navy officer say to another, 'I don't know why the Government should pander to a man who threw in his hand at the height of the battle. If I'd my way with Trenchard I'd have him shot.' Thanks to Winston Churchill, appointed Secretary of State for War and Secretary of State for Air in early 1919, Trenchard was reappointed Chief of the Air Staff. His struggle was now not with press barons, but senior officers in rival services and their friends in Westminster.

His genius was in proving incrementally that the RAF could police the Empire in peacetime and at minimal cost. In 1922, the RAF was given control of British forces in Iraq, after the role the force played in helping to put down a revolt of more than 100,000 armed tribesmen that broke out in the summer of 1920 and spread throughout the country. The RAF flew ops totalling 4,008 hours, dropped 97 tons of bombs and fired 183,861 rounds for the loss of nine men killed, seven wounded and eleven aircraft destroyed behind rebel lines. With the RAF in control, British military expenditure in Iraq fell from £23 million in 1921 to less than £4 million five years later – despite the fact that the Vickers Vernon troop carriers of 45 Squadron, fitted with bomb racks and led by Squadron Leader Arthur Harris, increased attacks on Iraqi targets.

Wing Commander J. A. Chamier, who in later life was a director of Vickers (Aviation) Ltd and the BBC's aviation correspondent, wrote, from experience, that the best way to demoralize rebels was to concentrate bombing on the 'most inaccessible village of the most prominent tribe which it is desired to punish. All available aircraft must be collected, the attack with bombs and machine guns must be relentless and unremitting and carried on continuously by day and night on houses, inhabitants, crops and cattle.' Or, as Squadron Leader Harris put it, 'The Arab and Kurd... now know what real bombing means... within 45 minutes a full-sized village can be practically wiped out and a third of its inhabitants killed or injured by four or five machines which offer them no real target, no opportunity for glory as warriors, no effective means of escape.'

Not by chance, when Harris was appointed chief of Bomber Command in 1942, his former 45 Squadron colleagues Ralph Cochrane, Roderick Hill and Robert Saundby became a part of his entourage. For two decades this formidable coterie had done their bit to drive the doctrine that – in words used by Stanley Baldwin, Conservative prime minister in 1923–24, 1924–29 and 1935–37 – 'the bomber will always get through.'

Because the RAF's policing of the Empire had been effective, its bombers were in the ascendancy until remarkably close to Hitler's takeover of Western Europe. This promotion of the bomber helps to explain Britain's confused and contrary official view of the Schneider contests, as by 1926 it had become clear that the aircraft involved were – more rather than less – high-speed military fighters in the making. The British government's hot-and-cold attitude towards the Schneider Trophy was also coloured by the ups and downs of economic circumstance.

The official Italian view of the Schneider Trophy and high-speed flight was deeply affected by the uncertainty of the country's political situation, although by the beginning of 1926

Mussolini had made himself dictator and set about modernizing Italy's roads, railways, architecture, town planning and, notably, its air force. In November that year, 30-year-old Italo Balbo, one of Mussolini's closest colleagues, was appointed Secretary of State for Air. He learned to fly, began building up the Regia Aeronautica Italiana, and was made an air force general in 1928 and Minister of the Air Force the following September. Balbo's precipitous rise personified a shift in focus in Italy from the concerns of civil aviation to those of the military.

Hanging from a ceiling in Munich's vast Deutsches Museum, Claude Dornier's Do A Libelle (Dragonfly) flying boat makes a pretty sight. With its streamlined hull and fin-like foils, this tiny, lightweight machine dating from 1921 seems as innocent as an aeroplane can be. It could take off and land on ice and snow. With 55 hp on tap, its top speed was 75 mph. Its wings could be folded back for easy transport. Examples were exported to Sweden, Belgium, New Zealand, Australia, Fiji and Japan. A little more than a decade later, Dornier was working on the design of his Do 17 high-speed 'mail plane'. This was, in fact, the 'flying pencil' light bomber brought into the service of the newly formed Luftwaffe, which had been created by the newly appointed Reich Commissar for Aviation Hermann Göring, the First World War fighter ace, and the Secretary of State Erhard Milch, son of a Jewish pharmacist and co-managing director of Deutsche Luft Hansa.

In the capable hands of Field Marshal Milch, working under architect-turned-armaments-minister Albert Speer, in March 1944 the Reich Aviation Ministry was transformed into

FOUR

Winged Lions: Venice, 1927

hen the British team arrived in Venice in September 1927, the Schneider Trophy was on display in St Mark's Square. Flags flew. Banners flapped. Striking Modernist posters heralded the great event, one showing seaplanes encircling the campanile of St Mark's. The Italians were in confident, carnival mood. So were the British. This time, their pilots were highly skilled RAF officers, members of the elite High Speed Flight formed in December 1926 with the single purpose of winning the Schneider Trophy. They were a formidable crew.

Their commanding officer, Squadron Leader Leonard Horatio Slatter DSC & Bar, DFC, was a South African civil engineer turned RNAS seaplane fighter pilot. He had shot down seven enemy aircraft in the Great War and had served in southern Russia fighting the Bolsheviks. In later life, Slatter led the battle against German U-boats over the Atlantic. Promoted to air marshal, his final posting was Commander-in-Chief RAF Coastal Command.

The pilots he chose for the Schneider contest were 27-year-old Flight Lieutenant Sidney Webster AFC & Bar; 29-year-old

Flight Lieutenant Oswald Worsley, an RNAS mechanic before he flew in combat; 30-year-old Flight Lieutenant Samuel Kinkead DSO, DSC & Bar, DFC & Bar, who scored 33 kills as an RNAS fighter pilot in the First World War and shot down three 'Red' Russian aircraft in 1919–20; and 27-year-old Flying Officer Harry Schofield, who built church organs for four years after the war – in which he had fought, initially with the RNAS, as a fighter pilot – before re-joining the RAF in 1922.

The team, accompanied by Air Vice Marshal Francis Scarlett, put up at the Excelsior Palace Hotel on the Lido, while their ground crews stayed at the Italian sergeants' mess at the San Andrea naval air station on another island in the Venetian Lagoon. The British aircraft came by sea on board SS *Heworth*, a cargo steamer (bombed and sunk 10 miles south of Aldeburgh, Suffolk, in July 1940), SS *Egyptian Prince* (later SS *Lorrain*, steaming under a French flag) and the aircraft carrier HMS *Eagle*, a converted dreadnought that would be sunk by a U-boat while escorting a convoy to Malta in August 1942. Four destroyers escorted the *Eagle*. The British were clearly out to make a show.

Aside from its smartly turned-out pilots in their blue uniforms, the British team had two very impressive new seaplane types to show: the blue and silver Supermarine S.5 and the blue and gold Gloster IV. These, and a solitary experimental white Short Crusader, had been ordered and paid for by the Air Ministry. Before agreeing to the cost, Winston Churchill, Chancellor of the Exchequer, had asked the ministry to explain the likely benefits. The answer was as comprehensive as it was compelling. Improvements in the power-to-weight ratio and the reliability of engines. Developments in propellers, radiators, carburation, lubrication, control mechanisms and floats. A challenge to manufacturers to up their game. Higher standards of airmanship.

The men from the ministry were, however, knocking on a door that was more than half open. Churchill had lost none of his enthusiasm for military aviation and, during the Second World War, would be proud to wear his RAF wings badge. It was said, although this might be little more than hearsay, that Churchill had prompted the design of the badge. In a discussion over the matter with Captain Murray Sueter, founder of the RNAS, he held a Napoleonic eagle brooch he had bought in Paris for his wife Clementine against the navy officer's sleeve, saying, 'Something like this?'

Churchill did, however, stress that government funding for the 1927 event was not to be taken as a precedent. Even so, it did allow British aircraft manufacturers to take a more scientific approach to design than they had before. The performance of airframes, airscrews, floats and wing radiators were tested using ¼-scale models in wind tunnels and water tanks at the National Physics Laboratory at Bushy Park, Teddington, and the RAE at Farnborough.

For Supermarine, the result was Mitchell's S.5. A smaller machine than the ill-fated S.4, the S.5's thin wing at the base of the slim fuselage was braced to prevent flutter at speed. The pilot sat amidships rather than a long way behind the engine, as had been the case with the S.4. The starboard float doubled up as a petrol tank, its weight counterbalancing the torque effect of the propeller on take-off. Straight-ahead vision was not ideal due to the size of the intrusive crankcases of the Napier Lion engine, although every possible move was made to lower its profile. Carburettors were sited at the back of the Lion. Spark plugs were shortened. The streamlined casing sheathed the engine tightly. What power this engine was now capable of! On a factory test bench, and with its compression upped to a high 10:1, Napier's engineers extracted 910 hp from the Lion VIIA at 3,300 rpm, or double that of the engine when first run in 1917.

After a first test flight with S.5 at Calshot in mid-July, Flight Lieutenant Webster recorded in his logbook, 'very very nice, no snags'. He did, however, find the tiny cockpit tricky, having to squeeze his frame in sideways before being able to sit down. But this aircraft, of course, was an out-and-out racer. Streamlining was all-important. The pilot had to make himself as small as possible. On take-off, the torque effect was noticeable, with the port float digging deep into the water. Without flaps, landing was a high-speed affair, the S.5 touching down on the backs of its floats.

In flight, Webster recorded 280–284 mph. The controls of the S.5 were positive, and the Supermarine could be turned very tightly. With practice and a machine like this, the team aimed for a Schneider circuit speed of just 3 per cent below the S.5's top speed.

Fitted with same Napier engine, Henry Folland's wooden Gloster IV biplane promised to be as fast as Mitchell's all-metal S.5. The view from the cockpit, however, was extremely limited by the top wing – mounted immediately in front of the pilot – and the crankshaft casings of the Lion. 'Very, very blind', noted

Webster in his logbook. Flying Officer Schofield dubbed it 'the Blind Wonder'.

To see their way, pilots were forced to rely on lateral vision and on bends when they tilted their aircraft. This was tricky – especially when the water below them was perfectly calm, as this made it hard for pilots to judge the aircraft's height above it. Small waves were better than no waves. Of course, the aircraft had altimeters, but in a contest and taking bends at great speed, pilots' eyes were not glued to the instruments. It would be better for everyone if they could see ahead clearly.

The view forward from the Short Crusader was not much better than either the Supermarine or the Gloster. This was a curious entry to the contest, given that it was very much slower than the two Napier-engine types. A spruce and mahogany veneered low-wing monoplane designed by Lieutenant Colonel Whiston Bristow, a consulting aero-engineer, and George Carter, ex-Sopwith and Hawker, the Crusader was a test bed for Bristol's upgraded and supercharged Mercury nine-cylinder radial engine.

Roy Fedden's achievement in advancing the power of this engine from a stock 420 hp to 960 hp on test was certainly impressive, and yet at the kind of speeds Schneider machines were now capable of attaining, radial engines were, at least for now, out of the running. They presented too great a frontal area to the wind, which slowed them down. With 808 hp on tap for the contest, the Crusader was coaxed up to 229 mph by Webster, who thought it nice to fly, and 240 mph by Schofield, although both pilots felt the engine misfiring and the fuel mixture to the supercharger playing up.

The Italian team, meanwhile, had been expecting great things of the new Macchi M.52, the only aircraft its pilots would be flying in the contest. They had been looking forward to an unbeatable top speed of 300 mph. The M.52 certainly looked the part. Smaller and lighter than the winning M.39 of the previous year, its wings were very slightly swept back. It looked extremely powerful, and it was. Its engine, the new 35.2-litre Fiat AS.3 V12, produced 1,000 hp, and with lightweight alloy pistons it weighed just 950 lbs. While this was something to crow about, there was a problem. Magnesium pistons proved to be poor conductors of heat. Unable to dissipate the tremendous heat generated in the cylinders at racing speeds, these light-weight components could buckle and seize up.

The stalling characteristics of the M.52 were also a matter of concern. On a training flight over Lake Varese, Lieutenant Salvatore Borra's M.52 had stalled and crashed. Borra was killed. The pilots' view of the M.52 was that it was fast but tempera-mental. Their main concern was the powerful but highly strung Fiat engine. Would it withstand seven 50-kilometre laps flat out over the Adriatic?

This time around, neither the Italians nor the British had to worry about the Americans. In one way this was odd, because US teams had won both the 1923 and 1925 events. If they entered and won the 1927 contest, the Americans would get to keep the Schneider Trophy for good. Lieutenant Alford Joseph Williams, a US Navy pilot, thought his government's decision not to challenge the British and Italians at Venice was wrong-headed – but since they refused to play ball, he would do so on his own.

Williams had form. Although he had not been chosen for the Schneider team in 1923, 1925 or 1926, he had won the Pulitzer Trophy race in 1923. An all-round sportsman, he had also been a pitcher for the New York Giants, a research test pilot and a combat instructor for the US Navy. With the support of navy colleagues and the Packard Motor Car Company, in March 1927 he formed the Mercury Flying Corporation to build a plane he would fly in Venice that September. The US Navy provided the mighty new 24-cylinder 1,200-hp Packard X-2775 engine – essentially a pair of V12s, one upright, the other inverted, both joined to a single camshaft – while former Curtiss employees now working for the Kirkham Products Corporation built the biplane in Garden City, Long Island.

Completed in mid-July, the Kirkham-Williams Racer was shipped to Manhasset Bay, Long Island, for testing. Painted blue and gold, it first flew on 25 August, which was certainly cutting it fine given that Schneider contest was less than a month away. This was also the first time the massive X-2775 had taken to the air. While the USS *Trenton*, a cruiser authorized by President Coolidge, stood ready to take pilot and aircraft to Venice full steam ahead, a combination of poor weather and technical snags prompted Williams to throw in the towel on 9 September. He promised to try again.

In Venice two days later, Flying Officer Schofield was very nearly killed in an accident with the Crusader. Presumably through incompetence rather than intentionally, the control wires of the Crusader's ailerons had been reversed when the aircraft was assembled at Sant Andrea. As Schofield accelerated away from rest on a test flight, a gust of wind caused his starboard wing to drop. His instinctive correction using the ailerons caused the wing to turn the machine over in the water. Until the Crusader broke in two under pressure, Schofield was trapped in the cockpit he had described earlier as a nailed coffin. Bruised black and blue, but with no bones broken, he clung to the Crusader's tail until rescued.

A week later, Flight Lieutenant Kinkead flew the circuit at a reputed average speed of 331 mph. If true, he was the first human being to exceed 300 mph. His flight was not timed officially, but whatever the case, the S.5 was clearly a very fast machine. The sight and sound of the blue monoplane roaring up and down the length of the Lido, close to the water and close to the beaches, must have been exhilarating.

And then, the weather turned. The contest was postponed from the weekend to Monday, 26 September. This was a pity, as about half the 250,000-strong crowd who had packed half-price trains and *vaporetti* from St Mark's to get to the Lido returned home so they could get to work or school the following day. A large contingent were Fiat workers from Turin, a five-hour train ride from Venice.

The weather at this time of year was normally warm – even hot – and sunny, while the Lido was perenially glamorous. There were, though, big cheers from the beaches and the hotel terraces and balconies on the Monday, as the Italian aircraft, Fascist insignia emblazoned on the flanks of their fuselages, arrived on barges in front of the Hotel Excelsior. And here were their pilots led by Major Mario de Bernardi, who had won for Italy the previous year. There was an especially big round of applause for Captain Arturo Ferrarin. Born and brought up in the Veneto,

Ferrarin was a highly decorated First World War fighter pilot who had competed in the 1926 Schneider contest. He had achieved national fame six years earlier when he flew the 5,000 miles from Rome to Tokyo with fellow pilot Guido Masiero in an Ansaldo SVA military biplane.

The British aircraft were towed on their floats, a confident display of their seaworthiness. As the three Macchis, two Supermarines and solitary Gloster took to the air, it began to rain. In what must have seemed their natural element – rain, sea, speed – the British set the pace. To the dismay of the crowd, Captain Ferrarin's Macchi was engulfed in flames and smoke as it crossed the starting line. Ferrarin turned low over the Excelsior in an attempt to get back to Sant Andrea. He was out of the race. Then Major de Bernardi's 1,000-hp Fiat engine gave up on the second lap when a connecting rod failed and punched a hole in the crankcase, or as Charles Grey put it in his report on the day in *The Aeroplane*, 'A connecting rod had come out of its crankcase for a breath of fresh air.' This left Lieutenant Frederico Guazetti flying the 800-hp AS.2-engined M.52, but the British machines outpaced him. On the sixth lap a fuel line split, spewing petrol in the pilot's face. Guazetti flew very close indeed over the domed roofline of the Excelsior before ditching in the lagoon.

On its sixth lap, the spinner of Flight Lieutenant Kinkead's Gloster worked itself loose, causing a strip of metal to wrap around the propeller. Sensing the vibration, Kinkead dropped out of the race. It was the right decision – the propeller gear was about to come apart. He had found the Gloster hard-going, not because he expected mechanical trouble but because for much of the time he was unable to see where he was going. He had to weave his way around the circuit and so was losing time, lap by lap, against the S.5s.

Webster and Worsley raced on, their Napier engines running well. In all the excitement, Webster forgot how many laps he had flown. The team's method of keeping count was to punch a hole in a board covered in a sheet of paper on the aircraft's dashboard, each time they flew past the Excelsior. At these speeds, though, and flying very low after the tightest of banked turns over and around Porto di Malamocco, Porto di Chioggia and Porto di Lido, it was easy to forget. Webster was also concerned with the thought that his engine cowling was working loose. He flew an eighth lap, one more than he needed, to win the contest at an average speed of 281.66 mph. Flight Lieutenant Worsley came in second at 273.01 mph.

Mario Castoldi was not amused. The Macchi designer turned to Fiat's engineer Tranquillo Zerbi and, thinking of the overstrained AS.3 engine, said, 'That wasn't horsepower. It was donkey power.' Zerbi himself had been concerned by the attempt to push the engine to 1,000 hp – but perhaps, as a committed Fascist determined that Italy must win the 1927 event, it had been the right thing to do. In Italy, unlike in England, the Schneider team was close-knit, from pilots and engineers to heads of government; to Italo Balbo, that is, and Mussolini himself. Balbo was to be one of the witnesses at Arturo Ferrarin's high society wedding to Adelaide Castiglioni in Milan in June 1931. The dashing Venetian pilot would go on to become a director of Avio Linee Italiane, a division of Fiat.

If Castoldi, Zerbi and the Italian team had been disappointed by their performance in the 1927 Schneider contest, Mario de Bernardi for one did not lose heart. Personally, he thought Castoldi was more to blame than Zerbi for the failure of the M.52s. He should have fitted smaller propellers and shorter wings. On 4 November, de Bernardi set a new world airspeed record with an AS.3 powered Macchi M.52 under 479.3 km/h (297.8 mph). On 30 March 1928, he beat his own record flying a lightened M.52R at 512.8 km/h (318.62 mph), and in doing so became the first pilot officially to break both the 300-mph and 500 km/h speed barriers.

Typically, this much-liked pilot had delayed the second of these two attempts at the airspeed record as a mark of respect for Flight Lieutenant Kinkead, killed flying a specially tuned S.5 while aiming for 300 mph. Kinkead had taken off from Calshot as mist began to form over a glass-smooth sea. Pulling out of a dive as he started his high-speed run and with no clear horizon ahead of him, Kinkead misjudged his height and smashed into the Solent. Fellow pilots around the world sent messages of condolence. Any of them might have made the same mistake.

A consummate professional, de Bernardi won the world aerobatics championship at Cleveland, Ohio, in 1931, flew the first Italian jet – the Caproni Campini C.C.2 – in 1940, and experimented with early military drones. Perhaps, though, his most remarkable flight was his very last. On 8 April 1959, de Bernardi suffered a heart attack while flying the tiny Partenavia Aeroscooter, his own design, in an aerobatic display at Rome's Urbe Airport. Landing quickly but safely, he died within minutes of being helped from his seat. One of those watching his final flight was his daughter Fiorenza, Italy's first female airline pilot.

A monument fixed that year to the entrance of the imposing apartment block de Bernardi lived in for many years, on Rome's Via Panama, marries classical Roman lettering and a bounding etched line evoking spirited flight. A quote from Gabriele d'Annunzio reads *'Che dell'ala fa l'emula della folgore'* ('That the wing emulates the lightning'). And yet, de Bernardi enjoyed making even the most daredevil aerial adventure seem, in his words, 'just as if I were flying on the wicker chair on which I usually have coffee at my house after lunch and dinner'.

It was this superficially insouciant spirit that allowed Schneider pilots to fly, to the delight of the festive crowds below, so very fast and so very low, pulling high Gs in turns taken at breakneck speed. If, though, the 1927 contest had made the Schneider Trophy the premier air event for speed, the aero-engines that powered the furiously fast seaplanes were under scrutiny. The Fiat AS.3 was too fragile even for what had become a 50-minute race, while the question of how much power could be mustered from the trustworthy Napier Lion was, as yet, unanswered. In any case, the W configuration of the Lion was proving to be a problem for both pilots and airframe designers. It was too bulky to allow a slimmer profile, while its three pronounced crankcases were hard to see around.

As engineers thought about these questions, it became increasingly clear that future Schneider seaplanes would need to be considered in a holistic way. If much higher speeds were to be achieved, it could no longer be a case of sticking the biggest and most powerful engine into an airframe and seeing what pilots could do with it. In future, engines, airframe, floats and radiators to dissipate the intense heat generated by even more powerful piston engines, would have to be integrated into a streamlined system.

These thoughts and demands were to challenge a very select breed of aircraft and aero-engineers between September 1927 and the next Schneider contest, which was scheduled to take place in September 1929. All parties had agreed to this two-year gap because of the need to rethink the aircraft and to plan ahead effectively.

FIVE

Chivalrous Sportsmanship: Calshot, 1929

On 7 September 1929, a day of glorious boating weather, a million people turned out on beaches, ships and foreshores around the Solent to witness the latest Schneider Trophy contest. Aviation was still thrilling and fashionable. And, this year, the British and Italian teams would fight an eagerly anticipated duel in the skies, in blood-red and marine-blue seaplanes of unprecedented power and presence.

After their disastrous performance in Venice two years before, the Italians were newly energized. A high-speed training centre, Scuola Alta Velocità – founded at the Regia Aeronautica seaplane base in Desenzano del Garda – had forged a tightly organized and highly driven team of pilots, engineers and mechanics under the command of Lieutenant Colonel Mario Bernasconi, a highly respected engineer and pilot. The Solent circuit had been mapped out on Lake Garda for Bernasconi's pilots, a wholly new team, to study and learn by rote.

There were four new types of Italian aircraft. Because of the poor performance of the Macchi M.52 in the 1927 contest,

Italo Balbo wanted three other manufacturers to show what they could do in 1929. The Macchi M.67 proved to be a further development of the M.39 and M.52, although this time around Castoldi chose an Isotta Fraschini engine instead of a Fiat. This was a herculean 57.3-litre W18, generating 1,800 hp and enormous heat. Radiators and oil coolers were installed in the aircraft's wings, under its nose and on each side of the fuselage. One of the aircraft had extra radiators on both the floats and the float struts.

The complexity of the M.67 meant that the first of these machines arrived for practice at Desenzano in August, just a month before the Schneider contest. Poor weather delayed high-speed testing and then, with a fortnight to go, Captain Giuseppe Motta was killed when, after taking the M.67 to 362 mph at 300 feet, he crashed into Lake Garda. The story made international headlines, with newspaper reports suggesting that breathing in exhaust fumes had caused Motta's death. This may well have been the case, as special ventilators were installed in the two remaining M.67s.

Fiat's offering was the tiny C.29. Weighing about half as much as the Macchi and fitted with a compact new 1,000-hp Fiat AS.5 V12, its power-to-weight ratio must have been one of the highest of all contemporary aircraft. The diminutive Fiat's enclosed cockpit was so small that only one team member, Sergeant Major Francesco Agello, could squeeze inside it. On his first test flight over Lake Garda, the Fiat's engine caught fire. Agello was forced to land.

On his second flight with the C.29, Agello bounced into the air after hitting the wash of a boat when attempting to land.

It dived vertically into the lake. Agello was thrown clear and rescued. Then, on 12 August, he was demonstrating the Fiat for the benefit of a British aviation journalist. Once, twice, Agello tried to unstick the floats from the water. No luck. On the third take-off run, the Fiat rose and dropped immediately. It sank to the bottom of the lake. Though unconscious when pulled from the water, Agello escaped alive.

A C.29 was shipped to England in time for the September contest, but did not compete. Today, one of the aircraft can be seen in the Italian Air Force Museum at Vigna di Valle on Lake Bracciano, just outside Rome. It appears to defy the old adage that what looks right is right, because it looks as if it wants to fly and might do so very well.

The same cannot be said of the Savoia-Marchetti S.65, a slender monoplane designed by Alessandro Marchetti with a pair of 1,050-hp Isotta Fraschini V12 engines mounted back to back in a streamlined nacelle above the wing. The pilot sat between them. This assembly was perched above long floats on slim struts and wires. It looked precarious. Engine problems dogged the S.65. It was shipped to Calshot, but stayed on the slipways there. When testing was resumed in 1930, the Savoia-Marchetti proved difficult to fly. It crashed, killing Warrant Officer Tommasso Dal Molin.

The fourth Italian aircraft was the oddest of all, and perhaps thankfully it was unable to lift itself from the water. This was the Piaggio P.c.7 designed by Giovanni Pegna. Nothing like this had been seen before – and, except in science-fiction comics, there has been nothing like it since. Instead of drag-inducing floats, this long and pencil-thin machine floated in the water like a strange winged boat. When its single Isotta Fraschini V12 was fired up, the pilot, sitting well to the rear, engaged a clutch to turn a boat-like propeller at its tail. Once up to speed on the water, and as the aircraft rose on a pair of hydrofoils, the pilot was to pull the clutch lever a second time to set the forward propeller spinning – and, in theory, the Piaggio would speed up and away. Despite the best efforts of Tommaso Dal Molin, it refused to do so. Even if it had, how would it have landed?

While it had been an interesting exercise to commission radical new designs from different manufacturers, in practice this meant that the Italian team was dependent on a pair of Macchi M.67s and a single M.52R powered by the AS.3 that had played up in 1927. Concerned, Italo Balbo asked the British Air Ministry, the Royal Aero Club and the FAI if they might delay the contest. The answer was a concerted 'no'. Italy then, announced Balbo, would take part anyway, 'to perform a gesture of chiv-alrous sportsmanship'. Privately, he must have known he had made a mistake. His one hope was that the powerful engines of the M.67 would last the Solent course.

There had been news of fresh competition from France and the United States. These rumours proved to be nothing for Balbo or the British team to be worried about. Under Raymond Poincaré's coalition government, France's economy had been on an upward curve. In the spring of 1928, the Marine Ministry ordered two new racing seaplanes from the Société des Avions Bernard and two from Nieuport-Delage, and appropriate engines from Hispano-Suiza, Lorraine and Gnome et Rhône. That September, a new Air Ministry was formed under the former First World War pilot, Laurent Eynac. Time, though, was pressing, and neither Bernard nor Nieuport-Delage were able to get brand-new machines designed, built and tested for the up-and-coming Schneider event. French pilots began training in biplane fighters while waiting for the racing seaplanes. Their spirit was dampened on 6 August when Bernard's chief test pilot, Lieutenant Florentin Bonnet, was killed at the lakeside airbase at Hourtin in the Gironde when attempting to loop-the-loop immediately after take-off in the latest Nieuport-Delage NiD.62 biplane fighter.

At the Naval Aircraft Factory in Philadelphia, a new Kirkham seaplane racer was under construction for Al Williams. Despite funding by the Mercury Flying Corporation, wind tunnel testing at the Washington Navy Yard, and a promise from the US Navy to ship the aircraft to England if it exceeded 318 mph on test, the project fell behind time and, as it did, Williams's personal capital was eaten up.

So the 1929 contest, the first following Jacques Schneider's death, would be between Italy and Great Britain, where both Supermarine and Gloster were working up designs of what, for the Italians, were two disquieting monoplanes. For Reginald Mitchell, who had now come very much into his own as a designer, the big question was not his ability to shape a winning airframe but what engine should power it. The Napier Lion had proved its worth time and again and would continue to do so with record-breaking boats and cars.

While the Napier had more to give in 1929, and it was Gloster's choice for the Schneider contest, Mitchell wanted something new and potentially much more powerful for his

Supermarine. He went to the Air Ministry to talk with Major G. P. Bulman, who was in charge of aircraft engine development. This led to discussions with Rolls-Royce. An apocryphal story tells of the Rolls-Royce engineers and Mitchell visiting Henry Royce at his home at West Wittering on the West Sussex coast. Royce suggested they go for a walk. Seated by a groyne in the sand dunes, the great man sketched the outline of a racing engine with his stick.

While this story was fiction, in reality Royce was keen. Rolls-Royce had studied the successful Curtiss D-12 some years ago and subsequently developed the V12 Kestrel, a project led by Arthur Rowledge, the Napier Lion's designer, who had joined Rolls-Royce in 1921. The upshot was the hugely powerful Rolls-Royce R, which promised to run for 80 minutes and more, flat out, while producing 1,900 hp.

While the Rolls-Royce team were able to provide Mitchell with a technical outline of the proposed engine in 1928, the government contract the company needed was only signed in February 1929. The pilots of the RAF's High Speed Flight team would have to practise for the September Schneider contest with the previous year's Supermarine S.5s. From a design engineering perspective, Mitchell's S.6 and the Rolls-Royce R were in all but name synonymous, with power plants and cooling systems distributed throughout the airframe.

Mitchell's S.6 was a daunting machine, bigger and considerably heavier than the S.5, but prodigiously powerful – and, as tests at Derby had proved by July 1929, reliably so. The young pilots of the High Speed Flight, re-formed in February under Squadron Leader Augustus 'Harry' Orlebar, had plenty to keep themselves occupied with while waiting for this latest Supermarine. Tactful, self-effacing, socially adept, supremely well-organized and kind, 32-year-old Harry Orlebar proved to be an ideal choice of leader. As a junior infantry officer he had landed at Gallipoli and been wounded by a Turkish sniper's bullet. Transferring to the RFC, he was a fine fighter pilot in the thick of action on the Western Front. As a post-war test pilot at the Aeroplane and Armament Experimental Establishment at Martlesham Heath, he commanded great respect.

Orlebar could hardly have had a better team. Thirty-year-old Flight Lieutenant George Stainforth was the quiet and serious son of a London solicitor, and a Sandhurst graduate, crack shot and cool-headed pilot. London-born Flying Officer Richard 'Dick' Waghorn, whose father was a civil engineer, was 24 years old, a conscientious and reserved young man who had been the top cadet of his year at RAF College Cranwell, a Sopwith Snipe fighter pilot and a flying instructor, before being posted in February 1929 to the Marine Aircraft Experimental Establishment at Felixstowe where he was selected for Orlebar's High Speed Flight. As for 25-year-old Flying Officer Richard 'Batchy' Atcherley, his career had been the mirror image of Dick Waghorn's. But unlike Waghorn, Batchy – son of Major General Sir Llewellyn Atcherley, Chief Constable of the West Riding of Yorkshire, and one of twins – was an outgoing character and, as Italo Balbo was to discover, a practical joker.

So, too, was Flight Lieutenant David D'Arcy Greig DFC, a lively 30-year-old Scot who had served as a fighter pilot during the war. When his Royal Aircraft Factory F.E.2b biplane was shot down over German lines, D'Arcy Greig made an emergency landing and, although he would need hospital treatment, walked 13 miles through German guns back to his 83 Squadron base. As an instructor with the Central Flying School, he teamed up with fellow pilot John Boothman to perform such daring and beautiful displays as the 'falling leaf', in which their biplanes twisted and tumbled gently in perfectly mirrored formation from the sky. During one of these displays, D'Arcy Greig's machine broke apart. As he had done in France in 1918, he walked away from the wreckage.

Remarkably, D'Arcy Greig did this yet again after bailing out of a powerful Gloster Gamecock biplane fighter that had got into an unrecoverable spin near Kenley Aerodrome, Surrey. D'Arcy Greig jumped, but not before the Gamecock had spun, he said, 27 times while falling 6,000 feet. He fell for some while before remembering to pull the ripcord of his parachute. The Gamecock, a notoriously tricky aircraft – 22 of the 90 operated by the RAF were lost to spins and hard-to-control landings – hit the ground near Riddlesdown, bursting into a tower of flame. Safely on the ground, D'Arcy Greig gathered his parachute and was directed by a young girl, Betty Knight, to the Hare and Hounds pub run by her mother in nearby Chelsham. Mrs Knight said the nearest telephone was at Colonel Arthur Daniell's house. It was. Within an hour of jumping from the Gamecock, D'Arcy Greig was back at RAF Kenley.

Most of Orlebar's team were non-smokers and teetotallers, or at least were while with the High Speed Flight. Cigarettes and aviation fuel had never been a good mix, while hangovers were not helpful when attempting to fly what had become the equal-fastest aircraft in the world in front of huge crowds, newspaper reporters and newsreel cameras, and close to water bobbing with boats and buoys. Newly arrived in Calshot for the Schneider contest, the team swam and also played tennis and, in D'Arcy Greig and Atcherley's case, practical jokes.

The crisply uniformed Italians had arrived at Calshot at lunchtime on 29 August with their own food and chefs. The two teams played snooker together that evening; D'Arcy Greig and Atcherley undermined General Balbo's virtuoso game by sticking chewing gum on the end of his cue. And when Balbo got into bed that evening, it was with a dead porpoise that had been washed up on the beach. Once removed, the porpoise was shifted surreptitiously from bed to bed during the night. To his great credit, Balbo, an Anglophile, found the antics of the British pilots amusing. How they could be so silly one moment and so serious at the controls of their machines the next was, though, something of a puzzle.

And what machines these were – the deep blue Supermarine and gold and Cambridge-blue Gloster monoplanes. The former was supremely purposeful, the latter arguably the most beautiful of all Schneider Trophy aircraft. The S.6 was Mitchell's first all-metal design. With its muscular Rolls-Royce engine – 60 per cent heavier than the S.5's Napier Lion – the S.6, fuelled and ready to fly, weighed 5,771 lbs compared to the S.5's 3,242 lbs. Internally and externally, pipes and radiator elements were caressed into fuselage and floats. Ingeniously, the tail fin doubled up as an oil tank and cooler. It was as if this machine had lungs, pores, arteries and veins. And it would need to breathe hard and sweat profusely; in human terms, it was an aircraft designed to run the equivalent of a 100-yard sprint over the length of a marathon.

Orlebar had taken the S.6 up first to put it through its paces before handing it over to his pilots. At first, the aircraft refused to lift from the water. With the much lighter S.5, Orlebar had kept the control column centred as it gathered speed and began to lift. With the S.6 he learned to pull hard back on the stick as if pulling the heavy machine into the air. This, though, was not before D'Arcy Greig had ploughed across the Solent for two and a half miles at take-off speed and boiled his engine. The first S.6 to arrive overheated in the air, too. The Supermarine team dealt with this by fitting extra cooling surfaces on the tops of the aircraft's floats, and air scoops under the wing radiators. When leaks were discovered in the wing radiators after test flights, the simple solution was to patch them with 'NeverLeak', the same sealant D'Arcy Greig used on the radiator of his 12-hp Austin Seven.

There was a discussion about reducing the size of the aircraft's propeller to get it to spin faster, and so raising the power output of the engine. This, though, would have created yet more heat while raising fuel consumption. The answer was a smaller prop and instructions to the pilots to fly, after take-off, at no more than 97 per cent full throttle. They would have to keep an eagle eye on the rev counter, and avoid the temptation to thrust the throttle lever to the limit of its throw in the heat of the contest.

The Gloster VI, despite its sleek outline and spare beauty, was not the aircraft Henry Folland had been thinking of when first planning for the 1929 contest. His intention was to design a biplane developed from the earlier IV. Such, though, was the weight of the supercharged Napier Lion VIID that a biplane's centre of gravity would be out of kilter. So Folland started from scratch and produced a machine that promised much but, after all the painstaking work that went into it, was let down by the 1,320-hp Napier. On Orlebar's first test flight, the engine failed immediately after take-off. On further runs, the Lion cut out on turns and continued to do so despite the best efforts of Napier mechanics and engineers. The two beautiful gold and blue Glosters – the first of these known as the *Golden Arrow* – were scratched from the contest. This was not without regret. Flight Lieutenant Stainforth, for one, preferred the Gloster to the Supermarine.

While the Supermarine's engine was beginning to perform as hoped, Rolls-Royce insisted that the racing R must not be run for longer than five hours. At that point, it would have to be stripped down and rebuilt at the company's works at Derby, some 200 miles north of Calshot. What to do? The answer was a specially adapted 7.7-litre Rolls-Royce Phantom I limousine transformed into a lorry of sorts, racing with spent and revived aero-engines between the two sites and mostly by night to avoid traffic. Rolls-Royce drivers were keen to discover how quickly they could do the trip. The Phantom lorry was supposedly stopped by police when caught speeding through Hampshire at 80 mph. What is certainly true is that its hard-pressed brakes had to be relined after every second round trip.

With so many men in uniform, it was clear that the Schneider contest had become a peacetime battle between rival governments and their air forces. The setting at Calshot was itself far distant – certainly in spirit – from the hedonistic Venice Lido. The hangars, workshops and messes of what had, since the war, been a military seaplane base were jammed at the end of a mile-long sand and shingle spit beside Calshot Castle. This squat fortress had been built in 1539–40 as part of Henry VIII's coastal defences, at a time when England feared invasion from France and Spain.

Remote from hotels and pleasure beaches, RAF Calshot was connected to the mainland by a two-foot gauge railway. RAF personnel called it the 'Calshot Express'. Curiously, while surviving Schneider planes sit silently in museums today, the locomotive of the Calshot Express, a 0-4-0 tank locomotive built by Andrew Barclay of Kilmarnock in 1918, is still very much at work. Donated to the Talyllyn Railway on the Mid-Wales coast in 1953, what is now No. 6 *Douglas* was repainted in RAF-blue livery complete with roundels in 2018, to commemorate the air force's centenary. Although RAF Calshot was closed in 1961, its buildings survive.

If Calshot lacked the deluxe comforts of the Lido, it had its own special glamour. During the contest the Prince of Wales came to visit, while a far more famous person could be seen deep in conversation at Spithead with General Balbo. What was remarkable is that he was dressed in the uniform of an aircraftman, the RAF's most junior rank. This, they must have known or learned very quickly, was none other than Lawrence of Arabia. While it was odd to see what appeared to be an ordinary aircraftman talking in Italian on a level with an Italian general and surrounded by British air marshals, the heir to the throne, leading politicians and assorted VIPs, Lawrence – or

Shaw, as he was known at time – was a part of the 1929 team and the work he undertook at Calshot was to prove not just helpful, but a lifesaver for RAF pilots in years to come.

Calshot was a busy place both on shore and on water. The Solent was criss-crossed by boats and ships of all scales, from dinghies and two-seat speedboats to freighters, ocean liners and warships. While attempting to land his M.67 on a test run, Lieutenant Giovanni Monti was faced with the daunting sight of HMS *Iron Duke* – all 622 feet and 30,000 tons of this veteran Royal Navy flagship – steaming across his path.

On shore and on boats bobbing in the Solent, press and cine-news photographers kept busy, too. With rival teams caught on film with the Prince of Wales, inspecting one another's aircraft, hands nonchalantly in uniform pockets – or sat with wives in cloche hats and Stainforth's cheery dog, or in front of an S.6 in the company of Reginald Mitchell and representatives from Rolls-Royce. The latter – several hundred in all – happened to be scattered in a number of local pubs the evening before the contest when a beady-eyed mechanic discovered a tiny fleck of metal on one of the spark plugs drawn from the cylinder head of the engine of Flying Officer Waghorn's S.6. Might the piston fail with the aircraft at full speed in mid-air? Very probably. Contest rules precluded an engine change at this stage. With the help of the local police, Rolls-Royce fitters with the requisite skills were tracked down and driven sharpish to Calshot. Overnight, they replaced the piston and had the engine running as it should before breakfast. It had been a close-run thing.

On the day of the contest, Dick Waghorn was first away from the starting point, Ryde Pier. His first lap was slower than hoped. The spray on take-off, the limited view ahead, and the intense and brightly coloured patchwork of boats on the water made it difficult to spot the pylons mounted on destroyers marking the turning points. There were four: at Seaview, south of Hayling Island, South Parade Pier and Cowes. Once in his stride and as the temperature of his cockpit rose, Waghorn increased his average speed to 331 mph. Among those cheering him on were members of the public who had booked space to watch the contest on board SS *Orontes*, the brand-new 20,000-ton Orient Line passenger ship built by Vickers-Armstrong, the engineering conglomerate that had swallowed Supermarine in 1928.

Dal Molin was off next in the M.52R but was unable to match the Supermarine's pace. D'Arcy Greig's S.5 was not quite as fast as Dal Molin's Macchi. Clouds of poisonous exhaust fumes caused Remo Cadringher, in the first of the two Macchi M.67s, to drop out on his second lap. He could neither see where he was going nor breathe without difficulty. The second M.67, flown by Giovanni Monti, failed on its second lap, too. Not only was Monti choked by exhaust fumes, his legs, arms and shoulders were badly scalded when a joint in the engine's cooling system gave way. Unable to see where he was going, at one point he had veered overland. He brought his Macchi down safely and was taken to hospital.

Dick Atcherley, who had taken off ahead of Monti, got into trouble when within seconds his goggles were spattered with oil. He had a spare pair, but found it impossible to put them on while keeping control of the rapidly accelerating aircraft as it approached its first turn. Ducking his head below the

Supermarine's token windscreen, he managed to turn but on the inside rather than the outside of the first pylon and was disqualified.

Waghorn entered what he thought was his final lap when his fearsome Rolls-Royce engine hesitated. Instinctively, he climbed from 150 feet or so to around 800 feet, aiming to glide across the finishing line if the engine continued to lose power. On the final leg, the engine stopped. Waghorn was forced to land with Ryde Pier close by. It is not difficult to imagine how he felt, and yet the crew of the launch he could see on its way to tow him back to shore were waving and shouting excitedly. Waghorn had miscounted. His final lap was his eighth. He had very nearly flown one too many. He had won with a time of 39 minutes and 42 seconds over 217.48 miles, at an average speed of 328.63 mph.

Dal Molin came in second, six minutes behind Waghorn's time, with D'Arcy Greig in third place, 21 seconds behind the Italian. 'We have obtained the results we expected,' General Balbo said at the post-race dinner in the French classical dining room of RMS *Orford*, another brand-new 20,000-ton Orient Line ship built by Vickers-Armstrong, 'but we have now finished playing our part as sportsmen. Tomorrow our work as competitors begins.'

There was little doubt then among the Italians that they had been overtaken in both the development of their aircraft and in the race itself. The Macchi M.67s had been a failure and it had been up to the veteran M.52 to take second place, 44.43 mph slower than Dick Waghorn's S.6. Even then, the Supermarine aircraft had been pushed to their limits, which is, of course, what they were designed to do – although perhaps without spraying oil in their pilots' faces.

A 'veteran' aircraft in a contest as intense as the Schneider Trophy meant one that was just two years old, so rapid was the progress made in the performance of these highly strung thoroughbreds. Progress meant taking risks, pushing the boundaries of flight and, in the pursuit, stretching the imaginations of designers, the science of engineers, the skills of manufacturers and mechanics, the resourcefulness of riggers and other ground staff – and, of course, jostling pilots into new realms of speed and forces of gravity.

Accelerometers and G recorders became increasingly essential tools to discover and measure the potentially lethal forces at work on pilots in what were now very fast machines indeed. Dick Atcherley recalled blacking out as he turned on a trial flight at unaccustomed speed above Calshot Castle:

> In my lapse of consciousness, I dreamt I was sitting in the housemaster's garden at Oundle in a deckchair... I could see the flowers – and hear the bees – the noise of which got angrier and angrier, until I started to wonder where I had heard that noise before. Then I realised it was the Napier engine in the S.5, and gradually came the frightening realisation that I was going like a bomb and might expect to hit the water at any second.

The day after Waghorn's win, Flight Lieutenant Stainforth had the Gloster VI up to a top speed of 351.3 mph while setting an official world speed record over four timed runs of 336.3

mph. A few days later, Squadron Leader Orlebar pushed the airspeed record with the S.6 to 357.7 mph. Within seven years, Mitchell's glorious Rolls-Royce–powered Supermarine Spitfire would reach and sustain this speed as a matter of course, while scything around bends with the grace and poised ease of a swift with the wind in its wings.

SIX

A Very Good Flight: Calshot, 1931

Quite what was going through the minds of the ministers of Ramsay MacDonald's Labour government in January 1930 remains in question. The Air Ministry had refused a request by the Royal Aero Club for funds to finance Britain's entry to the next Schneider Trophy contest, scheduled for the following year. Having won the past two races, in 1927 and 1929, Britain was in sight of capturing the trophy for good – and, with it, not just international prestige but a supercharged boost to the fortunes of its aviation industry.

While the Labour administration could claim it had other priorities, it seemed an odd and offhand decision given that Lord Thomson, MacDonald's first air minister, had been chairman of both the Royal Aero Club and the Royal Aeronautical Association. The former army officer, who had been a delegate at the Treaty of Versailles – which he thought a mistake – was also a patron of the Air League, a charity formed in 1909 to bring together different sectors of the aviation industry for various good causes, including that of the industry itself. He had, though, been killed the previous October, one of the 48 people who died when the government-sponsored dirigible R101 crashed in France on its maiden flight from London to Karachi.

Did this taint the government's view of major investment in radical new aircraft? Or was it that Thomson's successor, the Scottish barrister Lord Amulree, was just not interested in the Schneider Trophy – or, at least, could see little point in this flamboyant and glamorous international event?

To make its new stance clear, the Air Ministry also decreed that aircraft used in the 1929 event were forbidden to take part in the 1931 contest, that RAF pilots of the High Speed Flight would not be allowed to participate, and that the government would not help police the circuit around the Solent, with the help of the Royal Navy for example, even if a British team did find a way of entering.

While the Royal Aero Club, Conservative opposition and several newspapers protested, it seemed nothing could be done – until Lady Lucy Houston, Britain's richest woman, promised to write a personal cheque for £100,000 (around £7 million in 2020) on condition that the government lift its restrictions. This was the cost, reckoned the Royal Aero Club, of building two new racing aircraft and their engines. 'Every true Briton would rather sell his last shirt', declared Lady Houston, 'than admit that England could not afford to defend itself.'

It did seem odd that Britain's further involvement in a contest it had a very good chance of winning outright should be made possible only through the largesse of a single, if highly vocal, member of the public. What was all the more remarkable was the life and times of Lady Houston herself, both pre- and post-Schneider.

Born in Lower Kennington Green, Lambeth, in 1857, the daughter and ninth child of a south London warehouseman, Lucy Radmall was a chorus girl known as 'Poppy' when, at the age of 16, she ran off with a married man, Frederick Gretton. Twice her age, Gretton was a member of the Bass brewing family and immensely rich. The relationship broke down, but when he died in 1882, Gretton left Poppy £6,000 a year, or something like a million pounds today.

Poppy went on to marry again and yet again, acquiring further fortunes, an aristocratic title, and a damehood for her support for homes for nurses during the Second World War. Her third marriage to the 'hard, ruthless and unpleasant' shipping magnate and MP Sir Robert Houston saw her living either in tax exile in Jersey or aboard her husband's yacht *Liberty*. When he died on board *Liberty* in 1926, Lucy inherited £5.5 million, a colossal sum at the time.

So Lady Houston could well afford the £100,000 she gave to the Royal Aero Club in 1931 – allowing Reginald Mitchell to pursue the design and construction of the supremely fast Supermarine S.6B – but her generosity and what she saw as Britain's need to invest in its military and security were not to stop there. In 1932, she offered the government £200,000 to beef up the army and the Royal Navy. When this was turned down, she sailed around the coast of Britain with an electric sign bearing the message 'Down with MacDonald the Traitor' hung from *Liberty*'s rigging.

The following year, she financed the Houston–Mount Everest Flight Expedition, a part-scientific, part-quixotic adventure that saw two Scottish pilots from the Royal Auxiliary Air Force's 602 (City of Glasgow) Squadron conquer Everest in specially equipped and re-engined Westland PV-3 and PV-6 torpedo bombers. The pilots were Squadron Leader Douglas Douglas-Hamilton and Flight Lieutenant David Fowler McIntyre. McIntyre's aircraft was fitted with a small cabin behind its open cockpit; this was for Sidney Bonnett of Gaumont British News to fly in with his brand-new cameras.

Taking off from Purnia, a settlement founded by the East India Company in 1770, the team managed, with some difficulty, to crest Everest on their three-hour flight. Unfortunately, Bonnett blacked out when he mislaid his oxygen tube, and there was little usable film or photography. A second flight came back with photographs taken from McIntyre's PV-6 that were to help Tenzing Norgay and Edmund Hillary climb to the top of Mount Everest 20 years later. It also provided a wealth of information relating to high-altitude flight, from fuels to physiology.

It was Lucy Houston's enthusiasm for adventurous flight and the Schneider Trophy in particular – and how she liked to be photographed with the dashing young High Speed Flight pilots – that, in the face of government negativity and official indifference, was to fuel hugely significant advances in aviation and aircraft design and technology. Lady Houston was not going to let the British be beaten by foreigners, even if Lord Trenchard, the outgoing Chief of the Air Staff, had performed one last volte-face in his attitude towards Britain's further involvement in the contest. 'I can see nothing of value in it,' he boomed. On 25 September 1929, so soon after Dick Waghorn's victory, the Air Ministry issued its statement to the effect that the RAF would take no further part in the contest.

And yet, at the banquet on board RMS *Orford* to celebrate Britain and the RAF's success, the prime minister had said, 'We are going to do our best to win again.' When it was clear that MacDonald had gone back on his word, and before Lady Houston stepped in, Charles Grey, editor of *The Aeroplane*, let loose with all guns blazing:

The Government's attitude is a disgrace to the nation. To let us be beaten by a lot of Italians is selling the birthright of the Anglo-Saxon race. Governments have been put out of action for less... A Government which will give £80,000 to subsidise a lot of squalling foreigners at Covent Garden and will refuse £80,000 to win the World's greatest advertisement for British aircraft is unworthy of the nation.

'We are not worms to be trampled under the heel of Socialism,' chorused Lady Houston, 'but true Britons, with a heart for any fate except slavery and Socialism.' The Labour Party, she insisted, was nothing other than a hotbed of Bolshevism. Curiously, yet a sign of the times, Lady Houston was keen on Mussolini, and Grey, reputedly a kindly man away from his weekly editorial posturing, ended up supporting both Mussolini and Hitler.

For MacDonald and his Cabinet colleagues, the problem came down to money. Wall Street had crashed the month following the 1929 Schneider contest, and it was as if the plug had been pulled on the seas of global commerce. By January 1930 it was no longer possible to say the things he and his government had said in September 1929. Between these dates, so close together, was an ever-growing and global financial black hole. The government's initial response to Lady Houston's largesse was, however – even given the circumstances – peevish and blinkered. Her offer was, by any standards, a generous one.

This battle of wills endured until, with the press mostly on one side, the government on the other, Lady Houston played her famous trump card. She sent a telegram to 10 Downing Street. It read: 'To prevent the Socialist Government being spoilsports, Lady Houston will be responsible for all extra expenses necessary beyond what Sir Philip Sassoon [chairman of the Royal Aero Club] says can be found, so that Great Britain can take part in the race for the Schneider Trophy.'

Embarrassed and bowing to popular and media pressure, MacDonald expressed government approval as long as funds were made available from private sources. Sympathetic to the Schneider cause, the newly appointed Chief of the Air Staff, Air Chief Marshal Sir John Salmond – who had flown Sopwith Tabloids in action in the 1914–18 war – gave the go-ahead for RAF pilots to take part in the 1931 event.

The government's shilly-shallying meant there was no time for Supermarine to design a new racing seaplane for 1931. Nevertheless, Mitchell made a number of key improvements to the S.6 design, including longer and more streamlined floats, a flush riveted fuselage, yet more radiator surfaces, a longer and hinged windscreen, and streamlined balances to the ailerons. Work on the floats was essential because new FAI regulations – the French as keen on rules, regulations and decrees as ever – required contestants to perform a fully laden trial take-off and landing. The stress on the floats would be enormous.

The two S.6Bs were 300 lbs heavier than the S.6, but Rolls-Royce extracted a further 450 hp from its R engine. These stirring machines arrived at Calshot in the third week of July 1931. Squadron Leader Orlebar was first to try the new seaplane. In his words, the tremendous torque of the engine caused the aircraft to give 'a very good impression of a kitten chasing its tail'. Some kitten. Some tail.

While this skittish behaviour was under investigation, the High Speed Flight's youngest member, Lieutenant Jerry Brinton RN, was killed while attempting to take off at Calshot in S.6 N247, the aircraft flown by Waghorn that had won for Britain in 1929. Orlebar watched helplessly as it porpoised, climbed and dropped from 30 feet into the sea, its floats torn off. This had been 24-year-old Brinton's first flight with the S.6. His neck was broken.

The trick in getting the powerful S.6 – and the S6.B – successfully off the water was to keep the stick right back, even when its nose was pointing at a steep angle up into the sky and the aircraft felt as if it was hanging from its propeller. If the pilot sensed anything awry, he could close the throttle and, without releasing the stick, allow the machine to glide back down on to the water. In the heat of the moment and with insufficient experience and no height in which to recover, this was far easier said than done.

The previous month, Orlebar's other new recruit, Flight Lieutenant Eustace Linton Hope, had been caught in the heavy swell of a liner as he attempted to land after the engine cowling of his S.6 came loose. The Supermarine performed a cartwheel in the water. Hope managed to swim away from the stricken aircraft, but with a perforated eardrum he was out of the contest. He was an experienced wartime pilot who had excelled at long-distance flying and pioneered deck-landings on aircraft carriers at sea.

Accidents could happen to anyone out on the water. Even the meticulous Orlebar had pranged a barge with the first S6.B before its torque effects were brought under control. In his early forties, Group Captain Hope flew Hurricanes in action in the Second World War. He was shot down and killed over Normandy in August 1941, most probably by a German night-fighter while on an intruder mission deep into enemy territory. The quality of Orlebar's pilots was never in doubt.

As late as the end of August 1931, it looked as if the French might be back in the contest. While this promised to stimulate competition, nothing was going quite to plan on the other side of the Channel. The French government's STAé (Service Technique et Industriel de l'Aéronautique) commissioned three types of racing seaplanes for the 1931 contest – from Bernard, Nieuport-Delage and Dewoitine. Ideally, a single new engine by Marius Barbarou from Lorraine-Dietrich would power all three. This was the Lorraine 12Rer Radium, a supercharged – and possibly turbocharged – lightweight 28.7-litre V12 intended to develop 2,200 hp at 4,000 rpm. The inverted format, with the cylinders below rather than above the crankshaft, was chosen to give pilots a clear view ahead. Renault was tasked with producing a second, more conventional and heavier, engine of between 1,500 and 2,000 hp.

As time ticked by, the engines failed to appear. Mock-ups were sent to Bernard and Nieuport-Delage to help designers shape their Schneider seaplanes. Then a fully working engine was delivered to Dewoitine in July. The company expressed concerns over its airworthiness. Hurried plans were made to modify earlier aircraft, notably the Bernard H.V.120, but the French appeared to have lost heart – and especially so after the deaths of two key participants.

Antoine Paillard, the Bernard test pilot, died from peritonitis in mid-June. On 30 July, the Schneider contestant Lieutenant Georges Bougault was killed when his 1,500-hp Hispano-Suiza–powered H.V.120 dived into the Étang de Berre near Marseilles. No one has ever been sure why Bougault crashed. He was testing a new four-bladed propeller that may have broken up in the air, although it may have been a rogue spark plug breaking away from the engine and shooting into the cockpit that did for him. When the aircraft was pulled from the lake, its jammed speedometer needle indicated 363 mph.

Not long before Bougault's death, Fernand Lasne, an experienced test pilot, crashed the Nieuport-Delage NiD.450 that might have been a contender for the September Schneider contest into the Seine. Lasne escaped largely unhurt, but the NiD.450 would need extensive repairs. On 5 September, the French withdrew from the contest.

This left the Italians. Seven military pilots were selected for special training at the Reparto Alta Velocità (High Speed

Department) on Lake Garda. As they built up speed and confidence with existing seaplanes, performing landings at 125 mph, they awaited the stunning machine that would surely win the 1931 Schneider contest. This was the Macchi-Castoldi MC.72, a steel, wood and Duralumin projectile designed by Castoldi and powered by an outlandish supercharged 51.1-litre V24 engine by Tranquillo Zerbi, capable of short bursts of 3,100 hp. Weighing close to a ton and measuring 11 feet long, this operatic engine comprised a pair of Zerbi's new Fiat AS.6 V12s running in tandem. A pair of contra-rotating propellers would counteract the torque effect that had made Squadron Leader Orlebar's S6.B chase its tail like a kitten. Although colossally powerful, the MC.72 should take off in a civilized manner while spearing towards some unprecedented top speed.

General Balbo believed it was best to concentrate the team's efforts on a single aircraft design. While a sensible idea in theory, and in line with British thinking, the MC.72 proved to be a downright dangerous machine to fly. Castoldi's airframe was excellent, but was let down by Zerbi's temperamental engine. On 2 August, Captain Giovanni Monti was killed when his MC.72, being flown above representatives of Fiat and Macchi, exploded in mid-air and crashed. At a speed of something like 375 mph, a backfire in the engine had ignited a fuel-air mixture in the manifold. Captain Monti had flown the aircraft over the maintenance sheds at Desenzano so engineers and mechanics could listen first-hand and up close to the pops and bangs emanating from the irregular beat of his hot-running engine. The captain was a brave man. The duration of his final flight had been just two minutes.

Balbo asked the Royal Aero Club if it might consider delaying the contest, perhaps even until the following year, to allow the Italian team a sporting chance to compete. The answer was no, although in rejecting the Italians appeal, the British were hoping to push them into the contest. But, then, on 10 September, Lieutenant Stanislao Bellini, flying as fast as 394 mph, flew his MC.72 into low-lying ground on the shores of Lake Garda. When the remnants of the seaplane were examined, it was clear that the pilot had lost control only after an explosion in the engine had set fire to a fuel feed. Lieutenant Bellini would have been engulfed in flames in the moments before he died. Balbo withdrew from the Schneider contest.

All the British team had to do then on Saturday, 12 September, was to fly around the Solent circuit without engine failure or pilot error. This year, the triangular circuit – seven laps of 50 kilometres (31 miles) – had been plotted to bring competing aircraft close to the crowd and shores. From Ryde Pier, it extended out to a pylon on a destroyer anchored off St Helen's Point, and from there to the coast at West Wittering where Henry Royce would be watching. A 14-mile straight, covered in two minutes, led to a point midway between Cowes and Lee-on-Solent, and from there it was back to Ryde.

The crowd, a million strong, was to cheer on two aircraft – the Supermarine S6.Bs designated S.1595 and S.1596, flown by Flight Lieutenants John Boothman and George Stainforth. Boothman was to fly the circuit with the intention of capturing the Schneider Trophy for Britain. Later in the afternoon, Stainforth, the High Speed Flight's senior pilot, would attempt to break the world airspeed record.

Roads were jammed and trains packed on the Saturday when the contest was due to be held. Then the heavens opened. Torrential rain from sea clouds reduced visibility to next to zero in places. Many people had come down for the day, and trekked back disappointed to London and points east, west and north.

Those who stayed woke to a bright, clear morning. At ten-thirty, they watched an Armstrong Whitworth Atlas floatplane fly the circuit and then a Fairey Firefly. These were piloted and crewed by Squadron Leader Orlebar and members of the High Speed Flight. A gentle north wind gave a nice chop to the water. Conditions as Orlebar could see them were ideal. By midday, people were sunbathing on beaches, scoffing ice cream, tuning in to wirelesses, listening to loudspeaker announcements and getting in the mood for something special.

After the trial take-off and landing required by the new FIA rules, Boothman was away when the starting gun was fired at 1.02 p.m. from the deck of HMS *Medea*, a 540-ton coastal monitor and minelayer. Stick right back, full right rudder, a slight wiggle to see ahead, up Boothman went after a take-off run lasting 36 seconds.

His lithe blue aircraft flashed intense white-gold sunfire as it banked around the pylons. Boothman took these fairly wide to maintain a more or less constant speed. Revs 3,100 rpm. Engine temperature 95 degrees Celsius. His lap times were within 5 mph of one another, the fastest flown at 342.7 mph and the slowest – if that is the right word – at 337.7 mph. As Boothman made a textbook landing, the Jovian roar and lightning crackle of his Rolls-Royce engine was very nearly, if not quite, drowned out by ships' hooters, bells, sirens and whistles. It had taken just 47 minutes to fly 217.48 miles.

A motor launch ferried him from the seaplane to HMS *Medea*, where, still wearing his leather flying helmet and looking slightly embarrassed – almost as if he had made a mess of things rather than just won the coveted Schneider Trophy for Britain – he received the hearty congratulations of captain and crew. If Boothman's fleeting Supermarine had made a glorious sight and unforgettable sound as it tore around the Solent early that Sunday afternoon, perhaps there was a slight sense of anti-climax. There had, after all, been no competition. For everyone involved, it would surely have been a much more exciting event if the Italians had been there with their daunting Macchi-Castoldi MC.72s.

This, in part, is why George Stainforth took off in the afternoon aiming to set a new world airspeed record. His flight added extra excitement. While S.1596 was being prepared, Flying Officer Leonard Snaith, one of the reserve Schneider contest pilots, had the crowd oohing and aahing as he flew a daring stunt display in the High Speed Flight's Rolls-Royce Kestrel–powered Fairey Firefly II biplane fighter.

Taking off at 4 p.m., Stainforth made four runs over a three-kilometre course at an average speed of 379.05 mph. This was the new world record the crowd was rooting for. A Movietone newsreel shows Flight Lieutenant Stainforth being carried ashore from the Supermarine, where he meets his wife as three playful dogs weave around their legs. One of the dogs is seen in further footage of Stainforth and Boothman standing either side of Squadron Leader Orlebar as he announces the speeds his pilots have just achieved. Flight Lieutenant Boothman, he says with almost a chuckle, had 'a very good flight. No trouble. He flew exactly to instructions – what pleases me.' Even in this short run of film, it is possible to see that combination of playfulness, an inability to crow and a velvet-gloved steeliness that made these RAF pilots so very good at what they did.

The team received congratulations from the King, the prime minister Ramsay MacDonald and General Balbo. The following day they lunched with Lady Houston on board her yacht *Liberty*, and in October there was a formal banquet at Claridge's hosted by the Royal Aero Club to celebrate Britain's victory. That same month the team attended a celebratory lunch in honour of Reginald Mitchell – they all signed his menu – at Southampton's South Western Hotel. 'The credit', Orlebar later wrote, 'belongs to the brains which conceive, not to the hands which hold. But the hands had very good fun.' In between these revels, the High Speed Flight, knowing it was about to be disbanded, planned to go out in determinedly racy style.

Rolls-Royce prepared a sprint version of the R racing engine. By raising the boost pressure of its supercharger and fuelling with a cocktail devised by Rod Banks, mixing methanol, gasoline and ethanol, the power of the engine was raised to 2,530 hp. The plan had been to fit this to Stainforth's record-breaking S.1596. But after flying the aircraft from Calshot on 16 September with a new and shorter propeller at 385 mph, Stainforth swung on the water as he came in to land. He corrected the movement with the rudder but got his heel stuck under the pedal. Now overcorrected, the plane cartwheeled and capsized. With S.1596 out of action, the Trophy winner, S.1595, was fitted with the R27 sprint engine. After a frustrating day on 24 September when the engine refused to run up to power, Stainforth tried for an official new airspeed record five days later. Following a 43-second take-off run, S.1595 made four passes in opposing directions over a three-kilometre straight, averaging 407.5 mph. Touching down at 115 mph, it took Stainforth half a mile to stop. He was the first person to exceed 400 mph.

What did this feel like? 'This question is not easy to answer', wrote Stainforth in an account of his record-breaking flight published in 1934,

> because speed in a straight line produces no sensation in itself. It would feel almost the same to sit in the cockpit of a stationery aircraft in a 400mph wind tunnel... When going flat out, the S.6B is easy to control and quite comfortable, though a bit warm; there is no vibration, except for the sort one feels on a high-speed dynamo; and the noise is not painfully noticeable. There is practically no draught behind the tunnel-shape windscreen, but there is a wall of air doing over 400mph within 6 inches of one's face on each side... Such a flight is nearly all pleasure, though taking off is often uncomfortable. Of course, one felt subconsciously that if anything came adrift one couldn't do much about it.

On 31 October, Stainforth and Boothman went to Buckingham Palace and the King presented them both with the Air Force Cross, a medal awarded since 1918 for 'an act or acts of exemplary gallantry while flying, though not in active operations against the enemy'. As in the Movietone newsreel with Squadron Leader Orlebar, their very different characters are made clear in a photograph of the pair leaving Buckingham Palace, Stainforth seemingly so very self-assured, and Boothman, or so it seems, wanting to be anywhere but in the glare of cameras or the public gaze.

John Nelson Boothman – he flew close by Nelson's flagship HMS *Victory* seven times on his Schneider-winning flight – was born, the son of a railway clerk, in Harrow, Middlesex, in February 1901. The family spent holidays in France and John became fluent in French. At the age of 10 he flew as a passenger with Samuel Cody. Seven years later, and clearly an adventurous young man, he tried to join the army to fight in France, but was turned down for being too young. Undeterred, he joined the French Red Cross as an ambulance driver, serving as far afield as Salonica on the Macedonian Front. He was awarded the Croix de Guerre.

Back in England after the war, he took flying lessons and joined the RAF. His first post as a commissioned officer was with 4 Squadron in Constantinople. After serving as a flying instructor with the Central Flying School, Boothman joined 55 Squadron in Iraq, flying de Havilland DH.9A bombers on 'air policing' operations against rebellious tribesmen. An instructor again in England, his aerial stunts became the stuff of RAF legend. A test pilot with the Marine Aircraft Experimental Establishment, Felixstowe, in 1930, the following year he was made a member of Orlebar's High Speed Flight.

After his Schneider win and a subsequent long spell of ill health, he served as a test pilot in the Experimental Section, RAE Farnborough, and as chief flying instructor at the Central Flying School. Appointments followed with Coastal Command and RAF Far East, before he took command of 44 Squadron, Waddington, flying Bristol Blenheim and Handley Page Hampden light bombers. He was in Washington, DC in 1941 as adviser to the United States Army Air Forces (USAAF), and then commandant of the Aeroplane and Armament Experimental Establishment at Boscombe Down. In 1948, Air Vice Marshal Boothman was Air Officer Commanding, Air Headquarters, Iraq. Five years later he took over as Commander-in-Chief Coastal Command. Promoted to air chief marshal, he was knighted in 1954.

One of Boothman's proudest moments was the day in July 1944 when he and his son – his only child, and a fellow RAF officer – were both presented with the Distinguished Flying Cross at the same investiture. His son was killed two years later in a flying accident. Boothman retired in May 1956 and died the following year. He had joined Kelvin Hughes Ltd, manufacturers of navigation, radar and surveillance systems, as technical director, but his life had been one animated by flight. Outside the RAF it was as if the wings of this gifted and multitalented airman had been clipped. His DFC citation published in the *London Gazette* was very much a summary of who John Boothman was:

This officer has displayed the highest standard of skill, resolution and devotion to duty. In the early days of the war he undertook many sorties as pilot of aircraft. He participated in the initial attack against German naval vessels at Kiel and subsequently in numerous bombing missions against industrial targets. Air Commodore Boothman has completed many notable reconnaissances and his successes are a splendid tribute to his high skill and endurance. This officer has always displayed the greatest keenness for air operations and has only been prevented from participating in them more frequently by the pressure of his normal duties. He has set an example in keeping with the best traditions of the Royal Air Force.

As a new and independent military body, the RAF brought young men and women into its fold from a wide variety of backgrounds. Often thought of in its earlier days as a plaything for tally-ho public schoolboys, it was never really like this. The service needed and demanded specialist engineering skills and so drew on a new generation of technically literate would-be officers and other ranks from grammar and elementary schools. And to capture speed records and the public imagination, to push new aircraft to their limits, to win the Schneider Trophy barely able to see where your highly strung aircraft was heading, to make a biplane tumble like an autumn leaf at an air display or to pitch a Supermarine Spitfire into an armada of enemy aircraft – this demanded the sheer love of flying and the immeasurable and largely inexplicable fearlessness that was shared, in their different ways, by those two heroes of the 1931 Schneider contest, John Boothman and George Stainforth.

Another of the records George Stainforth set that year was flying upside down for 12 minutes. In those photographs and newsreels of 1931, there is a look of defiance in the eyes of Flight Lieutenant Stainforth. Unlike Boothman, he stares straight at the camera and without a hint of a smile.

Born in Dulwich in 1899, George Stainforth was raised by strict evangelical Christian parents. His father was a solicitor. One of George's early memories had nothing to do with the church or law, however. He had watched, open-eyed, as Samuel Cody flew over his prep school to land at nearby Crystal Palace. His grandfather's rectory happened to be near Brooklands, the Mecca or Jerusalem of early powered flight. George spent many hours there watching air displays with his younger brother Moxon.

George's mother, however, disapproved of aeroplanes. If God had intended her son to fly, he would have given George wings. After school – Dulwich followed by Weymouth College, Dorset, with its grimly ecclesiastical Victorian architecture – George was commissioned into the Buffs (Royal East Kent Regiment), but in 1923 was dismissed for bad behaviour. The RAF took him on. After serving at RAF Duxford with 19(F) Squadron, flying Sopwith Snipes and Gloster Grebes, George was assigned, like Boothman, to the Marine Aircraft Experimental Establishment, Felixstowe, and from there to the High Speed Flight.

A natural pilot, he was though – at least according to an account by Air Commodore Rodwell Banks, published in 1966 in the *Journal of the Royal Aeronautical Society* – a menace on the road:

Rolls-Royce gave a large party after the Schneider race and speed record affair had been wrapped up and I motored the pilots to Derby, except for Orlebar who went separately. I was driving the latest Buick and Stainforth particularly wished to try it. Nothwithstanding warnings from the others, I let him, but after ten minutes we had had enough and I reassumed control. It has always surprised me that a number of first-class pilots were such bad car drivers and Stainforth, who had first-class piloting judgement, had none in car. He was always in trouble with his little 7hp Austin at Calshot...

His behaviour in the years following the 1931 Schneider Trophy contest became rather eccentric. An incident involving him flying very low over Stonehenge in 1935 landed him with a non-flying position as RAF Adjutant on the aircraft carrier HMS *Glorious*. The ship was based at Alexandria, and it was here that George met Stella Deacon, a beautiful married woman who turned his head. This unsettling affair seems to have been the reason George was given command of 30 Squadron at RAF Habbaniya, a new military base the size of a town and a form of exile some 50 miles west of Baghdad.

After returning to England, George tested, among other aircraft, new-model Spitfires, exemplary flying machines designed by Reginald Mitchell and powered by Rolls-Royce V12s. In June 1940 he flew a captured Messerschmitt Bf 109E in mock dogfights over RAE Farnborough against Battle of Britain ace Bob Stanford-Tuck. As Officer Commanding 89 (Night Fighter) Squadron, Wing Commander Stainforth was posted to the Middle East to defend the Suez Canal. On 27 September 1942, he was killed in action flying a twin-engine Bristol Beaufighter at Gharib, near the Gulf of Suez.

These two very different RAF officers, John Boothman and George Stainforth, had flown into the history books under the guidance of a third, Squadron Leader Augustus Orlebar, who acted as their commanding officer, instructor and guardian angel.

Born in 1897 at Hinwick House in Podington, Bedfordshire, a handsome Queen Anne mansion built by John Hunt for Richard Orlebar between 1709 and 1714, Augustus was schooled at Rugby before joining the Bedfordshire Regiment. Thrown into action and wounded at Gallipoli, he was seconded to the RFC. As a fighter pilot flying B.E.12s, SPAD S.VIIs and Sopwith Camels over the Western Front, he scored seven kills. A test pilot at Martlesham Heath from 1919, he took on command of the High Speed Flight a decade later.

In 1939, Orlebar was the RAF's Director of Flying Training. Promoted to air vice marshal, he was Air Officer Commanding No. 10 (Fighter) Group from July 1941 and became Deputy Chief of Combined Operations, RAF Northolt, in March 1943, plotting raids against Nazi-occupied Europe. Cancer killed him in August 1943.

In September 1981, Christopher Orlebar – a British Airways Concorde pilot and distant cousin of Augustus Orlebar – and his wife Nicola chartered a Concorde to commemorate the fiftieth anniversary of the 1931 victory at Calshot. As Christopher Orlebar liked to say, the Rolls-Royce R engine of Boothman's S6.B had inspired the Merlin that powered the

Spitfire designed by Reginald Mitchell. The Merlin was super-charged to great effect by Stanley Hooker, who was key to the development of the Olympus engine that, further along the line, was to take Concorde to Mach 2.

Among those on board the 1981 Concorde flight were Air Commodore D'Arcy Greig and Group Captain Leonard Snaith, High Speed Flight veterans of the 1929 and 1931 Schneider contests. The Concorde, a machine able to fly from New York to London in three hours, retraced the 1931 circuit at exactly 340 mph. The experience was slightly more comfortable than it had been 50 years earlier.

If the Macchi-Castoldi MC.72 had been flying fit in September 1931, the stories of Orlebar, Stainforth and Boothman might have been very different. The Italian aircraft's backer, General Italo Balbo, had been a good loser in 1929 – and to his great credit he was again in 1931, not just congratulating the British team but attending several of the celebratory events. This was, and is, a reminder that the Schneider Trophy was an international event.

In its early days, cooperation between national teams was assured, given that British aircraft, for example, were dependent on French engines and manufacturers were keen to learn from one another. John Boothman spoke fluent French. Germany's Claude Dornier, who would have loved to compete, was the French-speaking son of a French wine merchant. Italo Balbo was an Anglophile who was to warn Mussolini against siding with Germany. While it was fun to wave flags and cheer on your home team patriotically, nationalism was

something else – a divisive force nurtured by a new generation of resentful European politicians with several chips on
their shoulders.

Balbo, a year older than Orlebar, was born in Quartesana,
Ferrara. His parents were both teachers: his mother the
daughter of a contessa, his father a frustrated soldier. Brought
up with a love of maps, boats, soldiery – 'Brave and bold on
the battlefield I'll be / There to win death or victory,' he sang
as a child – stories of Robinson Crusoe and Buffalo Bill, the
novels of Jules Verne, and the latest news of powered flight,
the young Italo was natural adventurer. A leader and rebel,
too. Most of all, he liked to go against the grain.

In 1910, when he was just 14, he attempted to join
Ricciotti Garibaldi's expedition to Albania to free the country
from Ottoman rule. The fourth son of the famous Giuseppe
Garibaldi, who had helped forge a unified Italy in the mid-
nineteenth century, Ricciotti had been brought up partly
in England, where his father was a much-feted hero. He
had fought with the French against the Prussians in 1870,
capturing the sole Prussian flag lost in the war, and had kept
to his father's promise of trying to liberate the Balkans. Italo
Balbo left home for Ancona, where Garibaldi was to set sail,
only to find that the mission had been called off.

As a student, Balbo campaigned vociferously for Italy
to join in the war against Germany, Austria-Hungary and
Ottoman Turkey. When it did, he fought bravely in Alpine
battalions, rising to the rank of captain. In 1918, he returned
to his studies in Florence, graduating with degrees in law
and social sciences. Siding with Benito Mussolini, he helped

lead the March on Rome in 1922 that brought the Fascists to power. He was appointed aviation minister in 1926. Balbo learned to fly. Appointed General of the Air Force in 1928, he became Minister of the Air Force the following year.

Between the 1929 and 1931 Schneider contests, Balbo led a flight of a dozen Savioa-Marchetti S.55 flying boats from the seaplane base at Orbetello, near Rome, to Rio de Janeiro. The expedition took place between 17 December 1930 and 15 January 1931, and was, in public relations terms, a *coup de théâtre*. The S.55, first flown in 1924, was a special and long-lived design. A catamaran monoplane, it featured twin passenger hulls with the cockpit mounted over and between them; a pair of 500-hp Isotta Fraschini V12s mounted in tandem in an upward-slanting nacelle; and a triple-finned tailplane. It was a gloriously futuristic design for its time, and successful, too. A total of 243 were built.

In July 1933, Balbo launched his 'Italian Air Armada' – a fleet of 24 S.55s, which flew on a round-trip from Orbetello to Chicago. The occasion was the Century of Progress World's Fair, an exhibition stretching along three and half miles of Lake Michigan shoreline. It ran from May 1933 to October 1934, attracting very nearly 50 million ticket-paying visitors. Focused on technological innovation, here was the place to see the latest in streamlined trains and cars, architecture, homes and product design. Balbo's armada flew in tight formation across the Atlantic via Holland, Ireland, Iceland and Canada. Mussolini, meanwhile, shipped an ancient Roman column with a newly carved base to Chicago. In English, its Italian inscription reads, 'This column twenty centuries old erected on the beach of Ostia, port of Imperial Rome, to safeguard the fortunes and victories of the Roman triremes. Fascist Italy, by command of Benito Mussolini, presents to Chicago [this] exaltation symbol memorial of the Atlantic Squadron led by Balbo that with Roman daring flew across the ocean in the 11th year of the Fascist Era.'

The Balbo Monument stands today in Chicago's Burnham Park, while Balbo Drive continues to connect Lake Shore Drive to Midtown Chicago. Although attempts have been made to remove both monument and street signs in recent years, a strong Italian-American lobby has maintained the status quo. Italo Balbo was no angel, and the question of whether or not he was responsible in some way for the brutal Italian war crimes committed in Libya and Abyssinia in the 1930s remains, say his critics, to be fully answered, although he did oppose Mussolini's three colonial wars and took no active part in them.

Accompanied by a 36-strong military escort, Balbo's armada flew on to New York. Here, the pilots enjoyed an open-top car parade through Manhattan. Balbo was invited to lunch with President Franklin Roosevelt, who presented him with the Distinguished Flying Cross. In Madison Square Garden, the general addressed a huge crowd of New York Italians: 'Be proud you are Italians. Mussolini has ended the era of humiliations.'

When he arrived back in Rome, Mussolini promoted Balbo to the newly created rank of Marshal of the Air Force. Although he had faced defeat at Calshot in September 1931 with good grace, Balbo still needed to prove that the Italian pilots and aircraft could beat the British. One way to do this was to topple George Stainforth's airspeed record.

The backfire from the giant Fiat engine was cured after Rod Banks, the British high-octane fuel expert, paid a visit to Desenzano. Up in the air over Lake Garda at speed on 15 June 1932, Lieutenant Ariosto Neri felt his MC.72 flutter. Guzzling Banks's potent cocktail, the engine was running well, but now there was a glitch somewhere in the control surfaces. Neri landed safely, but he was killed three months later flying one of the many hundreds of standard-issue 270 km/h (170 mph) Italian Air Force Fiat CR.20 biplane fighters. Great attention was paid to the workings of the MC.72 before, in April 1933, the press was told that a 700 km/h (435 mph) run was planned for the 10th of the month. The pilot was Warrant Officer Francesco Agello, whose recorded speed of 682 km/h (424 mph) fell a little short but was nevertheless a new world record.

The feeling of Colonel Mario Bernasconi, commander of the Reparto Alta Velocità, is that Agello could fly quite a bit faster than he had with the MC.72. Agello made several further flights that year, but was held back by disturbing vibrations and engine failure. His next attempt was pushed back to October 1934, by which time Italo Balbo had been appointed Governor-General of Libya.

Francesco Agello was now 32 years old and a test pilot with 12 years' military flying experience. Born in Casalpusterlengo, a small town in Lombardy, Agello had spent much of his youth playing sport. Anything went. Swimming. Gymnastics. Cycling. Football. Motorbikes. Small, lithe and as fit as a fiddle, he was an ideal pilot for racing seaplanes. Cockpits had grown ever smaller as the quest for speed and a concomitant need for improved aerodynamics grew. The RAF's Flight Lieutenant Stainforth, a perfectly trim fellow, had only been able to shoehorn himself into the seat of his record-breaking Supermarine S6.B by standing on the seat, turning sideways and wriggling himself down.

In April 1933, the Macchi's Fiat AS.6 had been tuned to give 2,500 hp. By autumn 1934, it was up to 3,100 hp. Agello made a fresh attempt at the airspeed record on 23 October. The event was filmed, so we can watch today as the Macchi-Castoldi seaplane is pushed out into Lake Garda by a team of men who are then, like Keystone Cops, soaked to the skin as Agello fires up and taxis towards the centre of the lake. Up he goes – a perfect, if long, take-off – climbing high and preparing for the measured runs. Agello clocked a maximum of 709.2 km/h (440.68 mph), a world record and the fastest a piston engine seaplane has ever flown. Here he is sitting on the nose of the aircraft and holding one of its propeller blades at the end of his run, before being carried high on the shoulders of his cheering colleagues.

It was at this point that the development of high-speed seaplanes stopped. Britain had won the Schneider Trophy for good. Italian honour had been restored. Neither air forces nor navies required machines like these. They might be the world's fastest aircraft, yet they were incapable of carrying bombs or of being fitted with machine guns, and in any case they were temperamental things. They were no use to civil aviation, either. They could barely fit a pilot let alone passengers, stewards and luggage. And as for range, they could hardly fly for an hour without running out of fuel or breaking down. They did, though, have lessons for both military and civil aviation.

Francesco Agello was commissioned a second lieutenant and awarded the Medaglia al Valore Aeronautico. As Captain Agello he was by 1938 Commander of the Reparto Alta Velocità, but flying war machines rather than record-breaking racers. Test-flying one of Mario Castoldi's Macchi C.202 fighters in foggy weather above Milan's Bresso Airfield in late November 1942, Agello collided with a second C.202 flown by Captain Guido Masiero, a First World War ace. Both pilots were killed.

Significantly, the engines of their fighters, although badged Alfa Romeo, were Daimler-Benz DB 601 V12s built under licence in Milan. These were the engines that drove Willy Messerschmitt's devilishly successful Bf 109 fighter. In March 1939, Captain Agello's world airspeed record was trumped by a specially prepared Heinkel He 100 that clocked 746.61 km/h (463.92 mph). The following month, a new record of 755.14 km/h (469.22 mph) was set by a Messerschmitt Me 209. Both aircraft were fitted with Daimler-Benz DB 601 engines. German design and engineering appeared to have triumphed, without the experience of the Schneider Trophy. Hitler was to invade Poland that September.

Mussolini told Air Marshal Balbo to his face at a meeting in Rome that the war would be over very soon. Germany would conquer Britain. Italy should have no fears. Back in Tripoli, the city he had done much to rebuild, Balbo said he felt caught between the British in Egypt and the French in Tunisia, 'like a slice of ham in a sandwich'. This was a war he did not want to fight.

On 28 June 1940, Balbo was flying a heavily laden tri-motor Savoia-Marchetti SM.79 light bomber to the Italian military base at Tobruk. This was very soon after nine British twin-engine Blenheim bombers had raided a nearby airbase. In the heat of the moment, Italian anti-aircraft gunners opened fire on Balbo's plane. How they cheered as, badly damaged, it crashed close to the harbour and exploded, killing all on board. Balbo's body was so badly burned that all that was left to identify him by were his teeth. Mussolini's reaction was to shrug his shoulders. By chance, Il Duce was rid of this turbulent airman.

The British response was quite different from that of the apparently indifferent Mussolini. On learning of Balbo's death, Air Chief Marshal Arthur Longmore, Commander-in-Chief RAF Middle East Command, dispatched an aircraft to drop a wreath over the site of the wreckage. A personal note attached read: 'The British Royal Air Force expresses its sympathy in the death of General Balbo, a great leader and gallant aviator, personally known to me, whom fate has placed on the other side.' Longmore had joined the RNAS as a seaplane pilot in 1912. For him, Italo Balbo was a fellow aviator and pioneer.

Adolf Hitler saw Balbo differently from Mussolini, too. In conversation over lunch two years later in his Ukrainian 'Werwolf' headquarters, he said, 'The death of Balbo was a great tragedy; there was a worthy successor of the Duce, a man who had something of the Renaissance in him! A man whose name alone was worth something! Balbo had the great advantage that he had equal influence with both Party and armed forces, and it is an ironic fate that he should have been shot down by Italian anti-aircraft guns.'

In Britain, Winston Churchill, another pilot, had been appointed prime minister a month before Balbo's death. He had witnessed first-hand the efficacy of Reginald Mitchell's Supermarine Spitfire. Shortly before Hitler's comment at Werwolf concerning Air Marshal Balbo, the Air Fighting Development Unit issued a report on the Mk IX Spitfire designed to take on the Luftwaffe's formidable Focke-Wulf Fw 190 fighter:

The performance of the Spitfire IX is outstandingly better than the Spitfire V especially at heights above 20,000 feet. On the level the Spitfire is considerably faster and climb is exceptionally good. It will climb easily to 38,000 feet and when levelled off there can be made to climb in stages to above 40,000 feet by building up speed on the level and a slight zoom. Its manoeuvrability is as good as a Spitfire V up to 30,000 feet and above is very much better. At 38,000 feet it is capable of a true speed of 368 mph and is still able to manoeuvre well for fighting.

By now, Ramsay MacDonald was a figure from ancient history. Lucy Houston was long dead. While her largesse had allowed Britain's entry to the 1931 Schneider contest and had led one way or another to that all-conquering Mk IX Spitfire 11 years later, she had become so frustrated with what she, and many others, saw as the fatal weakness of MacDonald and his Tory successor, Stanley Baldwin, that – aside from her well-known admiration of Mussolini and Hitler – she thought Britain should be led by a dictator, too.

PART TWO

The Legacy

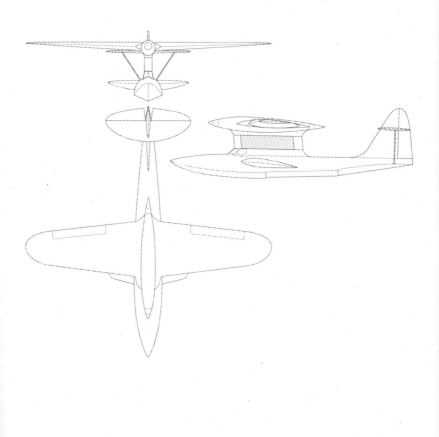

SEVEN

The Sea Shall Not Have Them

'I have been so curiously fortunate', wrote Aircraftman T. E. Shaw in 1935,

as to share in a little revolution we have made in boat design. People have thought we were at finality there, for since 1850 ships have merely got bigger. When I went into R.A.F. boats in 1929, every type was an Admiralty design. All were round-bottomed, derived from the first hollow tree, with only a fin, called a keel, to delay their rolling about and over. They progressed by pushing their own bulk of water aside.

Now, not one type of R.A.F. boat in production is naval... We have found, chosen, selected or derived our own sorts: they have (power for power) three times the speed of their predecessors, less weight, less cost, more room, more safety, more seaworthiness. As their speed increases, they rise out of the water and run over its face. They cannot roll, nor pitch, having no pendulum nor period, but a subtly modelled planning bottom and sharp edges.

The boats that Aircraftman Shaw helped develop between 1929 and his premature death in 1935 were to save the lives of some 13,000 British airmen in the Second World War. Flying on the crest of waves, what began life as a new type of RAF seaplane tender, and went on to become one of the finest air rescue boats of the twentieth century, was very much a product of the Schneider Trophy. The fact that Aircraftman Shaw – or Colonel T. E. Lawrence or Lawrence of Arabia, as he was known to press and public – was involved in the evolution and testing of these very fast and supremely seaworthy rescue boats adds immeasurably to the allure of their story. What makes their story doubly fascinating in terms of the Schneider Trophy is that they were invented, designed and built by Hubert Scott-Paine, who had named the flying boat company he bought in 1916 'Supermarine', employed Reginald Mitchell, inaugurated the first cross-Channel flying boat service and built the Sea Lion II that won the Schneider Trophy contest in 1922.

Scott-Paine sold Supermarine in 1923 and merged his British Marine Air Navigation Company into the newly formed Imperial Airways, of which he was a director. In 1927, he bought the Hythe Shipyard on Southampton Water, fully intending it to be the most modern of its kind in the world. During the First World War, Felixstowe flying boats had been built on a site at nearby Shore Road, where Lawrence was to rent a room at Myrtle Cottage in 1930. The Felixstowe F.1, a successful U-boat spotter, was designed by Lieutenant Commander John Porte, who before the war had teamed up with Glenn Curtiss to build a flying boat they planned to fly non-stop across the Atlantic and so win the *Daily Mail*'s £10,000 prize. The war intervened and the prize was finally won in 1919 by Alcock and Brown in a modified Vickers Vimy bomber.

Porte's Felixstowe was superseded in 1925 by the Supermarine Southampton, a highly successful design by the young Reginald Mitchell – who was to work there at Hythe on the Spitfire a decade later. There was, then, a symbiotic relationship of sorts between the development of flying boats, seaplanes, high-speed boats that flew across the water and the Spitfire. The Hythe works was also to serve as a maintenance depot for the Short Empire flying boats of Imperial Airways that, from 1936, operated services from Southampton to Singapore.

As the Schneider Trophy itself morphed year by year into an outright speed contest, fast boats were needed to rescue pilots in fast planes when accidents happened. 'Now, I do not claim to have made these boats', wrote Lawrence not long before he was killed in a motorbike accident near his hideaway cottage, Clouds Hill, near Bovington Camp, Dorset:

They have grown out of joint experience, skill and imaginations of many men. But I can (secretly) feel that they owe to me their opportunity and their acceptance. The pundits met them with a fierce hostility: all the R.A.F. sailors, and all the Navy, said that they would break, sink, wear out, be unmanageable. To-day we are advising the War Office in refitting the coast defences entirely with boats of our model, and the Admiralty has specified them for the modernised battleships: while the Germans, Chinese, Spanish and Portuguese Governments have adopted them! In inventing them we have had to make new engines, new auxiliaries, use new timbers, new metals, new materials. It has been five years of intense and co-ordinated progress. Nothing now hinders the application of our design to big ships – except the conservatism of man, of course. Patience. It cannot be stopped now.

Lawrence had long been fascinated by new machinery. During the desert war of 1917–18, he deployed Rolls-Royce armoured cars, Crossley and Ford tenders and worked closely with the RFC's 14 Squadron, which had sent a flight of Royal Aircraft Factory B.E.2c reconnaissance aircraft and Arab-speaking pilots to help with the campaign. Pilots and crews worked in extreme conditions. If the heat, thirst, mosquitoes, scorpions and shifting sands were not enough to try them, the Turks promised to crucify any airmen they captured. But in terms of reconnaissance and bombing raids disrupting Turkish movement and communications, the venture was a success.

Lawrence himself was a competent mechanic, very much at home in engineering workshops and with men on the shop floor. Unlike a number of his biographers, he had no difficulty in reconciling a life in which from year to year he might be making an archaeological dig, fighting a guerrilla war in Arabia, writing *Seven Pillars of Wisdom* or translating the *Odyssey* – or joining the RAF as an aircraftman when he had been a decorated army colonel. His instruction manual for the RAF 200 high-speed seaplane tender is a model of clear and useful prose. 'Every sentence in it', he wrote, 'is understandable, to a fitter.' Edward Garnett, the literary editor and first critic to read *Seven Pillars of Wisdom*, described it as 'a masterpiece of technology'.

Garnett tried hard to get Lawrence to write more. Of course, writing was important to Lawrence. In a letter of January 1933 he told his friend Ernest Altounyan, an Armenian doctor born in Aleppo and educated in England, who won the Military Cross as a high-ranking medical officer in France, 'Writing has been my inmost self all my life, and I can never put all my strength into anything else. Yet the same force, I know, put into action upon material things would move them, make me famous and effective. The everlasting effort to write is like trying to fight a feather-bed. In letters there is no room for strength.'

Lawrence understood and liked machines. He loved speed – on land, in the air and on water. He was also famously wiry, and happy to go out to sea in conditions that kept all but the bravest or maddest sailors safely in port. As such, it was hard for more conventional men like Lord Thomson to understand why this scruffy oik should not only be in deep conversation with General Balbo at Calshot in September 1929, but also giving orders to British airmen of senior rank – when not tinkering with engines, wading through water and generally getting his hands dirty. Unlike politicians, however, Colonel Lawrence had been right about the future of what became Syria and Iraq. And Aircraftman Shaw was right when he devoted four years of tireless effort to the development of the fast boat that would save the lives of, among others, those who flew Spitfires to defend Britain from the armed lust of Nazi Germany.

Shortly after buying Clouds Hill, Lawrence reported as Aircraftman T. E. Shaw to RAF Mount Batten, a seaplane base at Plymouth Sound, where his commanding officer was Squadron Leader Sydney Smith, an old friend who had accompanied his then superior officer to the 1921 Cairo Conference. Smith's wife later recalled, 'One cold March afternoon a shining and powerful Brough motor-bicycle roared to a standstill at the gates... On it was a small blue-clad figure, very neat and smart, with peaked cap, goggles, gauntlet gloves and small dispatch-case slung on his back.'

Aircraftman Shaw was recently returned from India, where he had chosen to be posted at the most remote RAF bases. He had found life idyllic at RAF Miramshah in Waziristan on the North-West Frontier, where he worked as a clerk to the base commander Squadron Leader Ian Brodie, who thought the world of the hard-working Shaw. Brodie's role was to keep raids by Waziri and Afghan tribesmen under control and, in the bigger picture, to show Russia that Britain was in charge there – although this was a particularly uncertain part of the Empire.

On one occasion, Brodie lost sight of the train he was detailed to escort. Its VIP passenger was Amanullah Khan, king of Afghanistan. Brodie and his colleagues circled the surrounding area for two hours before the train was found stuck in a tunnel. The king had pulled the emergency brake cord, mistaking it for the flush handle of his lavatory. This made Brodie and Lawrence laugh. Not so funny was an encrypted signal, deciphered by Lawrence, calling for his immediate return to England.

Nevertheless, life at Plymouth proved mostly idyllic, too. Smith took Shaw for flights in the de Havilland Moth seaplane he co-owned, while both Clare and Sydney were happy to talk books and adventures. Soon after Shaw's arrival, Smith was asked to help with the 1929 Schneider contest. He took Shaw as his clerk and, as the event unfolded, his jack of all trades.

Smith's friend Major Colin Cooper lent him the use of *Karen*, his impressive motor yacht. The yacht's tender was *Biscuit*, one of six Biscayne Baby two-seat speedboats built by the Purdy Boat Company of Port Washington, Long Island. This pretty boat – a sportscar on the water – featured a V-shaped prow that, as speed rose, lifted the hull so that it planed over the water rather than ploughing through it as existing Royal Navy tenders did. For Shaw, it was a revelation. Lithe, light and streamlined, *Biscuit* could scythe through the Solent at 40 mph. Its Achilles heel was its Detroit-built 100-hp, six-cylinder Scripps marine engine. Shaw, though, tinkered with this until it ran reliably.

After the British win at Calshot, Major Cooper made a present of *Biscuit* to Smith and Shaw. While Shaw made use of it as a pleasure boat, exploring the Tamar Estuary, Cornish coast and outlying islands with Clare Smith and a picnic basket, he was thinking of how the speedboat's design could be applied to a much larger boat, for service as a rescue tender with the RAF. On the morning of 4 February 1931, Shaw and Clare Smith were sitting below the seventeenth-century artillery tower – built during the English Commonwealth under Cromwell to keep the Dutch at bay – when one of RAF Mount Batten's Blackburn Iris III flying boats crashed while coming in to land on a perfectly smooth Plymouth Sound.

A harbour pilot, Wilfred Little, and his mate Harry Hole were sailing close by and were first on the scene, where they were able to rescue two men clinging to the wreckage. Shaw followed as quickly as he could in the RAF tender, and although he was able to bring two more men to shore – one fatally injured – he was deeply frustrated by the slowness of his boat. Giving evidence have been too slow. Might more crew members have been saved from drowning – assuming they were not killed outright as the aircraft hit the water at close to 70 mph – if Lawrence could only have got to them minutes earlier than he did? As for Schneider Trophy seaplanes that covered long distances on take-offs and landings, how could a plodding RAF tender possibly reach them in time? These launches had not been designed with speed in mind, because their primary duties were to transport men and equipment to moored flying boats. Now, though, there was a critical need for a new generation of high-speed launches.

At Hythe, Hubert Scott-Paine had been thinking much the same thing. In early 1930 he had approached Flight Lieutenant W. E. G. Beauforte-Greenwood, head of the Marine Equipment Branch at the Air Ministry, with a design for a 35-foot planing motorboat. A discussion between the two men over its ideal length and the need for a British engine led to the construction of a 37½-foot prototype powered by twin 100-hp Brooke marine engines made in Lowestoft. Its top speed was 23 knots. Beautifully made, the 4½-ton boat was constructed in elm, pine and mahogany, and although not as fast as it could be, it was clearly a design with great potential. To keep it away from prying eyes while undergoing service trials, Scott-Paine suggested these should take place far from the Solent.

Knowing of Lawrence's keen interest in the potential of high-speed rescue launches, Beauforte-Greenwood recommended RAF Mount Batten. With Lawrence on board, Scott-Paine's boat was taken out as far as the Scilly Isles. What they discovered was that it needed lighter and more powerful engines. The first of these, by Meadows of Wolverhampton, was tested successfully by Lawrence and Corporal Bradbury in an open launch on Plymouth Sound. The prototype 200 Class Sea Tender was returned to Hythe, fitted with a pair of the new engines and returned to Mount Batten. The trials went well, and nine boats were ordered for the 1931 Schneider contest. But on August Bank Holiday, a fire at the Hythe works destroyed them. Only the prototype was available. The energetic Scott-Paine had the works back in business that October. Production of the RAF 200 Class Seaplane Tender began.

Lawrence shuttled between Plymouth and Hythe, and was in talks with Scott-Paine about an altogether bigger and more powerful rescue boat. This was the RAF 100 High Speed Launch, powered by three Napier Sea Lion engines and capable of 35 knots. The ultimate development of the Scott-Paine design was the 21½-ton HSL 164 of 1941. With a range of 500 miles and equipped with a sick bay below deck and aircraft-style machine gun turrets and a 20mm Oerlikon cannon above, it proved to be a welcome sight to the pilots and crews of hundreds of RAF aircraft shot down into the seas around Britain during the Second World War.

In March 1933, Lawrence was busy off the Yorkshire coast testing an armoured version of the RAF 200 for use as a bombing target at sea. In April he was posted to the RAF Marine Aircraft Experimental Establishment at Felixstowe. In May he began travelling like a shuttlecock on RAF business between Hythe, East Cowes, London and Manchester. His last posting was at Bridlington in late 1934, in charge of overhauling the 10 RAF 200s stationed there. He retired from the RAF the following February and was dead that May. His work on the RAF rescue boats was one of his great achievements.

The influence of Britain's involvement in the Schneider Trophy contests on boat design continued apace with the wartime work of Hubert Scott-Paine, whose motor gunboats and motor torpedo boats were highly effective weapons in the armoury of the Royal Navy. They planed above and turned through water like marine versions of the racing planes that had skated around the Solent skies in 1929 and 1931. Their racing provenance could be traced, in part, to Scott-Paine's competition boats. His highly polished aluminium-clad *Miss Britain III*, built at Hythe in 1933, looked like some futuristic aircraft. Powered by a 1,350-hp supercharged Napier Lion aero-engine, it was the first boat to exceed 100 mph. In April 1933, *Miss Britain III* competed in the Harmsworth Trophy held at Algonac on the St Clair River, Michigan, against Garfield Wood's *Miss America X*. Wood won, by a very close margin, his 39-foot, 7-ton boat propelled by four Packard V12 engines. *Miss Britain III* was 24½ feet long, weighed 1½ tons and needed just the one engine.

Scott-Paine, whose Hythe works was bombed by the Luftwaffe, spent the Second World War in North America involved in the design and construction of motor torpedo boats built by US boatbuilders for the US Navy and by his Canadian Power Boat Company in Montreal for the Royal Canadian Navy. A team of designers from the US firm Elco had visited Scott-Paine at Hythe in early 1939. Impressed, they bought a 70-foot motor torpedo boat that became the blueprint of the company's wartime PT-series boats. The future president John F. Kennedy skippered one variation of the Elco MTBs.

When orders from the Royal Canadian Navy dried up, Scott-Paine manufactured plywood parts for the de Havilland

EIGHT

All That Mighty Heart

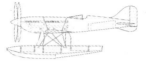

The noise of the Rolls-Royce R engine undergoing tests day and night at Derby in the spring of 1931 was so great that, understandably, local people complained. The mayor felt forced to ask for their understanding. This, after all, was a matter of national prestige. The tests, also involving three Rolls-Royce Kestrel engines to simulate air flow at 380 mph, cool the V12's crankcase and ventilate the workshop itself – a poisonous fug of hot castor oil, petrol and benzole sprayed on clothes and walls – were to last seven extremely trying months.

Today, one of the 19 racing R engines broods silently in the Science Museum in South Kensington. Close up, this imposing 8¼-foot-long coal-black machine looks as solid as a steel ingot. All of a piece, it represents pure mechanical muscle. And, in its day, it was the world's most potent aero-engine bar one: the V24 Fiat AS.6. These two imperious engines were the mechanical hearts of Mitchell's S.6B seaplane and Castoldi's rival Macchi MC. 72.

The Napier Lion, a 24-litre W12 engine that took Mitchell's Supermarine S.5 to victory in the 1927 Schneider race, had been in production since 1917 and, although it could be tuned to produce immense power for its era, its limit appeared to have been reached. Mitchell needed even more power. Rolls-Royce provided this in the guise of its supercharged 37-litre V12 R engine. It was designed for a brief – if especially intense – life, with lightweight aluminium components replacing many of the heavier and more durable bronze and steel parts of existing Rolls-Royce aero-engines.

It also required new and higher standards for ancillary components like spark plugs, while to squeeze the maximum possible power from the engine, fuel guru Rod Banks experimented with various fuel cocktails. George Stainforth's 400-plus-mph S.6B was to guzzle a heady mix of benzole, methanol, acetone and tetraethyl lead. If this had been fed into the cylinder heads of the fastest contemporary cars, like the 4½-litre 'Blower' Bentley or the Alfa Romeo 8C 2300, their engines would have burned out in minutes.

The combination of high-octane fuel and the 13-ton pressure of the engine's piston strokes under power meant that the Rolls-Royce R generated huge amounts of heat. To dissipate this, Mitchell and Rolls-Royce used the surfaces of the aircraft's wings and floats as heat exchangers. Coolant circulated from the engine and around the structure of the aircraft. Engine oil was cooled in much the same way using channels along the fuselage – which, by happy accident, helped make the S6 and S6.B look even faster than they were. Here were machines whose Futurist beauty was derived from pure functional necessity.

These cooling techniques were also vital because, in a bid to keep the Schneider aircraft as streamlined as possible, their engine cowlings fitted like sheaths. There was precious little room for cooling air to circulate around the formidable V12. Not for nothing were the S.6 seaplanes known as 'flying radiators'.

Hesitancy over government funding for the 1929 race meant that Rolls-Royce had just six months to ready the new engine. The team at Derby, however, was one of the very best Britain could muster. Its leader was Ernest Hives, who had worked with Charles Rolls, fixing his engines, from 1903. Wholly down to earth, Hives was a brilliant and practical engineer to whom Rolls-Royce and the free world owes the Merlin engine. Hives was to head Rolls-Royce's aero-engine division before being appointed chairman of the company in 1950, by which time he was leading the development of the gas-turbine engines that so many millions of us trust with our safety in the air today.

From 1923, and while head of the company's Experimental Department, Hives recruited one outstanding young engineer after another, among them Cyril Lovesey, Ray Dorey, Arthur Rubbra (the son of a Northampton watchmaker, he cycled all the way from home to take up an engineering scholarship at Bristol University), Stewart Tresilian and James Ellor, an expert in supercharging who had very nearly left RAE Farnborough for a well-paid job in the United States before Rolls-Royce made him an offer he was clearly unwilling to refuse.

Cyril Lovesey joined the Experimental Department in 1923 straight from Bristol University. Working on car and aero-engines, he was to have the responsibility of testing the R engine in flight. A pilot, his work on the racing engines led him on to the Merlin. In charge of its development from shortly before the Battle of Britain, he doubled the engine's power output during the Second World War while improving its reliability. In retirement, he was called on to help with the Rolls-Royce RB211 turbofan that powered many of the new Boeing 747 jumbo jets.

The son of a Peterborough bricklayer, Arthur Rowledge came up through the apprenticeship system and was appointed chief design engineer of Napier in 1913. Here he led the design of the hugely successful Lion engine. Moving to Rolls-Royce in 1921 as chief design assistant to Henry Royce, Rowledge led the design of the V12 Kestrel, a superb engine that prefigured the R, Merlin and Griffon. This was the engine that made the excellent Hawker Fury of 1931 the first fighter aircraft to exceed 200 mph in level flight. (With its Rolls-Royce R engine, the Supermarine S.6B flew twice as fast.) The Kestrel was the engine chosen for the prototype Messerschmitt Bf 109 and Junkers Ju 87 Stuka dive bomber at a time when German aero-engine manufacturers were lagging behind Germany's production of military airframes.

The Kestrel had been Rolls-Royce's response to an official request for an engine to compete with the Curtiss D-12. Charles Fairey, who had watched the Curtiss CR-3 racers in action at the 1923 Schneider contest at Cowes, had paid a visit soon afterwards to the Curtiss factory in upstate New York, returning with a D-12 which he kept in his ocean liner cabin on the way back to England. Fairey fitted this to his private-venture Fairey Fox biplane bomber. It was a revelation, 40 or 50 mph faster than contemporary RAF fighters. Rejecting Fairey's campaign for the bulk purchase of D-12s, the Air Ministry turned to Napier and Rolls-Royce. Napier declined, but a D-12 was dispatched to Derby where it was taken apart and analysed under the beady eye of Henry Royce.

The wizard himself was still very much at work at his handsome, if modest, eighteenth-century home at West Wittering when the Derby design team came down to the Sussex coast to discuss ideas for the racing engine with him. In Rolls-Royce legend, the guiding principles were laid down on the beach in sketches the great man made with his stick in the sand. Some of the design work on the R was, however, done in Royce's private studio.

Royce had promised Mitchell, face to face, an engine that would produce up to 1,900 hp – or 600 hp more than the Napier Lion had in 1927. The first R engine, completed at Derby in April 1929, was soon producing 1,500 hp at a cacophonous 2,750 rpm for 15 minutes, and then, very briefly, 1,686 hp at 3,000 rpm before failing. Successive engines pushed to their limits endured any number of technical mishaps. Main bearing failure after 17 minutes. Oil pressure lost after 22 minutes. Broken exhaust valves. Crankshaft failure. And so it went on. This, of course, was engine development at a time when the only way forward was to build the real thing and see what it would do. Rolls-Royce was working with new materials and new fuels, while making quantum leaps in terms of power and endurance. Intense noise, long hours, noxious fumes, frustration, strained muscles and bloodshot eyes were the price of technical mastery, mechanical efficiency and, ultimately, aviation wizardry.

It was the fourteenth engine that settled into a steady raucous growl, sustaining 1,850 hp for 1 hour and 40 minutes. The Rolls-Royce R was now ready for trials, shoehorned inside the long nose of Mitchell's S.6.

The maximum performance of the racing engine proved to be phenomenal. With tweaks to supercharger and fuel, the 'sprint' engine fitted in George Stainforth's S.6B S.1595 developed 2,350 hp at 3,200 rpm. In absolute terms, this power output was that of the most powerful contemporary British and European express passenger steam locomotives, a fact that would have interested Henry Royce, a one-time locomotive engineering apprentice with the Great Northern Railway at Doncaster. But where a 100-ton steam locomotive of such power would be expected to pull a 500-ton train with several hundred passengers at a maximum of 80 or 90 mph, the Supermarine S.6B weighed just 2.7 tons on take-off, had only the one seat and one singular purpose: to fly as fast as possible. And while a railway locomotive might have a useful working life of 30 or 40 years, the Supermarine seaplanes and their highly tuned engines had to survive just the one race.

Rolls-Royce engineers pushed the engine further to 2,783 hp at 3,400 rpm. This, though, was simply too much for the airframe of Mitchell's aircraft to withstand. In any case, given the engine's dipsomaniacal thirst for fuel – 3.5 gallons per mile in 2,350-hp tune – there was nowhere to store the extra fuel that would have been needed to sustain the engine in flight over the Schneider race course.

After the 1931 contest, the Rolls-Royce R helped break world speed records on land and water, too. On 3 September 1935, Malcolm Campbell sped the latest 4¾-ton R-powered version of his *Blue Bird* car designed by Reid Railton to just over 300 mph along the Bonneville Salt Flats in Utah. George Eyston took over where Malcolm Campbell left off after the latter's retirement from land-speed record breaking. Eyston's stunning *Thunderbolt* was a truly futuristic design of 1937, a streamlined machine longer and heavier than a London double-decker bus and designed to go a lot faster than *Blue Bird*. A pair of R engines were mounted side by side behind the cockpit. These engines – R25 and R27 – were the very same ones that had powered Boothman and Stainforth's trophy-winning and record-breaking Supermarine S.6Bs in 1931.

In 1938, Eyston set a new world land-speed record of 357.5 mph. The Rolls-Royce R had performed magnificently on land, as well as in the air. Eyston's record, however, was beaten by fellow Englishman John Cobb and his even more science fiction–like *Railton Special* powered by a brace of Napier Lions, the very engines the Rolls-Royce R had been designed to replace. At 369.7 mph, this was the world's fastest car before the Second World War.

On water, the world speed record was raised to 30.9 mph in September 1938 by Malcolm Campbell, who took this to 141.74 mph a year later in *Blue Bird K4*. A Rolls-Royce R powered both his boats. With Donald Campbell's failure to beat the record in 1951, although he was skimming over Coniston Water at 170 mph before a driveshaft from the engine failed, the mighty Rolls-Royce R fell silent.

If that magnificent V12 engine was noisy, then imagine what Fiat's AS.6 must have sounded like at full chat. This was the astonishing V24 aero-engine developed by Tranquillo Zerbi for the Macchi MC.72, the Italian aircraft that looked as if it might beat Supermarine's finest in 1931.

For the MC.72, Mario Castoldi needed an engine capable of 2,300 hp – and 2,800 hp in a sprint. Fiat was awarded the contract, although its most powerful engine to date was the 1,000-hp 12-cylinder AS.5 that had seen action in the Schneider races. This time around the Italians had to beat the British, otherwise they would lose the chance of winning the Schneider Trophy. The solution was a novel one at the time. Zerbi, Fiat's technical director, decided to connect a pair of AS.5s in tandem, their crankshafts driving contra-rotating propellers. This would guarantee the power Castoldi needed, and would counteract the torque effect that badly affected so many contesting Schneider aircraft under full power on take-off.

It was an ingenious arrangement, but the AS.6, though very powerful, was much heavier than the rival Rolls-Royce R. It was also a more complex engine, with more to go wrong. Although sharing a throttle linkage, the twin AS.5 units operated largely independently of one another. The rear engine – the first to start – drove the front propeller, and the front engine the rear propeller. The rear airscrew shaft ran through the hollowed centre of the front airscrew shaft.

This set-up meant that the blades could be shorter than a single propeller. In practice, this mean that they churned up much less sea spray on take-off than seaplanes with single propellers, much to the relief of pilots who could see very little if at all from the cockpits of Schneider racers as they committed to take-off.

In the race to get the AS.6 ready on time, Fiat engineers encountered difficulties with spark plugs, ignition, coolant flow, fuel metering, induction, exhaust valves, connecting rods and the supercharger at the rear of the twin engine. By April 1931, and only after a huge effort at resolving this legion of problems, the engine ran smoothly for an hour producing the 2,300 hp Castoldi needed.

Flight trials of five beautiful MC.72s began that summer. To everyone's initial satisfaction, the aircraft proved capable of 375 mph. But the engines began to backfire at high power and high speed. This seemed odd, as in Fiat's Turin workshops they had been running without a hiccup for some weeks. When the second MC.72 was flown, by Captain Giovanni Monti, over Lake Garda on 2 August 1931, a sudden backfire caused a volatile cocktail of fuel and air to explode in the engine's long induction manifold. The aircraft exploded and plunged into the lake, killing its pilot.

These technical difficulties proved to be overwhelming and the Italian team pulled out of the 1931 contest, leaving the British team, short of catastrophic failure or unhappy accident, with a clear run to victory and permanent possession of the Schneider Trophy. As a spoiler of sorts, however, the Italian team had decided to make an attempt on the world speed record on the day of the Schneider race at Calshot. On 10 September, Lieutenant Stansilao Bellini, timed at 394 mph, flew into a hillside after his engine caught fire and exploded.

This must have been a nightmare for Tranquillo Zerbi, the accomplished and inventive German-educated engineer who had been apprenticed at Sulzer in Switzerland before working for Franco Tosi Meccanica – where his boss was Ettore Maserati, a designer of diesel engines at the time and one of five brothers who would go on to set up their own famous racing and sports car company. Joining Fiat in 1919 at the time it was building its sensational Futurist factory at Lingotto – the one by Giacomo

Matté-Trucco with a racetrack on its roof – Zerbi became expert in early applications of supercharging and two-stroke engines. His six-cylinder 1.5-litre Type 451 two-stroke engine produced a highly impressive 152 hp at 6,500 rpm. It was also extremely noisy, and because of its unreliability it was never used in a production car.

Zerbi did, however, create one motoring masterpiece: the single-seat 12-cylinder 1.5-litre 806 racing car that won the 1927 Gran Premio de Milano at Monza, a 50-kilometre warm-up race on the same day as the 500-kilometre Italian Grand Prix. The highly advanced triple-camshaft engine Zerbi and his team developed produced 187 bhp at 8,500 rpm. With its low centre of gravity, the 806 handled well and boasted a top speed of 240 km/h (150 mph). In something of the same spirit as the AS.6, the engine comprised two half-blocks of six cylinders mounted in line to create a U12. What it also had in common with the early AS.6 was its complexity and the worry that it might not last the course.

So while the Fiat 806 was a progenitor of the great front-engine Grand Prix cars of the 1950s, it was considered too delicate to race over anything other than a short course. How the car and its engine might have developed we will never know, as in 1928 Giovanni Agnelli, the head of Fiat, decided to pull out of motor racing for good – and, as he did so, to destroy the company's racing cars.

In 1932, Rod Banks was invited back to Turin to discuss the issue of the AS.6's fatal backfire. What he discovered was that, when flying close to 400 mph, air rammed into the intake of the 50-litre engine thinned the fuel to the point of backfire.

Unlike Rolls-Royce at Derby, Fiat had not set up a test bed to simulate this condition. Once it had, under Banks's direction, and the engine was tuned to take high-speed induction airflow into account, the AS.6 ran smoothly. On 23 October 1934, Warrant Officer Franceso Agello set a new world airspeed record at 440.68 mph (709.3 km/h), his MC.72 fitted with a 3,100-hp sprint version of the AS.6. It performed faultlessly.

Revered by visitors to the Museo Storico dell'Aeronautica Militare today, the aircraft sits in a functionalist hangar against the backdrop of Lake Bracciano and alongside an AS.6. A second rare AS.6 can be seen at the Centro Storico Fiat, Turin, an Art Nouveau factory dating from 1907. This was the first purpose-built home of the Fabbrica Italiana Automobili Torino (Fiat). Here, both architecture and mechanical engineering are works of art.

Tranquillo Zerbi designed one last aero-engine that might just have been a masterpiece. This was his AS.8, a 2,250-hp, 34.5-litre V16 intended for Italy's Second World War fighters. On test it performed well, but perhaps for political as well as practical reasons – number one: insufficient time – the Regia Aeronautica became dependent on the Daimler-Benz DB 605 from Germany. Made the Grande Ufficiale della Corona d'Italia (Grand Officer of the Crown of Italy) in early 1939, Tranquillo Zerbi died of a heart attack that March. He was 48.

When, in the early days of the First World War, Rolls-Royce had been asked by the Royal Aircraft Factory to develop an aero-engine – its first – Henry Royce took apart a 7.3-litre water-cooled Daimler DF 80 V6 aero-engine that had been used in a racing car. This mechanical dissection helped spur on the design of the Rolls-Royce Eagle, the 20-litre V12 that – made in large numbers from 1915 – was to power John Alcock and Arthur Brown non-stop across the Atlantic in their Vickers Vimy in 1919. From the earliest days of the Schneider Trophy there had been a cross-flow of ideas and information from one manufacturer and one country to another.

Charles Kirkham's 400-hp K-12 V12 of 1916 for Curtiss led to his successor Arthur Nutt's Curtiss D-12, which gave the American company two first places in the Schneider contests, in 1923 and 1925, together with a third place for a Macchi M.33 in 1925. Daimler and Hispano-Suiza engines had influenced Kirkham's. Nutt's D-12 was hugely important in the development of the Rolls-Royce Kestrel – which, of course, was fitted to the prototype Messerschmitt Bf 109s that fought Merlin engines, developed from the Kestrel, in the Battle of Britain.

Of the 47 seaplanes and flying boats that made the starting grids of the Schneider Trophy contests, 40 per cent failed to make it round the course because their engines failed. At the outset of the contest in 1913, successful aero-engines were a very rare commodity indeed. The only one that made the grade was Laurent Seguin's air-cooled Gnome rotary that was manu-factured under licence in Britain as the Bentley BR.1 and in Germany as the Oberursel UR.1.

By the outbreak of the First World War, the only British engine made in anything like quantity was a Sunbeam, used by the RNAS and designed by French-born Louis Coatalen – who had drawn heavily on a Hispano-Suiza by the Swiss engineer Marc Birkigt, manufactured in Barcelona and under licence elsewhere in Europe. Engine-building then was, up to a point, an international affair. And, yet, in the case of the Rolls-Royce R and the Fiat AS.6 that marked the finale of the Schneider Trophy contests, it is hard not to see two very different and determined nations exemplified in two very different designs.

NINE

A Tale of Two Designers

Photographs of Mario Castoldi without a hat are rare. There is no photograph of Reginald Mitchell wearing one. Mitchell was slim and angular, Castoldi portly. Mitchell died, at the age of 42, from cancer, before his greatest creation, the Spitfire, took on Göring's Luftwaffe over the skies of Britain and won. Castoldi lived to see his country and the political system he served crushed. While Mitchell was cut off in his prime, Castoldi passed away after a long retirement.

The lives and careers of these two very different aero-engineers ran, however, more or less in parallel for a brief if intense spell, continuing even after Mitchell's death in 1937. Theirs was a professional rivalry to match that of their contemporaries Bentley and Bugatti on the racetrack, yet Mitchell and Castoldi were playing for much higher stakes and, by the end of the Schneider races, perhaps both had more than an inkling of this.

Mario Castoldi, the older of the two men, was born in 1888 in Zibido San Giacomo, a small town south-west of Milan. A graduate of the Politecnico di Milano, a university founded in 1863 and renowned for its faculties of architecture, design and engineering, he served as an aircraft engineer during the First

World War. In 1922, he joined Macchi at Varese, some 30 miles north-west of Milan. The factory, founded by Giulio Macchi in 1912 to build French Nieuport monoplanes under licence for the Italian military, faced Lake Varese. It was to specialize in flying boats and seaplanes, fighters, bombers, racers and passenger planes.

Macchi's chief engineer was Alessandro Tonini, although in 1925 Tonini left to join Officine Ferroviarie Meridionali (OFM), a Neapolitan railway rolling stock manufacturer that soon added aircraft to its remit. Tonini had overseen the design of the sleek Macchi M.7, a flying boat fighter that, with shortened wings for faster turns – designated M.7bis, and flown by Giovanni de Briganti – had won the 1921 Schneider contest. It was also the only machine to have lasted the course. An M.7bis took fourth place in 1922 behind an M.17, Macchi's first purpose-built racer, in third.

Up against the very fast and impressive Curtiss R3C-2s, de Briganti took third place in 1925 in a clean-lined M.33. His average speed, though, was about two-thirds that of the US Navy's Lieutenant James Doolittle in first. By now, Castoldi had certainly been taking a good look at the Curtiss machines. Equally, he was clearly intrigued by the Supermarine S.4, the stunning British monoplane designed by 30-year-old Reginald Mitchell. In 1926, Castoldi's new Macchi M.39, powered by the Fiat AS.2 V12 engine specially designed for the contest, beat the Americans and their Curtiss racers into first place and by a significant margin.

As the S.5 had been for Mitchell, so the M.39 was for Castoldi. What the design of this powerful-looking, cigar-shaped racer demonstrated was Castoldi's pragmatism as a designer and his intuition as an engineer. Mitchell had taken a calculated risk with the unbraced wings of the S.4. Castoldi braced the wings of the M.39. He also positioned the cockpit towards the centre of the aircraft rather than towards the tail as Mitchell had done, as if he were designing a racing car or a motorboat, and smoothed the windscreen seamlessly into the profile of the fuselage. Like the Curtiss machines, the M.39's wings were straight – unlike Mitchell's semi-ellipses. Like the Curtiss R3C-2, too, the M.39 was much shorter than the S.4, but with longer floats set further forward.

Although Castoldi was known for being secretive about his work and jealously protective of his designs, he was clearly willing to learn from others. As were the Fiat engineers whose 800-hp AS.2 was much influenced by the Curtiss D-12 that had done so well for the Americans. And yet, just as Mitchell's desire to create a faster and more forward-looking design with the S.4 led him to those unbraced and fluttering wings, so Fiat in a bid to lighten the new engine for racing chose magnesium-alloy over steel pistons. While these might be sufficiently resilient to the last the course of a Schneider contest, equally they might not. It was a gamble of sorts, yet engineers and designers were learning month by month how to balance lightness and strength, durability and power.

The M.39 displayed touches of vulpine genius. Wing surfaces were employed as low-drag radiators. To counteract the torque effect of the propeller on take-off, the floats had unequal buoyancy. The wings were of slightly unequal length to allow tighter turns in the Schneider circuit. (All turns were to the left.) At

Hampton Roads, Virginia, that November, the M.39 flown by Major Mario de Bernardi set a new world airspeed record while winning the contest. Four days later, de Bernardi broke his own record in the same plane.

Unsurprisingly, Castoldi's design for 1927, the Macchi M.52, was a reworking of the M.39 rather than a radical rethink. Lighter than the M.39 and with slightly swept-back wings, and with the 1,000-hp Fiat AS.3 engine very powerful, the M.52 was surely on form to take on the new Supermarine S.5. Engine failure, however, did for Italian hopes at Venice. Wisely, Mitchell had decided to go for the veteran Napier Lion once again because it was so well tested and proven.

Mitchell would, though, have taken to heart – even while feigning to dismiss it – the Eeyore-like warning of Charles Grey in *The Aeroplane* after the British triumph: 'We have an unfortunate tendency in this country when we have done anything good, to sit back and assume that we have done the very best that can be done, and that nobody else can do any better, instead of realising the plain cold fact that we have merely set a standard for somebody else to beat.'

When its engine was running well, the M.52 was able to show its paces. In March 1928, Major de Bernardi had been timed at a record 318.62 mph. What Castoldi needed, however, was a machine that could last the course at the Schneider Trophy and in 1929 take on both Mitchell's devastatingly powerful new Supermarine S.6 and the beautiful Gloster VI. His answer was the M.67, a design that was a further evolution of the M.39 but fitted with the enormous 57-litre Isotta Fraschini Asso 1000, a complex W18 engine. The M.67 would lose the September Schneider contest at Calshot. Italian honour was saved in the guise of the M.52R, entered as a backup for the much faster M.67s and flown into second place by Warrant Officer Tommaso Dal Molin. He was 44 mph slower than Flying Officer Waghorn's first-place Supermarine S.6.

While Castoldi's stunning MC.72 appeared to be the answer for the 1931 contest and a big step forward from earlier designs, the big seaplane was scuppered by yet another ambitious engine, this time Tranqillo Zerbi's V24 that refused to run smoothly and safely. If, however, interference at the highest state level had enforced the Fiat V24 on Castoldi, it is also true that the engineer had turned to Zerbi after his earlier frustration with Isotta Fraschini engines. Equally, Mussolini's personal enthusiasm for the MC.72, despite it not being ready for what proved to be the ultimate Schneider Trophy contest in 1931, prompted the investment needed to prepare Castoldi's machine for its attempts on the airspeed record.

One key feature of the MC.72 was its use of contra-rotating propellers. These were to become increasingly important as piston aero-engines grew to be extremely powerful and quite a handful for pilots when taking off. Even with a foot hard down on the opposite rudder, a pilot might struggle to cope with an aircraft seemingly determined to turn in a full circle rather than flying straight ahead on its take-off run. While Castoldi had tested his contra-rotating set-up at the Aeronautical Experimental Institute, Rome, the invention itself had been patented as early as 1907 by Frederick Lanchester, the English polymath inventor and engineer whose papers on the possibility of mechanical flight published from 1897 are as fascinating to read now as they were prescient at the time. Among descriptions of lift and drag, Lanchester pointed out, with the science to back him, that powered flight demanded engines with very high power-to-weight ratios; and he explained, when few were listening, the role that the aeroplane would play in future warfare. Late-mark Spitfires like the PR Mk XIX and the Seafire F Mk 47, powered by 37-litre Griffon engines, were to use contra-rotating propellers – as do the giant Russian Tupolev Tu-95 Bear reconnaissance turboprop bombers with their four 15,000-hp engines that have probed British air defences for potential weaknesses for many decades.

Significantly, though, when in 1936 Castoldi produced his 12-seat MC.94 flying boat for Ala Littoria, the new state airline, the first engines he selected were Wright 1820-F Cyclones, the powerful, smooth and reliable nine-cylinder radials also chosen for the Douglas DC-1 and DC-2 and early DC-3 airliners introduced to corporate, critical and public acclaim between 1933 and 1935. Wright Cyclones were also the engines that were to drive aerial fleets of Boeing B-17 Flying Fortress bombers over Nazi-occupied Europe, including Italy, to devastating effect during the Second World War. Later MC.94s were fitted with Alfa Romeo RC.10 nine-cylinder radials. These were modified Bristol Jupiter engines made under licence in Milan. The combination of the Italians' up-and-down experience with highly tuned and temperamental water-cooled V12s during the Schneider years and the dependable nature of powerful new radials played a role in the production of Italian military aircraft, including fighters, that eschewed the very type of inline V engines under urgent development in Britain and Germany.

Castoldi's MC.94 took a number of records in 1937, most notably a 2,000-kilometre closed-circuit flight with a payload of 1,000 kg (or 12 passengers) at very nearly 260 km/h (160 mph). If he had lived long enough, this, surely, was the kind of aircraft Jacques Schneider would have loved to have seen at work as a result of the trophy that bore his name. He would have been even more pleased to see the launch of Castoldi's MC.100, first flown in January 1939. This was a shoulder-wing cantilever monoplane flying boat with three 800-hp Alfa Romeo RC.10s mounted on struts above the wing. The main cabin seated 26 passengers. Sadly, war interrupted further production of this handsome civil flying boat, and just three were built. At least one flew in military service backwards and forwards between Rome and Tripoli. Italo Balbo would have been one of its passengers.

As war loomed, the Italian Air Force was woefully unprepared. The prevailing theory by the late 1930s was that if Italy were to fight a war in the near future, it would be against France. Military action would ideally be confined to the Mediterranean. Italy would reclaim and rebuild the Roman Empire. But when France fell to Hitler in June 1940 and, opportunistically, Mussolini sided with Nazi Germany and declared war on France and Britain, he had, aside from anything else, declared a fight in the air between the woefully inadequate Regia Aeronautica and the Royal Air Force – and, from 11 December 1941, the day of Italy's declaration of war against the United States, the US Army Air Forces, too.

Italo Balbo had already said that he could write an article called 'How we are getting ready to lose the future war', although there were those in the Italian military who believed Balbo had invested more time and money on propaganda than on building practical fighting aircraft. During its war against the Allies, Italy's air force had no long-range bomber, no torpedo bombers and no aircraft carrier in service. The former transatlantic liner *SS Roma* was in the process of being converted into an aircraft carrier in Genoa, but work was far behind schedule when Italy signed the Armistice of 8 September 1943. Most damagingly, the Regia Aeronautica lacked sufficient modern fighters.

Quite remarkably, as far as the RAF was concerned, the Italians joined in at the very end of the Battle of Britain – a fortnight after Hitler had cancelled Operation Sealion, the invasion of England – with a small number of Fiat CR.42 Falco (Falcon) and G.50 Freccia (Arrow) fighters. The former was an open-cockpit biplane; the latter an open-cockpit monoplane. Both were powered by Fiat radial engines. Both sported just a pair of machine guns. Up against Spitfires and Hurricanes, they seemed antique. Although the Italians had very little success against their Sydney Camm and Reginald Mitchell–designed rivals, the Fiats were nevertheless nimble and hard to shoot down.

In November 1940, a Fiat CR.42 flown by Sergeant Pietro Salvadori landed at Orford Ness on the Suffolk coast. It was later tested by Lieutenant Eric 'Winkle' Brown RN, Commanding Officer of the Captured Enemy Aircraft Flight, who was impressed by the biplane's top speed – 270 mph – and most of all by the fact that it was 'brilliantly manoeuvrable, an acrobatic gem, but under-gunned and very vulnerable to enemy fire'. In other words, while it must have been a hugely enjoyable machine to fly in air displays, it was not going to win the war for Mussolini.

Even the best Italian fighter of 1940 was insufficiently armed. This was the Macchi C.200 Saetta (Lightning). With slight tweaking, its metal airframe proved to be strong, with the aircraft achieving speeds of up to 800 km/h (500 mph) in steep dives. Castoldi would have liked to have given the C.200 a liquid-cooled V12 engine, but was held back by an Italian Air Ministry directive of 1932 ruling these out in favour of radials. At the time, it was more or less impossible to get as much power from a radial as from an inline piston engine. The most effective engine available was a Fiat A.74 radial, a reworking by Tranquillo Zerbi and Antonio Fessia of the Pratt & Whitney R-1830 Twin Wasp, more of which were to be manufactured than any other aero-engine, with a large number still in service in 2020.

To compete on a par with British rivals, Castoldi's wartime fighters needed greater power and speed. In July 1941 his 370-mph Macchi C.202 Folgore (Thunderbolt) went into action, its long, streamlined nose housing what was nominally an Alfa Romeo V12 but was in fact the same Daimler-Benz inverted V12 that powered the Luftwaffe's Messerschmitt Bf 109. The prototype C.202 was a private venture by Macchi. Castoldi and his team had wanted to demonstrate the need for inline engines against the frustrating official policy banning these in favour of radials. Who, though, could call the fuel-injected DB 601 anything other than dependable? But while the C.202 proved to be an excellent aircraft to fly, its construction was a much more laborious affair than that of the clip-together Bf 109. Production was ramped up, with Breda, the engineering colossus, manufacturing most of the aircraft, yet engines remained in short supply.

Experience gained in the Schneider contests prompted Castoldi to make the left wing of the new fighter longer than the right. This gave the left wing extra lift, helping to counteract torque effort on take-off without the added complexity of counter-rotating props. Allied fighter pilots facing C.202s over Malta and North Africa considered the Italian aircraft superior to their own Hurricane Mk IIs, Curtiss P-40 Kittyhawks and Mk V Spitfires. The C.202 could out-turn all three, and dive at immense speed. On test on 21 August 1941, Lieutenant Giulio Reiner was recorded at a maximum speed of 1,078.27 km/h (670 mph) in a vertical dive while pulling 5.8 Gs. While this was not strictly advisable, it was proof of the aircraft's sound aerodynamic design.

Too lightly armed, the C.202 was not the menace it might have been. It was, though, a tough aircraft, and fought on the Eastern Front in appalling conditions far from the Mediterranean and Mussolini's vainglorious new Roman Empire. To keep pace with enemy aircraft like the Spitfire Mk IX and North American P-51D Mustang, the Italian Air Force needed a more powerful, faster and more effectively armed version of Castoldi's C.202. This was the C.205 Veltro (Greyhound), a 400-mph fighter armed, variously, with 20mm cannons as well as 12.7mm Breda machine guns. Its engine was the new 35.7-litre Daimler-Benz DB 605 offering 1,775 hp on take-off and produced under licence as the Fiat RC.58 Tifone (Typhoon).

The C.205 was an impressive machine. Eric Brown went so far as to describe it as 'one of the finest aircraft I ever flew...

beautiful. And here you had the perfect combination of Italian styling and German engineering... It was really a delight to fly, and up to anything on the Allied programme.' Its problem was that it came into service late in the day, and, like its predecessor, took time to build when there was little time left. In the few weeks he flew a C.205, Adriano Visconti, Italy's highest-scoring Second World War ace, is said to have shot down 11 of the 26 enemy aircraft he is credited with.

Visconti continued to fly with the Aeronautica Nazionale Repubblicana (AZR), formed after the Armistice of September 1943 in defence of Italy against the Allies. Remarkably, he ferried fellow pilots after the Armistice from Sicily to northern Italy in the fuselage of a C.205. On 29 April 1945, Visconti surrendered to Communist partisans at Malpensa near Milan. He was taken with other AZR officers to a military barracks for what they assumed would be an interrogation. A Russian body-guard of the Italian partisan leaders killed Visconti, shooting him in the back.

In May 1945, Oberstleutnant (Lieutenant Colonel) Johannes Steinhoff, former commander of the Luftwaffe's JG 77 fighter wing, surrendered to American soldiers. In October–December 1943, JG 77 had been equipped with 23 C.205s while waiting for the latest Bf 109s. The Germans, unlike 'Winkle' Brown, were ambivalent. The 'Macchi is fast and has good flying character-istics, except for the tendency to lose control in sharp turns. The fighter is disadvantaged because its radio, while powerful, is far from reliable in action. Refuelling and rearming process is slow and difficult. It takes much time to make the fighters ready.' Pilot error caused the loss of five JG 77 Greyhounds. The throttle control of the C.205 worked in the opposite direction of German fighters – like their Allied enemies, German pilots were used to pushing throttle controls forward, not backwards, to gain speed. In the heat of the moment, it was an easy mistake to make.

Oberstleutnant Steinhoff, badly burned while attempting to take off in a Messerschmitt Me 262 jet fighter, would have his face reconstructed by a British surgeon. A veteran of 993 operational sorties dating from the German invasion of Poland to the very last days of the war, and with 176 kills to his name, Steinhoff made the right call in giving himself up to the Americans. A four-star general in the post-war Luftwaffe, he was appointed Commander Allied Forces Central Europe in 1965 and, six years later, Chairman of the NATO Military Committee. 'Wars', as his wartime and post-war colleague General Günther Rall (275 kills) told me, 'are stupid things caused by cretins but fought by brave people.'

Benito Mussolini, one of Rall's 'cretins', lost his war, his putative Roman Empire, and his life on 28 April 1945, executed by Communist partisans in the northern Italian village of Giulino di Mezzegra, along with his mistress Claretta Petacci. Their corpses were driven in a lorry to Milan's Piazzale Loreto, where after being abused by a crowd, they were strung up on meat hooks from a steel girder above a petrol station on the square. Two days later, Adolf Hitler killed himself.

Although Mario Castoldi was looked on as a technocrat, his connections with the Fascist state meant an inevitable fall from grace. At a late stage in Italy's war, he had been working on the C.207 – a C.205 with bigger wings and armed with four 20mm cannons designed to intercept Allied bombers at high altitude. Post-war, Macchi went on to produce civil and military training aircraft, one of which – the MB.308, first flown in 1947 – was available as a seaplane. Meanwhile, 15 C.205s were bought by the Egyptian Air Force and were briefly in action during the 1948–49 Israeli War of Independence.

Leaving Macchi in 1945, Castoldi soldiered on as a free-lance designer. A large-scale model of his C.208 two-seat piston-engine trainer for Agusta was shown at the 1950 Milan aeronautical fair, but nothing came of it. A year later, Castoldi produced a set of drawings for a jet trainer. Its engine was to have been the Rolls-Royce Avon. This was the axial-flow engine that powered the de Havilland Comet, the world's first jet airliner which flew the first transatlantic jet services. Although Castoldi's jet trainer was never more than a drawing-board project, there is something haunting, and almost touching, in the way that, after the horrors and sheer stupidity of years of war, a designer who had played such a key role in the Schneider Trophy contests had now embraced a wholly new generation of British engines that, ultimately, would make intercontinental travel safe and fast. Jet airliners, however, were to be flown exclusively from airports that, despite their name, were built on land covered in concrete. By the end of the Second World War, Jacques Schneider's distant dream of seaports around the world served by fast flying boats had all but evaporated.

Mario Castoldi died in 1968 at Trezzano sul Naviglio, some six miles from where he was born. He had outlived Reginald Mitchell by more than 30 years.

Mitchell, who was never to see his most famous design, the Spitfire, in fighting mode, had come from a very different background to his Italian counterpart's. Born in 1895, he was one of five children brought up in and around Stoke-on-Trent, a town best known for its industrial potteries and ceramics. His parents, Herbert and Elizabeth (née Brain) were both teachers, although later on his father set up a printing business. The young Reginald was crafting model gliders from strips of wood and glued paper at the very time the Wright Brothers made their giant leap from gliders to powered flight.

Instead of moving seamlessly from college to an aircraft research establishment as Castoldi had done, Mitchell was apprenticed at the age of 16 to the locomotive builders Kerr, Stuart & Co. in Stoke-on-Trent, studying engineering, mechanics and advanced mathematics at night school. At home, he used what little spare time he had to work at his own lathe in an effort to master practical engineering skills. In 1917, Hubert Scott-Paine took him on at Supermarine. Within three years of arriving in Southampton – and by now married to Florence Dayson, a head-mistress from back home in Stoke – Mitchell, or 'R. J.' as he was known at Supermarine, became the company's chief engineer. By the time Vickers took over Supermarine in 1928, Mitchell was the company's highly valued technical director.

Between 1920 and 1936 he was to design 24 different aircraft ranging from light seaplanes and powerful fighters to huge flying boats and a high-speed four-engine bomber. Not all of these went into production, yet they show the range of Mitchell's aerial ambition, and the depths of his skill as a designer. With this prodigious and prolific talent at the drawing board, Supermarine was to remain profitable throughout the great economic depression that sank so many businesses in the years following the Wall Street Crash of 1929.

Mitchell was an instinctive designer – not beyond making mistakes, but he learned from them quickly. Reserved (or shy), down to earth, quick-tempered and blunt, although a kind man at heart, Mitchell's earthiness is captured by the advice he gave to Spitfire test pilot Jeffrey Quill: 'If anybody ever tells you anything about an aeroplane which is so bloody complicated you can't understand it, take it from me, it's all balls.' His Spitfire remains a glorious and relatively easy aircraft to fly. It feels uncomplicated despite its design and engineering sophistication, and it is ideally and seamlessly paired with Rolls-Royce Merlin and Griffon engines. It would be impossible to imagine one without the other.

Castoldi, by comparison, was hampered by the complexity of the political situation that saw Italy as increasingly subservient to Germany. Even though Daimler-Benz promised Castoldi their finest engines for his fighter aircraft, supply of these built under licence by Italian manufacturers was limited and often delayed. Castoldi's final Second World War fighter, the C.207, never took off from the drawing board. By the end of the war, some 20,000 Spitfires had been built compared with little more than 1,400 Macchi C.202s and C.205s. While Castoldi faced frustration caused by official ineptitude, Mitchell, although his life was cut short, triumphed.

Many of Mitchell's more prosaic aircraft might surprise those who know him only for the Spitfire. The highly successful Supermarine Southampton and Stranraer flying boats were, for example, very much workaday machines. Rather ungainly-looking biplanes, they flew – low, slowly and well – around the world. The Southampton, although superficially obsolescent, flew with the RAF from 1925 to 1936, while its successor, the only slightly sleeker Stranraer, performed with the RAF and the RCAF (Royal Canadian Air Force) throughout the Second World War.

These flying boats represent a very important aspect of Mitchell's work: safety. He was one of the very few aircraft designers who learned to fly, and this showed in the way his aircraft handled both on the ground and in the sky. Fast and deadly though it was, the Spitfire was a very safe aircraft to fly. And many Second World War pilots were to be grateful to Mitchell, not just for the Spitfire they chased the enemy with, but also for his tough little Supermarine Walrus amphibian, first flown in 1933. One of these biplanes would often be there to rescue them when they were forced to bail out over water or ditch into the sea. The Walrus flew – with its top speed of just 145 mph at 4,750 feet – trouble-free throughout the Second World War. Even the Walrus, though, could be flown with surprising brio. Flight Lieutenant George Pickering, Supermarine's test pilot, made a point of looping-the-loop in new Walruses floated out from the factory. He liked to start his loops from as low as 300 feet; Mitchell, with a little help from his pilots, was truly a wizard of flight.

He was also fascinated by speed. The Schneider Trophy contests allowed him to move from flying boats trying to fly quickly, almost against their nature, to purpose-designed streamlined seaplanes that could fly very fast indeed. In

October 1931, a month after Mitchell's victory with the S.6B, the Air Ministry issued its specification number F.7/30 for a new RAF fighter armed with four .303 machine guns. Mitchell did not respond with some advanced military version of the S.6B. In fact, the resulting Supermarine Type 224 proved to be an ungainly inverted gull-wing monoplane with an open cockpit, fixed undercarriage and 660-hp steam-cooled Rolls-Royce Goshawk engine promising a top speed of 228 mph. It handled badly. Was the Type 224 really from the same hand and mind as the 400-plus-mph S.6B?

The answer is yes, of course, yet Mitchell was a designer who started brand-new projects with a clean sheet. Because the Type 224 was configured around the Goshawk, with its need to condense steam boiled from the engine and to return water to its cylinder cooling sleeves, its shape was different from that of an air-cooled or conventional water-cooled design. Even so, some of Mitchell's decisions seemed odd, then as now. Flapless wings meant that the Type 224 would have to land at speed – tricky at any time but especially in poor weather or in the dark.

On test from February 1934, the Type 224 performed poorly against its rivals, notably the 257-mph Gloster Gladiator. Powered by an 830-hp Bristol Mercury radial, this was the last RAF biplane fighter. It happened to be a very good one. As I wrote in my book *Spitfire: The Biography*:

It was as if the Type 224 had been a mirror of Mitchell's own less than happy condition. In May 1933 he had been diagnosed with bowel cancer. That August, he very nearly died on the operating table. And yet, well before the Air Ministry rejected the Type 224 in 1935, Mitchell, now patched up with a colostomy bag and often in pain, was more than busy at work on the Supermarine Type 300. Here was the giant leap of the imagination needed to supersede the RAF's Furies and Gladiators and, more importantly, to convince both the Air Ministry and the RAF that a modern, multi-gunned, high-speed monoplane fighter was an essential tool in a future war in which aircraft would play a leading role.

Many senior air officials, and notably Lord Trenchard, preached a doctrine of air power resolutely in favour of strategic bombing. This was still enshrined in Air Ministry dogma as late as 1936. According to Sir John Slessor, Deputy Director of Plans at the Air Ministry, it was 'a matter of faith'. It certainly was. The bomber, it was said, would always get through, and with new bombers like the Bristol Blenheim emerging in 1936 – with a top speed higher than that of a Gloster Gladiator fighter – the case seemed proven. But by the time Blenheims met well-armed, highly manoeuvrable 350-mph Messerschmitt Bf 109s flown by expert pilots, the wind had gone out of the sails of the argument.

Neville Chamberlain, the British prime minister long accused of appeasing Hitler and Mussolini, chose to listen to Air Chief Marshal Sir Hugh Dowding, Commander-in-Chief of Fighter Command since its inception in 1936. A former First World War fighter pilot who had gone solo in 1 hour and 40 minutes, 'Stuffy' Dowding was a precise, determined and quietly brilliant commander who ensured that suitable fighter aircraft and well-trained pilots and ground staff were available in just sufficient numbers in the summer of 1940 to prevent Hitler from launching his Operation Sealion.

A new type of fighter was needed, and the Schneider Trophy did help to show what they might be and what they might do. Designed for outright speed, the Schneider machines themselves would have made poor fighter planes. The pilots of the S.5 and S.6 racers had no forward view whatsoever from the cockpit, and, even if they leaned out to either side, streamlined casings over the long cylinder heads blocked slipstream views. Only by banking the aircraft could the pilot see where he was going. The big, pedigree engines that drove these aircraft to such great speeds needed to be stripped and rebuilt frequently. They were not designed to cope with the rough and tumble of war. And yet in the design of these rip-roaring inline engines lay the outcome of the Battle of Britain and, to a significant degree, the destiny of the free world. Mitchell saw this, although it has to be stressed that what became known as the Spitfire, despite Mitchell's famous put-down – 'It's the sort of bloody silly name they would give it' – began on a clean sheet of paper.

What it did owe to Mitchell's racing seaplanes was its lithe streamlined form and powerful, liquid-cooled V12 engine. But Mitchell was not a lone genius. He had around him a particularly fine team of draughtsmen, engineers and mechanics. After Mitchell's death, his chief draughtsman, Joseph Smith, was to develop the Spitfire into, arguably, not just the finest all-round fighter of the Second World War but one of the greatest and best-loved of all aircraft.

From 1926, Smith and what began as a team of 38 talented draughtsmen worked on the designs of all Mitchell's projects. In his quiet way, Smith must have loved the idea of an aircraft that was light yet strong, and one that could be – would have to be – flown into lethal action by young pilots straight from training school.

In 1914, while studying engineering at Birmingham Municipal Technical School, Smith signed up with the Royal Navy Volunteer Reserve, crewing motor launches in the Mediterranean. On completing his education he joined Austin Motors, where under John Kenworthy, the company's chief designer, he worked on the design of the Austin Whippet. A far cry from Castoldi's Greyhound, this was a tiny single-seat biplane 'designed for the Owner-Pilot'. With folding wings, it would fit into a garage measuring 8 feet wide, 18 feet long and 7 feet, 6 inches high. To be available with floats 'for sea or river use', the production model, powered by a 45-hp six-cylinder Anzani radial, promised a top speed of 95 mph and a range of two hours. A notably clean design, it was a lovely idea – an aircraft so small that you would have worn it as much as flown it – but money was tight and the market for the 'Owner-Pilot' largely non-existent. Austin, which had built S.E.5a fighters during the First World War, decided to focus on motorcars instead.

Austin's loss was Supermarine's gain. Smith arrived in Southampton as a senior draughtsman in 1921 and the production Spitfire was to a very large extent his work. He turned a very special prototype with immense potential into a highly effective fighting machine, and with an ever-growing team of engineers and draughtsmen continued to extend the reach of the Spitfire until 1947. The final RAF version, the F24 – in service until April 1955 – was almost another plane. In the words of the Royal Air Force Museum, Hendon, 'It is perhaps a mark of the propaganda value of the Spitfire name that this very different machine was not renamed.'

A graceful design, the F24 was more than twice as heavy as Mitchell's pretty blue 1936 prototype. Its Rolls-Royce Griffon engine was more than twice as powerful as the Rolls-Royce Merlin. The F24's top speed, at 26,000 feet, was 454 mph, compared to the prototype's 349 mph at 16,800 feet. It was armed with four wing-mounted 20mm Hispano cannons. The F24's magnificent elliptical wings could also carry rockets fired from racks mounted beneath them. The Spitfire had flown into a quite different world from that of the south coast of England and the lead-up to the Battle of Britain. In 1948, late-model Spitfires were strafing 'Charlie Tango', the 'communist terrorists' of the Malayan Races Liberation Army, formed largely of Chinese Malays who, keen on independence, had fought with Britain against the Japanese during the Second World War.

The genius of the Spitfire was rooted in the aircraft's sheer adaptability. And yet, even as it put on weight, it remained a balletic machine in flight. Although like Castoldi's C.200 series, it was not as easy to manufacture as a Messerschmitt Bf 109 or a Focke-Wulf Fw 190, the Spitfire made the most of minimal means to do what it needed to do. As Beverley Shenstone, the aerodynamicist who did much of the work on the Spitfire's wing, said, 'The ellipse was simply the shape that allowed us the thinnest possible wing with sufficient room inside to carry the necessary structure and the things we wanted to cram in' – like wheels, fuel tanks and guns.

Mitchell had employed Shenstone in 1932. For the three years prior, the young Canadian had worked in Germany, including a spell at Junkers. He had met and had held long discussions with that country's most forward-thinking aerodynamicists, including Alexander Lippisch and Ludwig Prandtl. He had also learned to fly gliders in Germany, and remained throughout his distinguished career a proponent of lightweight and human-powered flight. Mitchell had already considered elliptical wings in one form or another, but Shenstone did much to make these an essential element of the Spitfire. He was also Mitchell's ears and eyes in Germany, the United States and elsewhere, gathering information on the latest developments that might benefit Supermarine. Mitchell was always keen to learn of and to make use of new techniques, wherever they came from.

Shenstone was also very much involved in the design of Mitchell's Supermarine B.12/36 four-engine heavy bomber. Carrying bombs in its wings – with swept-back leading edges – as well as in a central bomb bay, this highly promising machine was expected to have a top speed of 350 mph, a ceiling of 30,000 feet and a range of 3,000 miles, figures way beyond those of the RAF's Stirling, Halifax and Lancaster heavy bombers. The B.12/36 would, in all probability, have gone into production had Mitchell not died in June 1937.

Mitchell had also, of course, worked closely with Rolls-Royce on the idea and development of the R engine. What the Spitfire needed was a smaller inline engine producing great power reliably and in combat conditions. Rolls-Royce had run the prototype of the ideal Spitfire engine in October 1933. This was the company's 27-litre PV-12 – Private Venture [V]12 [cylinder] – developed from the Kestrel by Arthur Rowledge's team of all-talents. By the time it became synonymous with Spitfire, the Merlin was a refined and reliable engine capable of further development. While not directly descended from the Schneider R engine, it shared a common engineering lineage stretching back to the Curtiss D-12 that powered Lieutenant David Rittenhouse to victory with his Curtiss CR-3 at the 1923 Schneider Trophy contest held at Cowes. The D-12 subsequently dissected by Henry Royce at Derby did much to inspire the Rolls-Royce Kestrel that led to both the Schneider racing R and the Merlin.

First flown from Eastleigh Airfield on 5 March 1936, by Vickers's chief test pilot, Captain 'Mutt' Summers, the prototype Spitfire K5054 was almost, if not quite, perfect from the word go. Summers clocked a disappointing top speed of 330 mph, found the rudder oversensitive and sensed a hint of wing flutter when he put the machine into a steep dive. Working at typically breakneck speed – and knowing that his life was side-slipping away – Mitchell had the Spitfire and Summers back in the air on 11 May. He monitored its aerial progress, and prowess, from the passenger seat of a Miles Falcon. Both men were satisfied.

At the end of the month, Summers flew K5054 to Martlesham Heath, where Flight Lieutenant Humphrey Edwardes-Jones – the future Air Marshal Sir Humphrey Edwardes-Jones, Commander-in-Chief RAF Germany –

climbed into the cockpit and into history. When he landed – having nearly forgotten to put the wheels down – Edwardes-Jones rang Air Vice Marshal Wilfrid Freeman at the Air Ministry to let him know what he made of the Supermarine prototype. A week later, Supermarine received an initial order of 310 Spitfires. The first production model emerged from Supermarine's Woolston works in July 1938, by which time Mitchell had been dead for over a year.

God only knows what Mitchell would have made of a film of his life and work being on show in fleapits around Britain from September 1942, after its premiere at the Leicester Square Theatre. Leslie Howard, who produced, directed and starred in *The First of the Few*, played Mitchell – 'Mitch' to his pilots – as a jolly decent and extremely well-mannered public school type. He was nothing of the sort. The film, of course, was propaganda. Mitchell did not meet Willy Messerschmitt in Germany. He did not persuade Henry Royce to build the Merlin. And yet, the film does contain superb flying sequences of a Spitfire Mk II performed by Jeffrey Quill, Mutt Summers's successor at Vickers; and footage, too, of real-life Battle of Britain pilots. Here's Tony Bartley, who married film star Deborah Kerr and moved to Hollywood where he became a film and television executive. Here's 'Bunny' Currant, who joined Hunting in Luton after the war and developed the Jet Provost trainer. And there's Brian Kingcome, who founded Kingcome Sofas and came for drinks a number of times with Brian Wilkins, the *Architectural Review*'s advertising manager, and me in The Bride of Denmark, the private pub of the architectural press secreted below the pavements of Queen Anne's Gate.

Mitchell had, of course, designed the Spitfire as a land-plane. But at the time of the German invasion of Norway in April 1940, a floatplane version became a priority. Even if the Germans seized key airfields – which they did – such a fighter could operate from fjords along the Norwegian coast. Folland Aircraft fitted a pair of floats to a Mk 1 Spitfire from a Fleet Air Arm carrier–based Blackburn B-25 Roc fighter. This did not bode well – as even when, in December 1939, the Roc had managed a stable flight with floats, its top speed fell to under 200 mph. A plan to equip a naval squadron with Roc float-planes had been dropped. The converted Spitfire, known as the 'Narvik Nightmare', did not fly well, but before further steps were taken, the Germans had overrun Norway and the project, however well intended, proved to be redundant.

A Mk VB Spitfire converted by Folland into a floatplane flew from Southampton Water in October 1942, reviving memories of the Schneider Trophy contests – not least because this time around the floats were by Arthur Shirvall, Mitchell's hydro-dynamicist, who had designed them for Supermarine's Schneider contest racers. After a number of modifications, the Mk VB floatplane was flown again from Glasgow in January 1943. Its test pilot, Jeffrey Quill, found it easy enough to fly. It handled well, and though at 340 mph it was slower than a standard aircraft, it was considered fast enough to serve as a sea-based fighter.

A further two Mk VBs were fitted with floats in the summer of 1943. The plan was to hide the three aircraft under netting around uninhabited Dodecanese islands off the Turkish coast. Unleashed, they would make surprise attacks on German transport aircraft supplying garrisons in the area. Crews would hide out in a submarine. A touch unrealistic, perhaps, and the project was scuppered when the Germans brought in heavy reinforcements. The pilots, who had got as far as RAF Fanara, an Egyptian seaplane base on the Suez Canal, were, however, happy enough with their Spitfires, although it proved next to impossible for them to take off in crosswinds at anything above 15 mph.

The idea of a Spitfire floatplane was resurrected in 1944, as such an aircraft could be useful in the Pacific theatre. Folland adapted a Mk IX, which performed well with a top speed of 377 mph, a service ceiling of 38,000 feet and a range of 460 miles. On a test flight made on 18 June, Jeffrey Quill found its handling on the water to be 'extremely good and its only unusual feature was a tendency to "tramp" from side to side on the floats, or to "waddle" a bit when at high speed in the plane'.

Would Mitchell have approved? Probably not. He would surely have designed a new, purpose-built seaplane fighter, although such aircraft would always be sitting targets as they made their long take-off runs. The Schneider seaplane contests had helped both Mitchell and Castoldi to design high-speed fighter aircraft best-suited to taking off from and landing on the ground rather than the sea.

Mitchell's reputation soars higher than Castoldi's for a number of reasons. He was on the right side. He was not prey to political circumstance in the way Castoldi was. In Rolls-Royce he had an ideal partner. He had, too, a sense of lightness and, as his work developed, an instinctive feel – even though he would say this was nonsense – for beautiful forms. Castoldi's very last post-war designs seem lacklustre, as if the spirit of the man who designed the arresting MC.72 had come down to cloying earth with a heavy thud. What Mitchell might have gone on to we cannot know. He died far too young.

TEN

Aftermath

The buzz around air races had clearly not quietened
when, early in the morning of 20 October 1934, a
crowd 60,000-strong gathered at the newly opened
RAF Mildenhall in Suffolk. At 6.30 a.m., the first of 20 aircraft
took off on the first leg of the 11,300-mile MacRobertson Air
Race to Melbourne. As long as there was no change of crew
along the way and stops were made at Baghdad, Allahabad,
Singapore, Darwin and Charleville, Queensland, aircraft of any
size or weight were welcome to compete for the £15,000 prize
(around £1 million in 2020 money) offered by Sir MacPherson
Robertson, the Australian confectionery magnate of Freddo
the Frog and Cherry Ripe chocolate fame.

The occasion was Melbourne's centenary. For wealthy or
sponsored private pilots, the race promised high adventure. For
aircraft manufacturers and airlines, it was an ideal opportunity
to test their latest designs to a new, and far extended, limit.

The first aircraft away was *Black Magic*, an ultra-modern
twin-engine de Havilland DH.88 Comet, its pilots the husband-
and-wife team Jim Mollison and Amy Johnson. After making
the fastest flight yet to India, as far as Karachi, the 'Flying

Sweethearts' made a navigational error and were forced to stop for fuel at Jabalpur. Petrol from a local bus depot caused a piston to seize in one of the Comet's Gipsy Six engines. Landing at Allahabad, they were out of the race.

A DH.88 Comet in British racing green, owned by Bernard Rubin – one of the 'Bentley Boys', and the winner with co-driver Woolf Barnato of Le Mans in 1928 – was flown by test pilot Ken Waller and Owen Cathcart-Jones, a former Royal Navy pilot. After a few hitches and running repairs along the way, they made Melbourne in 108 hours and were placed fourth. First place went to the third of the Comets, a lipstick-red machine named *Grosvenor House* after the Park Lane hotel owned by Arthur Edwards, who had bought the aircraft for a bargain £5,000 – as had the other owners of the Comets. De Havilland was out to win the race, not to make money. Flight Lieutenant Charles Scott, ex-RAF and Qantas, and Tom Campbell Black, a former RNAS and RAF pilot, took turns to fly 30 minutes at a time, smoking and sleeping in between. Despite cramp, a storm over the Bay of Bengal, fatigue that prompted them to hand over control to one another every 10 minutes, and a loss of power in one engine on the final leg over Australia, they landed at a rain-soaked Flemington Racecourse, Melbourne, in 70 hours 54 minutes and 18 seconds. They wore raincoats as they were congratulated on the podium in front of a large crowd, before being ferried to a hotel in a palatial Rolls-Royce.

Scott and Campbell Black had touched down at 3.33 p.m. local time on 23 October. In Italy that day, and as if the Schneider Trophy and its achievements were not to be upstaged, Warrant Officer Francesco Agello captured the world airspeed record at

Faster than the US military's top biplane fighters, the Boeing 247D was a revelation and perhaps even something of a shock when it made its streamlined debut in February 1933. A sleek, all-metal semi-monocoque cantilevered monoplane with retractable undercarriage, comprehensive instrumentation, autopilot, air conditioning, soundproofing, de-icing equipment and the ability to fly on just one of its two Pratt & Whitney Wasp radial engines, it was more than just a glimpse of the future even if it seated no more than 10 passengers – it was the real thing.

Due to demand, TWA (Transcontinental and Western Air) was unable to get hold of the new Boeing. So Jack Frye, the airline's president, asked five manufacturers to bid for a design to rival the Boeing. Don Douglas came back quickly with the DC-1 (Douglas Commercial 1), a 12-seat monoplane that was a step ahead of the 247. In fact, although only one DC-1 was built, the slightly bigger DC-2 flown from May 1934 led to the DC-3, of which 607 were in service by December 1941 when the United States joined in the Second World War. During that global conflict, more than 10,000 military versions of the DC-3 – known as the C-47 Skytrain in the US and the Dakota in Britain – were built. A further 4,937 were manufactured under licence as the Lisunov Li-2 in the Soviet Union and 487 in, of all countries, Japan. In 2020, DC-3s are still very much at work.

What was especially remarkable about the DC-2 named *Uiver* ('stork' in Dutch) that took second place in the MacRobertson Air Race was the fact that it was in service at the time with the Dutch airline KLM and carried passengers – admittedly just the three of them – and 420 lbs of mail all the way from England to Australia. True, it took almost 20 hours longer than *Grosvenor*

1. The Schneider Trophy itself, a silver-plated bronze casting by the French sculptor Ernest Gabard, sits on a decorative marble plinth in a case inside London's Science Museum. Overlooked, antique and even kitsch today, it nevertheless tells the story of how what became a hugely popular international contest began when the aircraft was a new invention and Art Nouveau still fashionable.

International
JACQUES SCHNEIDER CUP
R A C E S

BALTIMORE OCT. ·24· **U.S.A.**
1925
BAY SHORE PARK

2. Jesse Harrison Mason's poster advertising the 1925 Schneider event caught the spirit of the Trophy races well. Bright blue Curtiss seaplanes careering around a pylon over yachts and beach have a holiday air about them. Poster art like this helped draw crowds eager for an exciting day out. A million people may have turned out for the final two contests.

3. In between Schneider contests, the press generated excitement for air races and records. An April 1928 edition of *Illustrazione del Popolo* depicts Mario de Bernardi, winner of the 1926 event, breaking his own and the world's speed record at 513km/h (319mph) in a Macchi M.52R to the approval of a smartly garbed crowd lining the shore of the Venice Lido.

4. By 1931, art and design associated with the Schneider Trophy was far removed from Ernest Gabard's sculpture. This compelling advert by Adrian Hill for Amherst Villiers, makers of superchargers, appeared in the final Schneider Trophy programme. It evokes speed, energy and even, it appears, the breaking of the sound barrier. Years later, Hill presented BBC TV's equally compelling *Sketch Club*.

AMHERST VILLIERS

5. Aircraftman T. E. Shaw, or Lawrence of Arabia – seen here, centre – was intimately involved in the development of the RAF rescue launches designed and built by Hubert Scott-Paine, former owner of Supermarine and employer of Reginald Mitchell. Saving the lives of many Spitfire pilots, the launches rose from the water at speed, all but flying over the sea.

6. Although drawn up on a clean sheet of paper, Reginald Mitchell's Supermarine Spitfire, one of the most effective and agile of all warbirds, owed a debt to the designer's Rolls-Royce powered Schneider Trophy machines. This is MH434, a Mk IX Spitfire of 1943, a combat veteran with a top speed equal to George Stainforth's S.6B. It thrills crowds at airshows today.

7. The Spitfire's connection with the Supermarine Schneider racers was emphasised several times during the Second World War when Mk 1, Mk VB – illustrated here – and Mk IX aircraft were converted into seaplane fighters for operation in Norway, the Dodecanese and the Pacific. None saw combat but they were exciting machines that took to the water happily and flew well.

8. Significantly, for the future of long-distance commercial aviation, the aircraft that came second in the epic MacRobertson Trophy Air Race from London to Melbourne in 1934 was not a purpose-built racer, like the winning de Havilland DH.88 Comet, but a streamlined KLM Douglas DC-2 airliner flying a regular route with passengers largely overland. It had no need for floats.

9. Built at Cowes on the Isle of Wight, the twin-deck Saunders-Roe SR.45 Princess was a late attempt to prove that a luxurious long-distance airliner flying boat had a role in the post-war world. First flown in August 1952, the 360mph turboprop Princess was unable to compete with a new generation of turboprops and jetliners flying from much improved airports.

10. Howard Hughes's H-4 Hercules, or *Spruce Goose*, is the biggest-ever flying boat. Designed to transport 750 troops or a pair of Sherman tanks across the Atlantic, the giant aircraft – with Hughes at the helm – made its delayed maiden flight in November 1947, lifting 70-ft above the water for twenty-six seconds. Lovingly conserved, it has never flown again.

11. Where the flying boat proved indispensable in wartime was over the vast expanses of the Atlantic and Pacific Oceans. The herculean Short Sunderland, first flown in 1937, took on reconnaissance and rescue duties. It hunted and destroyed German U-boats. It transported troops and supplies. Armed to the teeth, it defended itself well. Post-war, some Sunderlands were pressed into passenger service.

12. It was this aircraft more than any other that set the pace for the Jet Age and sealed the fate of the flying boat airliners circumnavigating the globe dreamed of by Jacques Schneider. A prototype of the all-conquering Boeing 707 flew in 1954, production aircraft entering service with Pan-Am four years later. The last passenger 707 was built in 1978.

13. The Rolls-Royce-powered Saunders-Roe SR.N4 *Mountbatten* class hovercraft could fly across the English Channel in well under thirty minutes, loaded with up to 418 passengers and sixty cars. These impressive 80mph machines, in regular service on cross-Channel routes between 1968 and 2000, were deposed by competition from Channel Tunnel rail services. This is *The Princess Anne* entering Dover harbour in 1990.

14. A Beriev Be-200 *Altair* under power at Gelendzhik on the Black Sea. In production since 2003, the 430mph Be-200 is an amphibian jet. As well as carrying passengers and cargo, it is used as an air ambulance, for search and rescue missions, for maritime patrols and as a fire fighter, able to scoop water from the sea while in flight.

15. The lure of high-speed streamlined seaplanes has haunted generations ever since the final Schneider Trophy contest. During the six months of the Festival of Britain held on London's South Bank in 1951, millions of visitors had the opportunity to look up at a Supermarine S.6A, disguised as S.6B S.1596, appearing to dive down from the roof of the Transport Pavilion.

16. The joy and excitement of flying small seaplanes can be experienced today through lightweight contemporary aircraft like the amphibious Progressive Aerodyne SeaRey, designed and built by Kerry Richter in Tavares, Florida. It might be no faster than Maurice Prévost's Deperdussin of 1913, yet one of these machines has been flown around the world. This one is landing on Chesapeake Bay.

House, but the Comet had room for just a pair of pilots. The DC-2 had a crew, comfortable seats, a galley, a lavatory, soundproofing and air conditioning.

In June 1931, shortly before the 1931 Schneider contest and George Stainforth's record-breaking 407.5 mph with the Supermarine S.6B, Imperial Airways launched its latest passenger aircraft on its London to Paris route. This was the Handley Page H.P.45, a ponderous-looking unequal-span biplane. First flown by the happily named Squadron Leader Thomas Harold England, it had a maximum speed of 120 mph and cruised at 90–100 mph. These wallowing if luxuriously appointed aircraft remained in service until shortly before the outbreak of the Second World War. There were just the four of them. Four H.P.42s, a slight variation but with the same performance, were built for routes to India and South Africa. It does seem remarkable that these slow if notably safe aircraft flew the flag for Britain's airways abroad at the same time as DC-3s were sprinting west to east across the United States in just 15 hours with three stops along the way.

These two very different aircraft could carry the same number of passengers, yet where the H.P.42/45s were, at 92 feet long, 27 feet high and with wingspans of 130 feet, Edwardian country houses among the clouds, the compact and streamlined DC-3, measuring 65 feet long, 17 feet high and with a wingspan of 95 feet, was the aerial equivalent of Frank Lloyd Wright's Fallingwater. And where passenger flight in and from Britain was largely an exclusive affair for the well-heeled only, the democratization of flight was, albeit slowly at first, under way in the United States.

The US had been doing things differently. While the experience of the Schneider Trophy and the quest for speed had led the Americans by the time of the MacRobertson Air Race to fledgling airliners that could fly faster and were far more sophisticated than contemporary military aircraft, the British effort was directed more towards quick and nimble light aircraft and, in the drawing offices of Reginald Mitchell at Supermarine and Sydney Camm at Hawker, to very fast and highly aerobatic interceptor fighters. And whereas very fast British aircraft were powered at this time mostly by inline engines that drew on the Curtiss D-12, the Americans had developed the radial engine to new levels of power and, in streamlined airframes, speed.

The Douglas DC-3 and the de Havilland DH.91 Albatross went into service within a year of one another: the former, industrial design at its very best; the latter a work of aviation art. Its four de Havilland Gipsy Twelve V12 engines generating 2,100 hp gave the Albatross a top speed of 225 mph and an initial rate of climb of 700 feet a minute. The DC-3's two Pratt & Whitney R-1830 Twin Wasp radials gave 2,400 hp. The American aircraft had a top speed of 230 mph and could climb away from the ground at 1,130 feet a minute. The British aircraft was bigger, heavier and had a greater wing loading – meaning, among other things, that it needed more speed to take off and so longer runways.

From this technical perspective alone, it might be said that the Americans were doing more with less. This, though, is only one tiny corner of a much bigger canvas. Including two prototypes, just seven Albatrosses were built compared with more than 600 DC-3s and the nearly 16,000 military variants built at home and abroad. De Havilland built 95 Gipsy Twelve inline engines. The figure for Pratt & Whitney R-1830 Twin Wasp radials is 173,618. The last DH.91, seconded by the RAF, flew in 1943. Sixty years later, I flew in Buffalo Airways DC-3s in regular passenger service through snow above Alaska. Nearly 20 years on, DC-3s remain busy at work in different parts of the world.

Radial engines had become a stumbling block in Schneider Trophy contests. Presenting too great a surface to the slip-stream, they held top speeds down, while the power that could be squeezed out of them was significantly less than low-profile inline engines and especially the V12s, beginning with the Curtiss D-12 from the United States, that demonstrated their prowess in the 1923 Schneider contest. Radials, however, had several advantages over inline engines. Air-cooled, they were simpler, smaller and lighter. There was less to go wrong with a radial engine, and they took up precious little room. What if the radial could be made much more powerful than it had been between the First World War and the mid-1920s, and what if it could be streamlined into airframes?

The Americans did indeed break the inline orthodoxy, despite the fact that they had done so well in the Schneider contests with the Curtiss V12s, persuading European engine makers to go the same way. On 5 September 1932, a 55,000-strong crowd at the Cleveland Airfield, Ohio, witnessed a thrilling race between daredevil pilots banking around 50-foot pylons on the tightest of 10-mile circuits. This was Labor Day, a national holiday in the States, and the event was the fourth annual Thompson Trophy contest sponsored by Thompson Products, the Cleveland firm specializing in engine valves that had made the sodium-cooled valves that helped Charles Lindbergh to fly the Atlantic in his Wright Whirlwind radial–powered Ryan monoplane.

The contest was a free-for-all, an aerial rodeo, with bucking aircraft and their variously skilled sky-riders taking off one behind the other from the same starting line at 10-second intervals. Prize money was generous and, in Depression-era America, it was well worth having a go even if the stakes were set high.

The most striking aircraft in this unnerving sky was a stubby red and white machine that looked rather like a pumped-up jelly bean with tiny wings. This was the Gee Bee Model R Super Sportster flown by Major Jimmy Doolittle in shirtsleeves and tie. Careering around the circuit and lapping the pack, Doolittle – the 'Human Bullet' – won the race at an average speed of 252.68 mph. Earlier in the event, he had set a new world speed record for landplanes of 296 mph with the Gee Bee. Doolittle told the *Springfield Union*, 'She is the sweetest ship I've ever flown. She is perfect in every respect... It never missed a beat and has lots of stuff in it yet. I think this proves that the Granville brothers up in Springfield [Massachusetts] build the very best speed ships in America today.'

Designed by Howell 'Pete' Miller and Zantford 'Granny' Granville, who had set up Granville Brothers Aircraft at Springfield Airport in 1929 to build dedicated pylon racers, the foreshortened shape of Doolittle's Model R was deceiving. If looked at from above – in plan – its shape was that of a teardrop. In wind tunnel tests at New York University conducted by Professor Alexander Klemin, dean of the Guggenheim School of Aeronautics, it proved highly aerodynamic. And this despite its bulbous nose concealing a highly tuned nine-cylinder Pratt & Whitney R-1340 Wasp. Clearly, the shape of the fuselage from nose cone to tail worked. The research, begun the previous year by Robert Hall, Granville's chief engineer, suggested that radial engine aircraft could, after all, be very fast indeed.

Hall had been responsible for the design of the Gee Bee Model Z that won the 1931 Thompson Trophy at Cleveland at 236.2 mph with Lowell Bayles, who liked to fly barefoot to get a better feel of the rudder, at the controls. The day before, Hall had flown the yellow and black Gee Bee Z – yes, it did look like an enormous bee – to victory at the General Tire and Rubber Trophy Race. A few years later, Hall joined Grumman, where as a senior engineer and lead test pilot he worked on the design of some of the finest US Navy carrier-based fighters, including the F6F Hellcat of 1942 and F8F Bearcat of 1944. The Hellcat was a heavily armoured and well-armed machine that was easy to build, fly and maintain, and it performed magnificently in the Pacific against Japanese opposition. A total of 12,275 were built in two years. They shot down 5,223 enemy aircraft, more than any other Allied naval fighter. Powered by a Pratt & Whitney 2,000-hp R-2800 Double Wasp, the Hellcat had a top speed in level flight of 400 mph.

US Navy pilots, however, wanted a yet-more-powerful version of the Hellcat with greater climbing ability. While the Hellcat was, for the most part, more than a match for the Japanese Navy's renowned Mitsubishi Zero fighter, the Nakajima Ki-84 Hayate (Gale) first seen in action in November 1944 was a new threat. Rather luckily, this single-seat fighter's engine, a 2,000-hp 18-cylinder double-row radial, tended to play up without meticulous maintenance. On a good day, the Gale could climb high enough to intercept Boeing B-29 Superfortress bombers, the aircraft type that finally put an end to the war in the Pacific by dropping atomic bombs in August 1945 on the port cities of Nagasaki and Hiroshima.

As the most powerful piston engine available to Grumman was the Pratt & Whitney R-2800, the Bearcat was designed to be a smaller and lighter aircraft than the Hellcat. With its truncated wings and bubble canopy, it had the look of some military racer. Just too late to see service before VJ Day, the F8F was 20 per cent lighter than the F6F, had a 30 per cent faster rate of climb, and was more than 50 mph faster in level flight. Quicker and more able than many early military jets, the Bearcat was to become a favourite post-war racer.

On 21 August 1989, Lyle Shelton, a Texan airline pilot, set a world airspeed record for piston-engine aircraft in level flight of 528.33 mph in *Rare Bear*, an F8F fitted with a Wright R-3350, the engine used by B-29 Superfortress bombers. Shelton set a second piston-engine record by climbing *Rare Bear* from rest to 10,000 feet in 91.9 seconds. Who, in 1931, would have thought radial-engine aircraft capable of such spectacular feats? While *Rare Bear*'s speed record was finally beaten, unofficially, on 2 September 2017 by *Voodoo*, a modified Merlin-engine P-51 Mustang flown by Steve Hinton Jr at 531.53 mph over a three-kilometre test course – with a top speed of 554.69 mph – it had been by less than 1 per cent and so, by the rules, *Rare Bear*'s record stood.

Observed in plan, both the Bearcat and Hellcat bear a remarkably close resemblance to a Gee Bee racer. One big difference is the location of the cockpit, set right back in the Gee Bees and merging into the tailplane. While this gives those aircraft their cartoonish appearance, there was a good reason to design the aircraft this way. It allowed pilots to fly very close to the pylons around the Thompson Trophy circuit.

The Gee Bee pilots included several women. The daughter of James Tait, one of the owners of Springfield Airport, Maude Tait was a schoolteacher before the desire to fly lifted her out of her classroom and up into the air above Springfield in a Gee Bee Model Y Super Senior Sportster. She won the 1931 Cleveland Pneumatic Aero Trophy Race for Women at 187.6 mph, her Gee Bee adorned with a Filaloola bird on the fuselage. This comic-book character had a tendency to turn in ever-decreasing circles until it flew into its own tail feathers.

Charismatic but dangerous to fly if mishandled – with such short wings, the aircraft could turn quickly yet all too easily roll – the Gee Bee racers were hugely influential aircraft, even if just 24 were built and nearly all lost in crashes. Among those killed flying them was Lowell Bayles, during an attempt at the world airspeed record in December 1931. His accident was recorded on film. What seems to have happened is that the fuel cap of his Model Z came undone, flew back and knocked him unconscious. The Gee Bee pitched up, its right wing folded in half, the aircraft spun, hit the ground and exploded.

Another high-profile death was that of Florence Klingensmith from Minnesota, who had decided she had to fly when, in 1928, Charles Lindbergh visited Fargo. Persuading local businessmen to stump up the money to buy her a Monocoupe, she barnstormed around the state. In front of a 50,000-strong crowd and

NAA (National Aeuronatics Association) officials, on 22 June 1931 Klingensmith made 1,078 loops in four and half hours above Wold Chamberlain Airfield, Minneapolis. Competing against men in the 1933 Frank Phillips Trophy Race, Chicago, she tried to land when the fabric covering the fuselage of her Gee Bee Y tore, but flipped and crashed into a ploughed field.

These and other deaths and accidents eventually killed off Granville Brothers Aircraft, as with each loss the company stood to lose more of the prize money it relied on to survive. To keep manufacturing costs down, the Gee Bee team had bought off-the-shelf components to build the planes. If you looked carefully and were in the know, you would find a gear-shift knob from a 1928 Chevrolet crowning the throttle lever, a throttle handgrip from a 1931 Indian motorbike, and, inside the fuselage, aileron controls fashioned from Ford Model T steering rods.

Shortly after the firm went bankrupt in October 1933, Granny Granville was working on a design for an aircraft for Jacqueline Cochran to fly in the MacRobertson Air Race. Cochran was to become a famous American pilot – as a racer, as head of WASP (Women Airforce Service Pilots) during the Second World War, and as the first woman to break the sound barrier with an F-86 Sabre 3 in May 1953. While delivering a Gee Bee E Sportster to raise money for the new company that would build Cochran's Granville R-6H *Q.E.D.* (*Quod Erat Demonstrandum*), Granville spotted a construction crew walking onto the landing area. As he pulled up, the engine of the Gee Bee cut out. The aircraft crashed. Granville died in an ambulance on the way to hospital.

In the 1934 MacRobertson race, Cochran and her co-pilot Wesley Smith, a First World War US Army Air Service veteran and a long-serving pilot with the Post Office Department Air Mail Service, got as far from RAF Mildenhall as Bucharest in their bright green and orange Granville racer – it was sponsored by the Lucky Strike cigarette company – before its flaps gave up. Bought by the Mexican pilot Francisco Sarabia, repainted white and red and renamed *Conquistador del Cielo*, the Granville brothers' final aircraft made several record-setting flights including Sarabia's 10 hour 47 minutes from Mexico City to New York City. On the return to Mexico City following the fastest flight yet made from there to Washington, DC, Sarabia crashed into the Potomac after, it seems, a rag blocked the carburettor of the Gee Bee's Pratt & Whitney Hornet. Sarabia was killed, but his *Conquistador* was pulled from the river and repatriated to Mexico. It can be seen today in a circular museum pavilion, built as a gateway to the city of Ciudad Lerdo in Sarabia's memory.

The pilot of the Boeing 247 that came third in the epic MacRobertson race was Roscoe Turner. Turner, one of America's great barnstorming pilots, had come third to Jimmy Doolittle in the 1932 Thompson Trophy at Cleveland. Turner won the last two pre-war Thompson races in 1938 (283.4 mph) and 1939 (282.5 mph) flying his Laird-Turner Meteor, a clean-cut monoplane with a cockpit above the wing, powered by a 1,000-hp Pratt & Whitney Wasp.

A farmer's son from Corinth, Mississippi, Roscoe Turner was every inch the all-American showman, from his riding boots and faux-military uniform to his all-purpose grin. In 1930, the Gilmore Oil Company gave him the money to buy a lion cub from Goebel's Wild Animal Farm, supplier of exotic animals to Hollywood. The oil company's logo was a red lion and its slogan, 'Roar with Gilmore'. Over the following five years the lion, named Gilmore, flew 25,000 miles with Turner. By then the animal had grown rather large and even the normally unflappable Turner found its behaviour in the air a touch disconcerting. Both pilot and lion lived to a good age, something that cannot be said for all too many American racing pilots.

Jimmy Doolittle gave up pure air racing the day he won the 1932 Thompson Trophy. 'I have yet to hear of anyone engaged in this work dying of old age,' he said. Doolittle lived to 96. And yet if any pilot was to show why adventurous flying was important – it would save many more lives in the future than it lost in a dangerous present – it was Doolittle. His career was extraordinary.

Born in California in 1896 and raised in Alaska, Doolittle interrupted his studies at the University of California, Berkeley, in 1917 to sign up with the Signal Corps Reserve. The Corp's aeronautical surveillance work led to Doolittle's training as a military pilot. A regular officer after the First World War, he completed his bachelor's degree at Berkeley and began pioneering flights to test aircraft instruments. As a test pilot and aeronautical engineer he completed a master's degree and a doctorate at MIT (Massachusetts Institute of Technology).

In 1929, Doolittle was the first pilot to take off, fly and land an aircraft relying wholly on the readings of cockpit instruments. He also tested the artificial horizon and directional gyroscope he had helped invent. Working for Shell in the 1930s, while holding the rank of major in the Air Reserve Corps,

Doolittle encouraged the development of high-octane fuels necessary for high-speed flight. In 1940, he was elected president of the Institute of Aeronautical Science. On 18 April 1942, this pilot-engineer-racer-scientist led 16 North American B-25 Mitchell twin-engine bombers crewed by volunteers from the aircraft carrier USS *Hornet* on the Americans' first retaliatory raid on Japan after Pearl Harbor.

Having bombed assigned targets in mainland Japan, Doolittle led his Mitchells to China. Running out of fuel after 12 hours flying, in storms and in the dark, Doolittle parachuted into a paddy field. Having found all members of his crew, he was helped to safety from behind Japanese lines by friendly Chinese. Not everyone made it home, but it had been an extraordinary mission, rocking Japanese confidence and boosting American morale.

Even while privy to the breaking of the German Ultra code, Major General Doolittle continued to fly in action over German-occupied Italy as commander of the Fifteenth Air Force. From January 1944 until the end of the war, he was based in England as a lieutenant general in command of the Eighth Air Force. He freed fighter pilots from having to stick close by bombers at all times, meaning that his formidable new 440-mph P51-D Mustangs – powered by Packard-built Rolls-Royce Merlin 61 engines – could clear air space ahead of the bomber fleets. Their pilots were free to intercept the enemy as they saw fit, and to attack airfields and other ground targets.

A successful Anglo-American collaboration, the Mustang emerged from talks between teams led by Sir Henry Self, air representative of the wartime British Purchasing Commission, and James Kindelberger, head of North American Aviation. The British had wanted North American to build Curtiss P-40 Kittyhawks, but Edgar Schmued, Kindelberger's chief designer, suggested a new and more able fighter. When, though, the P51 went into RAF service, it was found lacking in high-altitude performance. Ronald Harker, a Rolls-Royce test pilot, thought it needed the same engine as the highly effective Spitfire Mk IX. Rolls-Royce installed a Merlin 61 in a P51, and Kindelberger and Schmued redesigned their fighter around the British engine. The result was one of the finest fighters of all time. It had the range to escort bombers into the heart of Germany and the ability to dogfight with the Luftwaffe's finest while it was there. As Hermann Göring said, 'When I saw Mustangs over Berlin, I knew the jig was up.'

Eric 'Winkle' Brown tested a brand-new P51-D at RAE Farnborough in March 1944. He later recalled:

The Mustang was a good fighter and the best escort due to its incredible range, make no mistake about it. It was also the best American dogfighter... It could not by any means out-turn a Spitfire. No way. It had a good rate-of-roll, better than the Spitfire, so I would say the plusses to the Spitfire and the Mustang just about equate. If I were in a dogfight, I'd prefer to be flying the Spitfire. The problem was I wouldn't like to be in a dogfight near Berlin, because I could never get home to Britain in a Spitfire!

Did Göring know that a German had designed the Mustang? Born in Bavaria in 1899, Edgar Schmued had left for Brazil in the early 1920s when the German economy was on its knees. His later designs included the acclaimed F-86 Sabre and F-100 Super Sabre jet fighters. And James 'Dutch' Kindelberger was the son of German immigrants, his American nickname a corruption of *Deutsch*. Aviation has rarely been a purely national game.

By D-Day in June 1944, and working in close collaboration with land forces, Doolittle had 200,000 American men and women at his command, along with 2,000 bombers and 1,000 fighters operating from 76 British airfields. Fighting against resolute opposition, the Eighth Air Force suffered the loss of 26,000 lives, but could boast 261 fighter aces as well as 305 gunner aces battling the latest German aircraft from their bomber gun emplacements.

Post-war, Jimmy Doolittle was kept busy, especially by President Dwight D. Eisenhower, former Supreme Commander of the Allied Expeditionary Force in Europe, with matters concerning military intelligence, aeronautics and space. Although he turned down the job of first head of NASA, Doolittle viewed aviation as a matter of ever onwards and upwards. In October 1967, the North American X-15 rocket plane achieved a speed of 4,520 mph, the highest ever recorded by a crewed and powered aircraft. This was more than 10 times as fast as the Mustangs Doolittle commanded in 1944–45, and 20 times faster than the Curtiss he had flown in the Schneider Trophy.

The quest for pure speed did not die with John Boothman's Schneider victory in 1931 and George Stainforth's 407.5 mph with the Supermarine S.6B. Nor even with Francesco Agello's 440.68 mph in 1934 with the Macchi-Castoldi MC.72. Far from it. The Schneider contests had established records that were there to be broken. German, French and American manufacturers, pilots and air forces were noticeably keen to set new airspeed records, partly because they had either dropped out of the Schneider contests or been unable, as with Germany, to take part. The British and the Italians had ridden high. Who could beat them?

One man thought he could. This was Howard Hughes, the precocious Texan-born American business magnate, film-maker and pilot. In 1927, the 21-year-old began filming *Hell's Angels*, a First World War epic finally released three years later. With its spectacular aerial sequences, directed from the air by Hughes, the movie cost $2.8 million to make – a fortune at the time – and won an Academy Award for Best Cinematography. Real First World War aircraft fought the dogfights on the screen, and while the script and acting left much to be desired, the flying sequences remain exciting 90 years on. Many of the pilots had flown in action in the war. Three died in crashes during the film. Flying a dangerous diving sequence himself, Hughes crashed, too, but survived. In Martin Scorsese's acclaimed biopic, *The Aviator*, Roscoe Turner and Gilmore the lion make an appearance at the premiere of *Hell's Angels* at Grauman's Chinese Theatre on Hollywood Boulevard.

Turner was to finish third in the MacRobertson Air Race in 1934, but although it was a sign of things to come in terms of commercial flight, his Boeing 247D's top speed was 200 mph and Hughes was planning to fly much faster than that. And where Turner's Boeing was sponsored by, among others, Heinz, the Macmillan Oil Company and Warner Brothers, Hughes would go it alone – making an attempt on the world airspeed record in the purest of aircraft.

This was the Hughes H-1 Racer, a lean, spare and graceful monoplane built in secret to sketch designs by Hughes and a working design by Richard 'Dick' Palmer, a Caltech graduate and former Lockheed project engineer who had helped Hughes tune his Boeing 100 biplane for greater speed. Palmer had only recently started a promising new job with Jerry Vultee's Aircraft Development Corporation, but a telegram he received from Hughes made him jump ship. It read, 'Would you like to help design the fastest plane in the world?'

Glenn Odekirk would build it. An accomplished aircraft mechanic, Odekirk had been hired by Hughes to maintain the 130 First World War machines used in the filming of *Hell's Angels*. Together, Odekirk, Hughes and Palmer shaped a racing plane that was, in every way, polished. To ensure optimum aerodynamic efficiency, aluminium sections were butted together, rather than overlapping (as was standard practice), while rivets were flush with the bodywork. The wings were made of wood and two sets were prepared, one shorter for the attempt on the world speed record, the other longer for long-distance flight.

The engine was a brand-new design, the Pratt & Whitney R-1535 Twin Wasp Junior, a supercharged twin-row 14-cylinder radial rated at 700 hp. With a higher compression ratio and 100-octane fuel, the H-1's engine produced at least 1,000 hp.

Press interest was intense. When would anyone get a look at the custom-built aircraft they called the 'Silver Bullet' and the 'Mystery Ship'? The answer was at Martin Field near Santa Ana,

California, on Friday, 13 September 1935, when Hughes made his attempt on the speed record.

High-speed cameras and officials from the FAI on the ground – as well as Amelia Earhart in the air in her red Lockheed Vega – were there to monitor proceedings. Up Hughes went, his H-1 Racer clearly a very fast and nimble machine. His average speed over four timed runs was 352.4 mph, a new world record for land-planes. Intoxicated by the sheer thrill of it all, Hughes made two further runs and was entering his seventh when the engine cut out. He had run out of fuel, having taken on a minimal amount to keep the weight of his aircraft as low as possible. Hughes made a successful emergency landing, with no time to lower the wheels, on a field of either beetroot or beans. He was found sat on top of the H-1 making notes. 'She'll go faster,' he said when he looked up.

On 19 January 1937, Hughes flew the H-1 non-stop over the 2,490 miles from the Union Air Terminal, Los Angeles, to Newark Municipal Airport in an unprecedented 7 hours, 28 minutes and 25 seconds at an average speed of 322 mph. Maintaining an altitude of 14,000 feet for much of the way, he reported a maximum speed of 370 mph. It had been an aston-ishing if exhausting flight. 'My next record,' he told reporters in New Jersey, 'will be some seriously long-distance sleep.'

While he slept, the *Seattle Daily Times* printed a letter from 1828, found by one of its readers, from the school board of Lancaster, Ohio, to someone trying to organize a discussion about the coming of the railroads. It said:

You are welcome to the use of the school house to debate all proper questions, but such things as railroads and telegraphs are impossibilities and rank infidelity. There is nothing in the Word of God about them. If God had designed that His intelligent creatures should travel at the frightful speed of fifteen miles an hour, by steam, He would have clearly foretold it through His holy prophets. It is a device of Satan to lead immortal souls down to Hell.

Hughes must have had Lucifer and all his legions of dark angels with him.

What he had achieved was truly impressive: a transcontinental flight made at a speed not far off that of John Boothman's winning Schneider Trophy run over 217 miles six years earlier. Hughes had hopes that the USAAF might order a military version of the H-1, but partly through conservatism and partly perhaps because the record-breaker was a one-off made by a small company, it kept to its increasingly outmoded biplanes. Hughes would have been heartened to read a transcript of a lecture entitled 'The Problems of High Speed Flight', given by Willy Messerschmitt in November 1937 to the German Academy of Aviation Research: 'We need pure experimental aircraft in the development of which the designer must be completely unfettered; he must not be bound by restrictions, by considerations regarding available tools and equipment, by regulations and preconceptions, by the need for a practical application of the experimental aircraft to the end user.'

In the meantime, Hughes's focus shifted to commercial aviation. In July 1938, he made a record around-the-world flight with a 14-seat twin-engine Lockheed Super Electra, a rival to the Boeing 247 and Douglas DC-2. At the same time,

German scientists and engineers were indeed thinking of new ways of flying both theoretically, which they were very good at, and practically, at which they were equally good. Alexander Lippisch, a brilliant German aerodynamicist and engineer who had watched Orville Wright fly at Berlin's Tempelhof Airport in 1909, had already developed a tail-less delta-wing glider as early as 1931, a proposal for a delta-wing fighter with a pusher propeller in 1934, and by 1937 was thinking of a rocket-powered fighter that would emerge as the Messerschmitt Me 163 Komet in 1941. He also designed a supersonic delta-wing ramjet fighter that got no further than model stage before the end of the Second World War and his move via Operation Paperclip to the United States. In wind tunnel tests, a model of the ramjet fighter proved stable at Mach 2.6.

Germany captured the world airspeed record for land-planes for the first time on 11 November 1937 not with a Lippisch design, but when Messerschmitt's chief test pilot Dr Hermann Wurster flew a measured course above the Augsberg–Kaufbeuren railway line in a specially prepared Bf 109 V13, its DB 601 engine boosted to 1,700 hp, at 610.95 km/h (379.63 mph).

Heinkel responded the following June with its He 100 single-seat fighter, a highly promising new design by Walter and Siegfried Günter. Piloted by Ernst Udet, the Luftwaffe's director of research and development, it maintained an average speed of 634.73 km/h (394.4 mph) over 100 kilometres. Fitted with a short-life racing version of the DB 601 that produced a whopping 2,770 hp during a bench test, and with Hans Dieterle at the controls, on 30 March 1939 the He 100 peaked at 746.61 km/h (463.92 mph).

Heinkel had high hopes of getting the He 100 into mass production. It was a more modern and, in all likelihood, better fighter than the Bf 109; but, for whatever reason, the vast majority of DB 601 engines were assigned to Messerschmitt, leaving a question mark over what engine would power a mass-produced He 100.

Perhaps to assure the ascendancy of his own aircraft, Willy Messerschmitt had produced a one-off racing machine first flown in August 1938. Designated Me 209, its code name suggested it might be some new version of the combat-tested Bf 109. This, though, was a small racing machine, its wings doubling up as part of its engine's cooling system and with no room for guns. With its cockpit set far back towards the tailplane, the Me 209 had the look of slim pylon racer. On 26 April, 23-year-old Fritz Wendel flew the feisty Messerschmitt to 755.14 km/h (469.22 mph) and a world record for a piston-engine aircraft that was not to be broken for many years. In 1938–39, German landplanes had decisively taken the world airspeed record from the seaplanes nurtured by the Schneider Trophy.

No British aircraft could get near the speeds set by Dieterle and Wendel. An unofficially tested, flush-riveted and highly tuned Mk 1 Spitfire, its Merlin uprated to 2,100 hp for short bursts, flew at 407.6 mph in spring 1939, but though this equalled George Stainforth's record with an S.6B in 1931, it was some way behind the Germans. The British did try for the world speed record again and, intriguingly, the attempt was made in June 1940, just a month before the Battle of Britain.

The contender was a purpose-built machine, the Napier-Heston Racer designed by George Cornwall of Heston Aircraft and Napier's Arthur Hagg. With its timber fuselage and knife-edge wings hand-finished with 20 coats of lacquer, the Napier-Heston was a strikingly smooth machine that certainly looked as if it might fly very fast indeed. Although the Air Ministry had been interested in the project, this was mostly to get a handle on its engine, the new 2,450-hp H-24 Napier Sabre. In the event, it was left to William Morris – Lord Nuffield – to fund the aircraft.

All looked promising on 12 June 1940 as Squadron Leader G. L. G. Richmond opened up the 24-cylinder engine and, after a slight bump, was up in the air over Heston Aerodrome. Would the Napier-Heston reach 480 mph as its designers intended? Within five minutes, the complex engine overheated and for some reason Richmond stalled the aircraft, crashing down to earth from 30 feet and breaking it in two. Richmond, although burned, survived. The Napier-Heston was written off.

The French, seemingly out of the high-speed picture for a long while, had in fact attempted to break the world speed record on several occasions. One of the two Bernard H.V.120 seaplanes meant to have competed in the 1931 Schneider Trophy contest was converted into a landplane. Strong winds held the newly designated Bernard V.4 back on what was meant to have been a record-breaking flight just after Christmas 1933, while problems with its Hispano-Suiza W18 engine and the withdrawal of government funding put paid to further assaults on the speed record.

In September 1936, Michel Détroyat flew one of the speedy little Caudron C.460 aircraft – their distinctly Gallic noses were almost improbably long – to victory in the Thompson Trophy at Los Angeles. Détroyat was the only non-American to win this challenging pylon race. The Caudron, though, was never powerful enough to fly at truly high speeds. A final pre-war Caudron designed by Georges Otfinovsky, and with the same elongated nose, was built around the new 900-hp Renault 12R Spécial 12-cylinder engine; but, again, it seems unlikely that with such limited power it would have flown anywhere near as fast as the Germans. When war broke out, it was hidden in the cellar underneath the Renault exhibition hall. The Germans must have goose-stepped past hundreds of times, but never caught sight of the blue-black C.714R that is now in the care of the Musée de l'Air.

The one French aircraft that did seem to be a contender was the radical Bugatti 100P. This futuristic machine, looking like something from *Dan Dare* or *Star Wars*, was like no other aircraft of its time. Assembled in a Paris furniture factory, it was designed for Ettore Bugatti, the famous Italian-born Alsace car manufacturer, by Louis de Monge, a highly inventive Belgian aero-engineer.

Bugatti, whose cars had won many races over the years, was keen to have a crack at the world airspeed record using his own engines. De Monge placed a pair of canted Type 50 Bugatti engines – 4.9-litre straight-eights – side by side in the slimmest-possible fuselage behind the aircraft's cockpit. Each engine drove one of a pair of contra-rotating propellers. The wings of this wooden wonder, fabricated from balsa ply, were swept forward. The tailplane was V-formed. The 100P was light, and so the 900-hp produced by its twin engines would be enough,

Bugatti and de Monge believed, to propel this lithe royal-blue machine to 830 km/h (516 mph).

By the time the 100P was nearing completion, the Germans marched into Paris. Bugatti had the machine disassembled and packed off to his Château d'Ermenonville, where it was stored in a barn. Many years later the parts were brought to the United States where the aircraft can now be seen in the EAA (Experimental Aircraft Association) Aviation Museum in Oshkosh, Wisconsin. Because he and so many other aviation enthusiasts were keen to know how the 100P would have flown, Scotty Wilson, an ex-USAF jet fighter pilot, decided to build a replica using modern materials and a pair of Suzuki Hayabusa motorbike engines. On 6 August 2016, the replica made three very brief test flights from near Clinton-Sherman Air Force Base, Oklahoma. On the third run, Wilson had been flying for less than a minute when his 100P banked and ploughed into a field. He was killed and the aircraft destroyed.

Untroubled by the threat of a German invasion – for the time being at least – might Italy have produced the post-Schneider dream machine, a piston-engine aircraft capable of 500 mph in level flight? Giovanni Agnelli, president of Fiat, certainly thought so. Agnelli asked Umberto Savoia, head of Fiat's aviation department, to look into the matter. With his aircraft designers working flat out on military projects, Savoia offered the job to CMASA (Costruzioni Meccaniche Aeronautiche Società Anonima), a company with its factory in Marina di Pisa at the mouth of the River Arno. It had been acquired by Fiat in 1934.

In April 1939, Manlio Stiavelli, who had worked on the design of seaplanes since the First World War, unveiled the

CS.15 (Corsa Stiavelli), a spectacular, lightweight, mid-wing, all-metal monoplane with semi-elliptical wings and its cockpit merged into a long fin. It had something of the look of a racing speedboat, and it is easy to imagine the blood-red CS.15 perched on suitably streamlined floats and competing in some Schneider-style contest. A youthful design, the CS.15 owed much to Lucio Lazzarino, Stiavelli's 25-year-old assistant who, when I went to see him in the late 1980s, was director of the Aerospace Engineering Department at the University of Pisa.

The CS.15's engine held great promise. A new design by Antonio Fessia and Carlo Bona – Tranquillo Zerbi, who died in March 1939, had been involved at the outset of the project – this 34.5-litre V16 produced a reliable 2,250 hp at 3,200 rpm. Driving a pair of contra-rotating propellers, its heat was dispelled through a condensation cooling system that took up most of the wing surface. Tested in wind tunnels, the CS.15 promised a top speed of 850 km/h (528 mph). Hopes were dashed, though, when Mussolini declared war on France and Britain. Work on the racer dragged to a halt. The Germans, it seems, may well have damaged or destroyed the airframe, although the CS.15's engine is on display at the Museo Storico dell'Aeronautica Militare at Vigna di Valle.

Any number of exciting and imaginative designs for high-speed and record-breaking aircraft had been made on drawing boards in France, Italy, Germany and Britain – and in the Soviet Union and Japan, too – as the world headed towards the terrible confrontation of 1939–45. And while, in terms of aircraft design and technology, the Second World War witnessed the first successful flights of rocket- and jet-powered planes, it also produced one extremely beautiful and rather forgotten piston-engine aircraft that could fly at 500 mph. This was no 30-minute racer, but a machine with a cruising range of 1,500 miles, an aircraft loved by those who flew it. This was the de Havilland DH.103 Hornet, designed as a successor to the Mosquito for long-range operations in the Pacific against Japan.

Although just too late for service in the Second World War, the Hornet flew in action in Malaya and took part in a number of post-war air races. The prototype made its first flight on 28 July 1944, the day after the RAF took the Gloster Meteor jet fighter into operational service. With its twin 2,070-hp Rolls-Royce Merlins, the Hornet clocked 492 mph – more than 30 mph faster than the first-generation Meteor. With just a nudge down on the stick, the Hornet would reach 500 mph. While by November 1945 the Meteor F.3 had gone on to take the world's first accredited jet airspeed record, at 606 mph over Herne Bay in Kent, the Hornet was the more enjoyable aircraft to fly.

Testing a brand-new Royal Navy Sea Hornet, Eric Brown reported:

> The view from the cockpit, positioned right forward in the nose... was truly magnificent. The Sea Hornet was easy to taxi, with powerful brakes... the takeoff... was remarkable...
>
> For aerobatics the Sea Hornet was absolute bliss. The excess of power was such that manoeuvres in the vertical plane can only be described as rocket-like. Even with one propeller feathered the Hornet could loop with the best single-engine fighter, and its aerodynamic cleanliness was such that I delighted in its demonstration by diving with

both engines at full bore and feathering both propellers before pulling up into a loop...

I revelled in its sleek form and the immense surge of power always to hand... in my book the Sea Hornet ranks second to none for harmony of control, performance characteristics and, perhaps most important, in inspiring confidence in its pilot. For sheer exhilarating flying enjoyment, no aircraft has ever made a deeper impression on me than did this outstanding filly from the de Havilland stable.

Schneider Trophy pilots could only have dreamed of such an aircraft. The Jet Age, however, had arrived, and by the time it was decommissioned in the mid-1950s, the Hornet was rather like what a fast clipper would have been in the early days of long-distance steam ships, or my Canon A-1 camera is in the era of smartphones and Instagram: truly excellent, yet pushed aside by overwhelming new technologies.The global roar of the Jet Age was to drown out the rhythmic sounds of both Hornets and flying boats.

ELEVEN

Sky Galleons

Imagine yourself at Southampton harbour in the late 1950s. A number of launches are lined up, waiting to take you and several hundred other passengers from the terminal to your P&O 'ship' bound for Australia. There she is, sitting out on the water beyond the Cunard's *Queen Elizabeth*. Your 'ship' is, of course, one of the new P&O Saunders-Roe P.192 Queens, an immense five-storey flying boat. She is 318 feet long, has a wingspan of 313 feet, weighs 440,000 lbs and carries up to 1,000 passengers, many of them 'Ten Pound Poms' – British citizens, that is, emigrating to Australia for an adult fare of £10 (about £240 in 2020). Children go free.

It takes some while to board the P&O Queen, but the 40-strong cabin crew is on hand to show passengers to their cabins. These are not unlike compartments of railway carriages, with seats that convert into beds for the night. The first-class deck is spacious, with its grand dining room, cocktail bars and generous 'bathrooms'. An electric dumb waiter brings food from the spacious galley to all decks.

No fewer than 24 Rolls-Royce Conway gas turbine engines are housed inside the P.192's huge wing. It is sufficiently deep to allow the flight engineer and his deputy to walk inside to check the engines if need be. The jets themselves, mounted well away from the hull to avoid the intake of sea spray on take-off, provide a total thrust of 444,000 lbs, enough to allow the giant flying boat to cruise at 454 mph at 40,000 feet. On the passage to Australia, the aircraft will call at Alexandria, Karachi, Calcutta, Singapore and Darwin.

What will it be like to take off in this Brobdingnagian machine? No one, in fact, would ever know. The Saunders-Roe P.192 was to remain a drawing-board project. For a brief while, however, it had been a serious proposition. Like other passenger shipping lines in the latter half of the 1950s, P&O was concerned for the future of its liners. They were under threat from the new 'jetliners', and in particular the long-range Boeing 707. What if it could offer passengers a jet airliner with something of the comfort and style of its ocean liners?

Without government assistance, the cost of building the P.192 would have been prohibitive, and there would have been no economies of scale once production was under way at Cowes, because P&O would only want five of the flying boats. While eyebrows were raised and a certain pleasure was taken in the outlandish daring of the project, beyond P&O there was no commercial interest in the Saunders-Roe Queen. Sheer scale – and complexity – aside, it would have been, at best, a time-consuming business getting so many people on board and off. Most of all, though, while it would surely have been possible to build the Queen and make her fly elegantly and safely halfway around the world and back, the flying boat was on its way out.

Since the end of the war, scores of ex-bomber bases in Britain, Europe and elsewhere had been transformed into civil airfields. For airlines, landplanes were the profitable way to go, not least because jet airliners proved to be fast – so not only could they fly long distances quickly, without the need for dining rooms, but they could also be turned around quickly and sent packing back to where they had come from in double-quick time.

There had been, though, a brief moment when it did look as if Jacques Schneider's dream might come true and the flying boat would be the future for long-distance and rapid travel by air. It certainly made sense for VIPs, or simply wealthy passengers flying from England in the 1930s to major ports of call across the British Empire and its dominions. Those very cities the P&O Queen flying boats would have called at on their way to and from Sydney were seaports. The Short S.23C Empire flying boats, designed by Arthur Gouge and built by Short Brothers at Rochester on the River Medway, made their debut seven months after the Douglas DC-3 in California. While the DC-3 was a harbinger of future global air travel, few passengers on board an Empire flying boat making its impeccably mannered way from port to lake to port all the way to Singapore, where a Qantas S.23 might take them on to Sydney, would have thought anything of such a proposition.

In any event, Imperial Airways was not concerned solely with passenger flight. One of its key roles was flying newspapers, post and, increasingly, newsreels around the world. The desire, on both sides of the Atlantic, to run newsreels on cinema screens as quickly as possible was difficult to realize at a time when there were no aircraft that could fly the Atlantic non-stop from east to west into the powerful headwinds that had helped Alcock and Brown and Lindberg to cross non-stop from west to east years before the Short S.23 took to the air.

In 1937, and working in tandem and in great secrecy with Major Robert Mayo, technical general manager of Imperial Airways, Arthur Gouge and his team at Rochester produced the Short-Mayo Composite, a modified S.23 carrying a stream-lined four-engine mail seaplane piggyback-style on the top of its fuselage. The theory was that an aircraft launched in flight would be able to lift a much greater payload into the air than one fighting to take off from either land or water. In practice, the idea worked well.

Filmed by Movietone, the S.20 seaplane *Mercury* was detached from its host, *Maia*, over Foynes Harbour on the Shannon Estuary, and was flown non-stop by Captain Don Bennett from there to Montreal – 2,930 miles in 13½ hours. Powered by four 365-hp H-16 Napier Rapier radial engines, *Mercury* carried a 1,000-lb payload in its watertight floats. With 1,200 gallons of fuel in its wings, this good-looking aircraft had a range of 3,900 miles. Captain Bennett's flight, a marvel in many ways, was the first made non-stop over the Atlantic east-to-west by a heavier-than-air machine.

Until the outbreak of war in September 1939, *Maia* and *Mercury* flew a regular mail route from Southampton to Alexandria, Egypt. When *Maia* was destroyed in a German bombing raid on Poole Harbour in May 1941, *Mercury* was seconded to 320 (Netherlands) Squadron. Operating from RAF Pembroke Dock on reconnaissance and anti-submarine patrols with Dutch Fokker T.VIII seaplanes, 320 Squadron was posted to RAF Leuchars, Fife, in autumn 1941 and re-equipped with American Lockheed Hudsons. Now redundant, *Mercury* was returned to Short Brothers at Rochester and broken up, its metal components recycled. It remains one of those aircraft that dearly deserved to be kept for future generations.

With a war on, the Short S.23 flying boats disappeared, too, along with their intended replacements – the three bigger and more powerful S.26s that were to have been the first batch of a fleet of new flying boats for BOAC (British Overseas Airways Corporation, successor to Imperial Airways) and its regular passenger service from Southampton to New York. Flying an S.23 – if not from Southampton to New York, then from Southampton to Singapore – would have been an unforgettable and, for many, a delightful experience, yet by 1945 the kind of luxury travel that Empire flying boats offered for the very few was out of kilter and out of fashion. The Second World War had been a great leveller, with English country houses turned into barracks and military hospitals, luxurious flying boats like the S.23 pressed into RAF service, spacious ocean liners turned into jam-packed troopships, and entire cities, of course, blitzed into ash heaps.

During the war, flying boats played key roles in reconnaissance, rescue and anti-submarine patrols. The Short S.25 Sunderland, designed by Arthur Gouge, was, unlike its civil siblings, produced in large numbers. First flown in 1938, this large and sturdy flying boat was known by Germans as the 'flying porcupine'. Bristling with 16 Browning .303 machine guns, the Sunderland was good at looking after itself on long and lonely ocean patrols. On 2 June 1943, eight Junkers Ju

88C twin-engine fighters intercepted a Sunderland Mk III of 461 Squadron RAAF (Royal Australian Air Force) skippered by Flight Lieutenant Colin Walker over the Bay of Biscay. In an extraordinary fight, the Sunderland's gunners shot down three of the fast and agile German aircraft, damaged others and sent them packing. Flying on three engines, Walker nursed the bullet-riddled flying boat 350 miles to land at Praa Sands, Cornwall. Ten of the Sunderland's crew of 11 survived, wading to shore.

Post-war, a number of brand-new Sunderlands with no future role to play were scuppered at sea. Others were converted for civil use into Short Sandringhams flown in the Far East, Australia and New Zealand. In 1947, BOAC began flights with Sandringhams from Southampton to Hong Kong, but Lockheed Constellations ousted these just two years later. These were the fast, long-distance piston-engine airliners with a porpoise-shaped fuselage and pressurized cabins Howard Hughes had helped to develop.

An excellent aircraft, the Constellation was also responsible for the rapid demise of the Boeing 314 Clipper, the heavyweight transatlantic and trans-Pacific Pan Am flying boat of which just 12 were built, between 1938 and 1941. Twice the weight of a Short Brothers S.23, the Boeing 314 was a luxurious, silver-service aircraft, but the inaugural Pan Am Clipper flight from Southampton to Port Washington, New York, was made less than 10 weeks before Hitler invaded Poland and Britain went to war with Germany. While Pan Am Clippers flew the lucky few from San Francisco to Honolulu throughout 1940, the transatlantic service looked doomed from the start and Pan Am cancelled orders for new Clippers. Three were sold to BOAC, and it was on board one of these, G-AGCA *Berwick*, that in January 1942 Winston Churchill became the first head of government to fly the Atlantic. Six years later, *Berwick* was scrapped.

For all their grandeur, flying boats were expensive to operate. Impressive catering and more-than-generous legroom aside, these aircraft demanded the very best and most experienced pilots, and even they were not convinced by the supposed virtues of these much-courted aircraft. As Pan Am Clipper pilot Horace Brock recalled, 'I argued daily for eliminating all flying boats. The landplanes were much safer. No one in the operations department... had any idea of the hazards of flying boat operations. The main problem... was the lack of the very high level of experience and competence required of seaplane pilots.' Because they were ships when on water, pilots had to be sailors, too. In foggy conditions, they would land their Clippers out to sea, guiding them into port on water.

It was, though, Howard Hughes – champion of the Lockheed Constellation – who devoted much time during and after the Second World War to the creation of the world's biggest flying boat, the Hughes H-4 Hercules. Best known as the *Spruce Goose*, a name Hughes did not approve of, this huge aircraft may have seemed like the daydream of an American multimillionaire with a compulsion to shape the fastest aeroplane, the most epic film and now the biggest flying boat, and yet the initial brief for the Hughes H-4 made good sense.

In 1942, the US War Department had called for designs for an aircraft that could cross the Atlantic with a heavy payload. The Battle of the Atlantic was fought from the very first until the German surrender in May 1945. Allied convoys crossing the ocean were under sustained attacks by German U-boats. Altogether, some 3,500 merchant vessels – British, American, Canadian, Brazilian and Norwegian for the most part – 36,000 merchant seamen, 175 warships and 36,200 sailors were lost, mostly to U-boats. True, 783 U-boats and 17 Italian submarines were destroyed, with the loss of over 30,000 lives, yet for a while it looked as if the Kriegsmarine might take complete control of the 'Atlantic Bridge' between the United States, Britain and the Soviet Union. An aircraft that could carry war personnel and materiel at speed, high above the fray, could only be a good thing.

Henry J. Kaiser, the shipbuilder, whose parents were German immigrants, had come up with initial thoughts for a truly giant air-freighter. Capable of ferrying 750 fully equipped troops, or two 30-ton Sherman tanks, it would be the largest aircraft ever built. Kaiser certainly knew how to think big. He built many of the mass-produced 10,500-ton Liberty ships that maintained the supply line across the Atlantic. In a spectacular publicity stunt for the US war effort, in November 1942 his shipyard at Richmond, California, laid down, assembled and launched an entire Liberty ship, SS *Robert E. Peary*, in just four days and 15½ hours. No matter how many freighters were sunk by U-boats, the US would keep them coming at a prodigious rate. What if Henry J. Kaiser could do the same thing with a flying cargo 'ship'?

Kaiser turned to Hughes, who entrusted the design to Glenn Odekirk. But Kaiser pulled out of the project months later, partly in frustration at the slow pace of development. While materials and components were in short supply – the *Spruce Goose* would have to be made of wood because of the demand on aluminium and other metals – Hughes, ever the perfectionist, wanted to build the best-possible flying cargo ship, even while less-than-perfect Liberty ships were being built across 18 American shipyards at a rate of three every two days.

Meanwhile, the American M4 Sherman tank manufactured by automobile plants and railway locomotive works may have been no match in one-to-one combat with the highly sophisticated, heavily armoured and pugnacious German Tiger tank from Henschel and Krupp, yet while fewer than 2,000 Tigers had been built by the end of the war, the figure for the M4 Sherman stood at 49,324. By 1945, the first Hughes H-4 Hercules had yet to be completed.

Called to testify before the Senate War Investigating Committee in August 1947 over the use of government funds during the development and construction of the giant aircraft, Hughes said, 'The Hercules was a monumental undertaking. It is the largest aircraft ever built. It is over five stories tall with a wingspan longer than a football field. That's more than a city block. Now, I put the sweat of my life into this thing. I have my reputation all rolled up in it and I have stated several times that if it's a failure, I'll probably leave this country and never come back. And I mean it.' Evidently, it had been all about him.

On 2 November 1947, between hearings, Hughes piloted the $2.5-million *Spruce Goose* (about $300 million in 2020, the price of a Boeing 747-400 jumbo jet) on its maiden flight. With 36 people on board including co-pilot, two flight engineers, 16 mechanics, and a clutch of journalists and aviation industry representatives, the flying boat gathered speed to the accompanying whirr of its eight 3,000-hp Pratt & Whitney 28-cylinder Wasp Major engines. Up it went, flying at 135 mph for 26 seconds at 70 feet above the Californian water. And that was it. Hughes landed the flying boat. Although meticulously maintained in a climate-controlled hangar at Long Beach, California, until Hughes's death in 1976, the *Spruce Goose* never flew again.

If it had, Hughes's H-4 was to have cruised over the Atlantic at a steady 250 mph, carrying payloads that could be handled far more cheaply by peacetime freighters ploughing across the ocean below. Had it been built quickly, though, the H-4 Hercules might have made a valuable contribution to the war effort. In practice, Hughes's freighter had been a case of too big, too late. On display today at the Evergreen Aviation & Space Museum in McMinnville, Oregon, the birchwood-ply *Spruce Goose* is a daunting sight. Inside, its spacious flight deck and long empty fuselage call to mind something of the feel and structure of the even-bigger transatlantic German airships of the 1930s. Looking up at the *Spruce Goose*'s squadron of engines, it is hard not to think of how jets might have made this leviathan a more realistic proposition. From the Dornier Do X of 1929 onwards, large flying boats needed all the engines they could feasibly fit to break from the surface of the water, lift into the air and maintain a reasonable cruising speed once there.

Redundant by the time it flew, the *Spruce Goose* raises the question of which, if any, flying boat – this side of the Consolidated PBY Catalina, a truly multipurpose though slow-flying aircraft in use today as a fire-fighter – had a commercial or military purpose at the end of the Second World War and the dawn of the Jet Age.

One British company remained almost defiantly optimistic. This was Saunders-Roe (formerly S. E. Saunders), the aero and marine engineering company founded by Samuel Saunders and renowned for its racing yachts and the occasional seaplanes made at its shipyard at East Cowes. Saunders, of course, had gone out of his way to help with the Schneider Trophy contests held in the Solent. When the company was taken over by Avro in 1929, it focused more than it had before on aircraft. During the Second World War, it built Reginald Mitchell's Supermarine Walrus and the Sea Otter, a bigger version of the Walrus launched in 1938. The Sea Otter was the company's last flying boat.

A fascinating new project came Saunders-Roe's way in spring 1944, with an Air Ministry specification for a sea-based jet fighter. The idea made a certain sense. In part, the war in the Pacific was fought from one small island to another. If a high-performance fighter could operate from shallow and even undetected bays, it could surprise Japanese fighters. Aircraft carriers were vulnerable to attack, especially with the launch of *kamikaze* ('divine wind') suicide missions flown by volunteer Japanese pilots in the sealed cockpits of Mitsubishi Zero fighters and, from early 1945, Yokosuka Ohka (Cherry Blossom) rocket-powered attack aircraft.

With no need for prepared airbases, a jet-fighter flying boat might make a highly effective surprise weapon in the prolonged Pacific War. Once again, though, time proved to be Saunders-Roe's greatest enemy. The prototype SR.A/1 was finally flown on 16 July 1947. Too late for action against Japan, it was never-theless the world's first jet-propelled water-based aircraft. Its specification was impressive. A pressurized cockpit. Retractable flaps. The first Martin-Baker ejection seats. And, on test, with 7,770 lbs thrust from a pair of Metropolitan-Vickers Beryl MVB.2 turbojets, a top speed of 520 mph at 40,000 feet. Armed with four 20mm cannons, eight underwing rockets and two 1,000-lb bombs, it handled well and was fully aerobatic.

At the 1948 Farnborough Air Show, test pilot Geoffrey Tyson wowed the crowds with what *Flight* magazine called 'One of the most dramatic pieces of demonstration flying ever witnessed in this country.' Captured on film, the SR.A/1 is seen flying upside down at considerable speed. Those in the know would have recalled how Tyson had celebrated the twenty-fifth anniversary of Blériot's flight from Calais to Dover across the English Channel, when he flew a Tiger Moth inverted all the way in the opposite direction. This barnstorming pilot was also responsible for saving the life of fellow test pilot Eric Brown, who struck a log hidden under the water while landing a second SR.A/1 prototype in the Solent off Cowes in August 1949. Quick on the scene, Tyson jumped from a launch and pulled an uncon-scious Brown from the wreck of the flying boat. Brown thought Tyson 'the most gifted aviator I have seen'. These two brave and daring test pilots were to lead long lives. The same cannot be said of the SR.A/1. Just three were built.

Soon enough, though, Geoffrey Tyson was back at the controls of another bold Saunders-Roe flying boat. This was the SR.45 Princess, a 150-foot-long double-decker with a wing span of 219 feet that promised to fly 100 passengers or 200 troops for 5,720 miles before refuelling. Powered by four Bristol Coupled Proteus 5,000-hp turboprops, the Princess would cruise at 360 mph. A cutaway colour drawing in the *Eagle* revealed the Princess in all its glory. Sleeper berths, a cocktail bar on the lower deck and restaurant above, a purser's room, staff dormitory and prom-enade; well-dressed and, obviously, courteous passengers and crew: these were all aspects of air travel that were about to be stripped away as the Jet Age got into its all-conquering global stride. The economics of a Princess flying boat would never have made sense, and certainly not by the mid-1950s.

Between the first test flight of the Princess in August 1952 and the last in 1954, BOAC, which would have been the main customer for the flying boat, decided it would fly the Atlantic and other long-distance routes by land-based jets. Just the one Princess flew. Geoffrey Tyson put on impressive displays at the 1952 and 1953 Farnborough Air Shows, but there was still a lot of work to be done to ready this complex aircraft for commer-cial service. In any case, the development programme of the Bristol Proteus ran late, while the idea of carrying two crews aboard one flight seemed if not decadent then wasteful. The three Princesses were mothballed. Various parties – including Aero Spacelines, the American company that transported parts of Saturn V rockets by air, and the United States Navy – showed interest in buying and recommissioning the flying boats, but by 1967 they showed extensive signs of corrosion and were broken up.

Saunders-Roe went on to make hovercraft, a new form of low-flying boat invented by Christopher Cockerell in the mid-1950s. The first production model, SR.N1 ('N' for Nautical) was shown to the public in June 1959. On 25 July, the fiftieth anniversary of Blériot's first cross-Channel flight – and with the inventor on board – the SR.N1 flew successfully from Calais to Dover. The flight took two hours and three minutes.

Before it was swallowed in various mergers, Saunders-Roe had initiated the SR.N4, the largest hovercraft yet put into commercial service. I rode several times on board *Princess Anne*, a stretched version of the first of the class. She was 185 feet long, weighed 320 tons, and carried up to 418 passengers and 60 cars. Powered by four Rolls-Royce Proteus gas turbines driving lift fans and steerable propulsion airscrews, *Princess Anne* had a top speed of 95 mph and flew across the Channel in a spray of water, the occasional bump and an insistent turbine whine. She could certainly move. Although a regular flight from Dover to Boulogne took 35 minutes for the 22-mile crossing, free of passengers and cars *Princess Anne* made one trip in a record 15 minutes and 23 seconds. Christopher Cockerell spoke of a future generation of giant nuclear-powered hovercraft – a Queen class perhaps – that would race across the Atlantic.

The big SR.N4 flew on until 2000, by which time Eurostar trains and 'Le Shuttle' car ferries sprinting on rails through the Channel Tunnel had made the hovercraft redundant. In Russia, however, the mighty and well-armed Zubr-class military hovercraft, in production since 1988 and even bigger than *Princess Anne*, can carry three tanks – one more than the *Spruce Goose* – and 375 troops.

A quarter of a century before *Princess Anne*'s retirement, the world's last regular traditional flying boat service was withdrawn. This was Ansett's regular 2½-hour flight, operated by a pair of Short Sandringham flying boats from Rose Bay, Sydney, to the sparsely populated Lord Howe Island in the Tasman Sea. The Sandringhams flew this 500-mile route from the early 1960s until 10 September 1974. Charles F. Blair Jr bought the two aircraft for his Antilles Air Boats operating in the Virgin Islands.

During the Second World War, Blair, a hugely experienced military, commercial and test pilot, had flown a Sikorsky VS-44 – a four-engine flying boat smaller and faster than its contemporary and rival, the Boeing 314 – backwards and forwards across the Atlantic. In January 1951, he flew a P-51C Mustang owned by Pan Am 3,478 miles from New York to London in 7 hours and 48 minutes at an average speed of 446 mph, a record for a piston-engine aircraft. His experience with pushing so many different aircraft types to their limits led him to becoming a consultant to NASA.

For Blair, Antilles Air Boats must have been as much a hobby as a business – flying a collection of wartime floatplanes. In 1967 he added the very Sikorsky VS-44 he had flown across the Atlantic so many times, and then, seven years later, the two Sandringhams. All this made the circumstances of Blair's death in September 1978 somewhat odd. While piloting a Grumman G21 Goose, a popular 1930s twin-engine amphibian, from St Croix to St Thomas, the port engine failed. Blair brought the stricken Goose down from 1,700 feet towards the water, yet failed to turn it into the wind, lower his flaps, cut power and tell his 10 passengers to prepare for an emergency landing. When it touched the water, the Grumman cartwheeled, landed upside down and promptly sank. Although no one was killed on impact, Blair and three of his passengers drowned.

TWELVE

Seaspray

B uying a sound second-hand floatplane is not a difficult thing to do today – especially if you live in the United States, where there are plenty of opportunities and places to fly them. If you happen to have between $35,000 and $350,000 to spare, there are any number of Cessna floatplanes and Cessna amphibians on the market dating from the early 1960s, along with more ambitious de Havilland DHC-2 Beavers with their sonorous Pratt & Whitney Wasp Junior radial engine. You can even find such radical aircraft as the Republic RC-3 Seabee, a post-war 'less is more' amphibian that was the personal choice of the American inventor and designer Buckminster Fuller.

Purebred flying boats are harder to come by. This is partly because so few have ever been built, and partly because amphibians allow pilots to fly from landing strips as well as from coasts and rivers. In recent years, a new generation of lightweight American amphibians have allowed amateur pilots with little flying experience, or even no flying experience when they make their purchase, to take to the air from the warm beaches of Florida and California, and increasingly from Australian, Scandinavian and Chinese waters, too.

The two outstanding amphibians on sale in 2020 are the Progressive Aerodyne SeaRey made in Tavares, Florida – 'America's Seaplane City' – and the A5 from ICON Aircraft of Vacaville, California. Although quite different designs, these light sports aircraft offer would-be Boothmans, Stainforths and Agellos the chance to play Schneider Trophy pilot, albeit at a quarter of those record-breaking speeds; and, more realistically, to enjoy the freedom of flight in beautiful and relaxed settings over and by the sea. Kerry Richter founded Progressive Aerodyne in 1991, having previously worked with his father, Wayne Richter, building ultra-lightweight aircraft – beginning in 1978 with the Advanced Aviation Hi-Nuski. The Hi-Nuski was sold as a kit, and the SeaRey can be bought as one today, requiring between 600 and 1,000 hours to complete.

With its high wing supported by struts and a pusher prop, the SeaRey has the air of some early racing flying boat. The difference is its lightness. The basic Adventure model's Rotax 912 100-hp engine provides entertaining performance. Essentially spin-resistant, the SeaRey is safe for relatively inexperienced pilots to fly. It is also easy to transport, its wings folded, by trailer, or to stow, as many are, on the decks of yachts.

Proof that the SeaRey is far more than a beach toy came when Michael Smith, owner of the Sun Theatre, Melbourne – a late 1930s cinema he brought back to life over five years from 1998 – decided to trace the route of Qantas and Imperial Airway's flying boats from Australia to England. Setting off on 12 April 2015 in his silver SeaRey, *Southern Sun*, Smith flew for 60½ days to a safe landing at Damyns Hall Aerodrome near Upminster, Essex.

Why not carry on, his wife suggested, and fly the rest of the way around the world, back home to Melbourne? Michael Smith did just that, although his Atlantic crossing was not entirely a piece of cake. As he told the *Herald Sun* shortly after getting back home on 11 November, 'I did have a moment when it was a bit scary. I was in thick cloud coming into Canada... and I couldn't see a thing. For a moment I really thought it was all over and the first thing that popped into my mind was my family. Just as I thought about my family, I saw a speck of light and was able to steer into it and out of the cloud.'

In an account in the *Sydney Morning Herald* nearly a year on, it became clear that the situation over the Canadian coast had been extremely frightening: 'He didn't know which way was up or which way was down. His plane spun out of control and reached such velocity his speedo rocketed into the red, way over its maximum reading of 120 knots [138 mph]. His perspex windscreen began caving in.' Guided by that speck of sunlight, Smith followed a river that took him to Goose Bay and its airport. He flew on to Manhattan, landing on the Hudson River. Heading south, 'He "Huck Finned" the entire length of the Mississippi River, tying up to trees and sleeping nights bobbing on the river.'

Smith flew for eight hours at a time with no guarantee of a place to land. Refused permission to fly over Russia, he made a long journey over the sea to Japan. To make this possible, he had to fly separately from Alaska to store fuel on the abandoned island of Attu. The westernmost of the Aleutian Islands, this once-inhabited Alaskan territory had been the scene of brutal hand-to-hand fighting in May 1943 when the Americans took it back from the Japanese. From Attu, Smith plotted a course south-east via the Philippines, Indonesia and Horn Island, Queensland, and made his final landing at the Royal Yacht Club of Victoria at Williamstown, Melbourne. He had completed the first around-the-world flight in a single-engine flying boat.

In November 2016, Smith was presented with the Australian Geographical Society's Adventurer of the Year award. Although, as he told the *Sydney Morning Herald*, he 'wouldn't do it again', he had written a new and exciting chapter in the story of the post-Schneider flying boat. On his trip round the world, Smith had also visited 68 cinemas. They ought to have shown newsreels of his adventure.

All of a piece, as if sculpted from carbon fibre, the ICON A5 is a very modern-looking machine. First flown in July 2014, the production model received widespread media coverage, and understandably so. Here was a small amphibian flying boat designed to look, as well as to be, as easy to fly as possible. Styled by Randy Rodriguez of Nissan Design (he moved to Tesla in 2016), and with a svelte car-like cockpit and instrument panel by BMW, the A5 makes it clear that if you happen to enjoy driving a sports convertible along the Californian coast, then you might just want to jump into this lightweight aircraft and do the same trip from the air, dropping into beach resorts along the way.

Easy to fly? The A5's low-set 'dashboard' features a centrally mounted angle-of-attack indicator. By keeping its needle in the green sector of the dial, a pilot knows the aircraft will fly securely as it dips, turns, twists and climbs. Powered by the same reliable Austrian 100-hp four-cylinder Rotax 912 fuel-injected engine as the SeaRey, the A5 is a nippy and responsive 'seat of the pants' machine.

Kirk Hawkins and Steen Strand, who met at Stanford University in a product design class, founded ICON Aircraft in 2006. Hawkins joined the USAF, flying supersonic F-16 Fighting Falcons, before moving on to captain Boeing 757s for American Airlines. After Stanford, Steen set up Freebord, an innovative skateboard company. They both wanted to create an aircraft that could be flown instinctively and, as far as possible, by touch and feel. Agello and Stainforth could certainly have told them a thing or two about that.

When Jon Karkow joined the company, the ICON team seemed complete. Born near Baltimore, Maryland, in 1962, as a schoolboy Karkow mowed lawns to pay for flying lessons. At home, he built his own first aircraft from a kit of parts. In 1986 he joined Burt Rutan's Scaled Composites in Mojave, California, where he worked on the design of two remarkable aircraft, the Virgin Atlantic GlobalFlyer and the Virgin Galactic SpaceShipTwo, made under the auspices of Rutan and Richard Branson's Spaceship Company. In February 2006, the former, an ultra-light carbon-fibre jet – with businessman and adventurer Steve Fossett at the controls – made the longest flight ever, covering 25,766 miles non-stop from the Kennedy Space Center, Florida, to Bournemouth Airport, Dorset. The latter aircraft will, soon enough, take tourists on flights into space.

For all his achievements and knowledge of flight, in May 2017 Karkow flew an ICON A5 into the wall of a narrow canyon in Napa County while executing what appears to have been a sudden 180-degree turn. He and his passenger, fellow Scaled

Composites engineer Cagri Sever, were killed. Karkow's and other A5 accidents seem to have been caused by pilot error. While the Supermarine S.6B would have been a lethal machine to fly in the hands of a pilot with less experience than John Boothman or George Stainforth, an aircraft that is very easy to fly can instil a sense of overconfidence in much less experienced pilots. Any pilot, though, can make a fatal mistake.

New flying boats bigger than the A5 and the SeaRey have been very thin in the air. One promising design, the Dornier Seastar by Claudius Dornier Jr, first flown in August 1984, has been in abeyance since the first two examples were built, although production might yet restart in 2021. Constructed from largely composite materials, this good-looking reimagining of the record-breaking Dornier Do 18 flying boat of 1935 is much lighter than its predecessor, with lighter turboprop engines, too – although of much the same power as the older aircraft's twin six-cylinder Junkers Jumo diesels. The Seastar may yet find roles in, for example, air-sea rescue, security, exploration and environmental monitoring, and it is in these capacities that flying boats have a future.

Perhaps, though, the most impressive utility flying boat of recent years is the Russian Beriev Be-200 Altair, an altogether-bigger aircraft designed by Alexander Yavkin as a passenger or cargo plane, as well as for long-range search and rescue missions, anti-submarine warfare, and as an ambulance or fire-fighter. The twin-engine jet can scoop water at 90–95 per cent of take-off speed – a truly impressive achievement – and since 2004 the Be-200 has been successfully in action dowsing forest fires in Sardinia, Portugal, Greece, Russia, Azerbaijan, Israel and

The technology underpinning and defining this massive Soviet GEV was not unknown to the Americans; and certainly not to Alexander Lippisch, who designed and built a prototype, the Collins X-112, while working for the aviation division of the Collins Radio Company in Cedar Rapids, Iowa. With its big inverted delta wing, this small machine – its gross take-off weight was just 710 lbs – flew successfully in 1963 at speeds of up to 77 mph. Lippisch developed his bigger and more powerful X-113 in Germany with Rhein-Flugzeugbau. On test from 1970, the X-113 was able to climb to 1,500 feet to avoid obstacles, and flew safely over the North Sea in choppy conditions. Lippisch built one further prototype, his X-114, in 1977. This flew happily over trees, low-lying ground and waterfalls, proving its worth, but crashed on test. Pilot error again. By this time, Lippisch was dead and the project came to an end.

A year before Lippisch's death in 1976, the Black Sea Fleet of the Soviet Navy began trials with a new sea monster. This was the Lun (Harrier) *ekranoplan*. About half the weight of the earlier KM, and powered by eight Kuznetsov turbofans mounted on canards – small forewings ahead of the main wings – the Lun was armed with six P-270 Moskit 'Sunburn' missile launchers and two gun turrets armed with pairs of 23mm cannons. Since the early 1990s, the Lun has been marooned at the Caspian Sea port of Kaspiysk. The Lun was a second attempt at this new type of warship by Rostislav Alexeyev, whose early work on hydrofoil boats at the Red Sormovo shipbuilding factory on the banks of the Volga River near Nizhny Novgorod had been undermined by the German invasion of the Soviet Union in June 1941. Alexeyev supervised the construction of tanks, until he was posted to the

Soviet Navy to work on the design of military hydrofoils. It was at the Central Hydrofoil Design Bureau, post-war, that Alexeyev began work on his *ekranoplans*. Injured when a new *ekranoplan* he was testing to show at the 1980 Moscow Olympics crashed, Alexeyev was immediately removed from his job. He died from his injuries soon afterwards.

Like some mechanical stingray, the fast AirFish 8, a six- to eight-seat GEV made by Wigetworks of Singapore, keeps the flag flying for civil versions of these intriguing machines. Suhartono Setiawan, the firm's engineering manager, describes them as 'plane-boat-chimeras'. He means hybrid, of course, although a chimera is also an illusion.

Fresh ideas for how the seaplane and flying boat might yet develop continue to bubble away. There is an enduring fondness for the very idea of aircraft that belong to both seaways and skyways – the very sight of a seaplane taking off, however great or small, is never less than memorable – and the thought remains that, as ever more and ever bigger airports become increasingly unacceptable for a litany of reasons from noise and congestion to visual pollution, water-based aircraft offer an alternative way of flying.

In 2015, *The Engineer*, a magazine founded in 1856 by Edward Charles Healey, a friend of Robert Stephenson and Isambard Kingdom Brunel, reported on a design concept for a new transatlantic flying boat. The research project had been conducted by the Department of Aeronautics at Imperial College, London. Howard Hughes, for one, would have been pleased to learn that biggest was found to be best. The most dramatic proposal for a flying boat was a design for a

2,000-seat model with a range of 9,500 miles. Slightly longer than a double-deck Airbus A380, its wingspan was more than double that of the airliner. The scale and mass of the Imperial College design was, in part, to allow the aircraft to take off, land and manoeuvre in the kind of rough waters that held back earlier generations of flying boats. With a wing blended into the fuselage, research showed, the flying boat would be free of the need for tip floats, or stabilizers, at the ends of its wings, thus saving weight and reducing drag. Adapting the technology of GEVs, the flying boat could come to land gently rather than with a very big splash. As to the question of fuel, the Imperial College team were thinking of hydrogen, among other possibilities.

On Boxing Day 2019, the *New York Times* published an article on a battery-powered seaplane. This was not some experimental and futuristic design, but a reworking of a 63-year-old six-seat de Havilland DHC-2 Beaver flown by Harbour Air in Vancouver. Greg McDougall, Harbour Air's founder and chief executive, told the paper's Mike Arnot, 'I was an early adopter of the Tesla car and so impressed by their innovation. When I got the car five years ago, I wondered if we could transfer similar electric engine technology to our planes. Someone was going to do it someday, so it may as well be us.'

The Beaver's electric motor has been developed and made by magniX, a company founded in Australia in 2009. Since 2017, its headquarters have been just outside Seattle, Washington. As Harbour Air operates mostly 30-minute flights between Vancouver, Seattle and coastal communities in British Columbia, battery power seems realistic. And, given that power would be drawn from the regional hydroelectricity grid, the reborn Beaver promises to be an aircraft even Greta Thunberg might be persuaded to fly in.

On 10 December 2019, the electric Beaver took off from the Fraser River, Vancouver, and flew for four minutes. These, as everyone involved knows full well, are early days. The number of lithium-iron batteries needed to get the Beaver into the air spells maximum take-off weight. The 750-hp magni500 motor is more powerful than the seaplane's original Pratt & Whitney Wasp Junior, but at present the battery charge is sufficient for flights of no more than 30 minutes, with a 30-minute safety reserve. In due course, Harbour Air plans to convert its 40-strong fleet to battery-electric power. The idea is appealing, although everyone involved – and indeed the aviation industry as a whole – is still looking for the breakthrough in battery technology that, one day, may allow airliners to cross the Atlantic or Pacific comfortably on a single charge.

During the year I lived on the Venice Lido, I tried my best to stir interest in the rehabilitation and renewal of the abandoned Ospedale al Mare. This once-magnificent complex, first opened as the Hospice Marino in 1868, was rebuilt between 1921 and 1933 at the time of the Schneider Trophy contests. Facing beaches and the Adriatic, the hospital provided treatments for TB and polio, among them hydrotherapy, heliotherapy and thalassotherapy – the use of seawater for healing – along with an Art Nouveau–style theatre where patients could enjoy concerts, films and opera. Children from the poorest parts of Italy were sent here to recover. From beach, balconies and rooftops, some of them would have watched the Schneider contests as the brightly coloured and crackling seaplanes raced up and down the Lido and out over the Adriatic.

In 2003, the Ospedale al Mare was abandoned. By the time I got to step carefully through its corridors, wards, surgeries and theatre, it was as if the complex had been bombed in a war I had, for some unfathomable reason, been unaware of. The whole place stank. It was a home, of sorts, to rats, cats, drug addicts, the homeless, and those washed up unwanted on the shores of Venice. An attempt had been made to transform the Ospedale into an enormous marina, but this foundered in a turbulent sea of city politics, deals, counter-deals, accusations, counter-accusations and, as usual in Venice, the culture of *far niente* ('doing nothing'). No one seemed to want to get up and make things work.

To the immediate north of the wreckage of the Ospedale al Mare is Nicelli Airport, a small and elegant airfield sporting a grass airstrip pointing towards the lagoon. A singularly handsome terminal building dating from 1935 features a grand piano at its core as well as murals of contemporary aircraft by the Futurist artist Tato (Guglielmo Sansoni), whose exciting paintings include depictions of Schneider Trophy seaplanes. This was a curiously glamorous place. It clearly had such potential and yet was used by just a few private light planes and small helicopters taking tourists on flights around Venice.

First opened in 1915 as a military airbase to safeguard Venice from attack by the Austrians, Nicelli was an alluring place, its French pilots residing in the Albergo Paradiso and socializing with Italian and English royalty – the Prince of Wales came to visit – as well as Venetian aristocracy, artists, writers and intellectuals. Italian pilots who flew seaplanes in action from the neighbouring island of Sant'Andrea da Varriale joined them.

From the 1920s, there were scheduled flights from Nicelli to major Italian cities as well as over the Alps to Graz, Vienna and Munich. The airport lost its way in 1960 when Venice Marco Polo opened and jet airliners from around the world thundered over La Serenissima. But what, I thought, if the airport could host some new festival of flight? It was the perfect setting for a gathering of both historic and experimental light aircraft, and the long stretch of the Lido itself a natural theatre for air displays and races. What if the Ospedale al Mare were renovated as a health hydro for the world's wealthy and fashionable, a holiday home for children of less well-off Italian families and an exemplary local clinic? Imagine this wreck alive again, and as glamorous as the Lido was in those years when the hugely popular Schneider contests were held here.

I did try, but it was hopeless. Despite meetings with nominally interested parties, and an expenditure of energy sufficient to make a Macchi MC.72 fly right around the Lido at 440 mph, it proved impossible to get things off the ground. Whether from Nicelli Airport, the balcony of my house, the bar of the Excelsior or the woods at the southern tip of the Lido, I could see and hear in my imagination beautiful aeroplanes skimming along and over the islands.

Perhaps they might do so one day, but first Venice and the Lido need to cure themselves, to believe in a creative and joyous future. Not once while living in the Lido did I see a seaplane or a flying boat, much less a racing machine dicing with wind and waves.

Each a Glimpse

The English comedian and satirist Peter Cook invented a character named Sir Arthur Streeb-Greebling. One of Sir Arthur's lifelong quests was to teach ravens to swim underwater. When asked by his make-believe television interviewer, played by Dudley Moore, 'Is it difficult to get ravens to fly underwater?' Sir Arthur replied, 'Well, I think the word "difficult" is an awfully good one here. Yes, it is. It's well nigh impossible... God, in his infinite wisdom and mercy, designed these creatures to fly in the air... rather than through the watery substances... it's a disastrous experience for them... not a single success in the whole forty years of training.'

Racing seaplanes were not exactly ravens trying to swim underwater, and yet, without knowing the backstory of the Schneider Trophy, they might still seem something of an anomaly. And yet, how they flew and how they set the pace for future generations of aircraft – and notably so those designed to fly, as ravens should, from land into the air. The era of seaplane racers was brief and far fewer were built than flying boats, which although never less than rare, have served many different purposes and, here and there around the world, continue to do so. Where, though, did those chimerical Schneider racers and their highly specialized world go?

Early one July morning, I walked in the shadows of Bernini's arcade to Rome's San Pietro railway station. It was already hot and humid by the time the delayed 0727hrs train to Bracciano – a double-deck suburban electric – arrived. Its grubby carriages were forensically lit by rows of flyspecked fluorescent tubes. Greasy windows were etched crudely with dirty-minded graffiti. Grey steel frames with unfinished welds supported hard and lurid-blue plastic seats. The speckled blue lino floor served as a litterbin. The train rumbled slowly through tunnels between stations with flickering lamps and peeling acid-green paintwork. They bore bravura names – Valle Aurelia, Ottavia, San Filippo Neri – yet looked wilfully neglected and even war-damaged. Gaps between tunnels revealed determinedly glum high-rise apartment blocks, grim petrol stations and half-built block-work houses untouched by architecture.

With five more of the fifteen stops to go, and under a thunderous sky, the train ambled into a landscape beyond Rome's suburbs, of unkempt farmland punctuated by pylons and communications antennae that finally surrendered to rolling fields, hay bales, trees as if painted by Claude and, just visible though the smeared windows, a level lake stretching to a sun-gold horizon. From Bracciano, a taxi took me to the gates of the Museo Storico dell'Aeronautica Militare where I waited for them to open in the shade of scented pines, in the company of tireless ants, basking lizards and the busy hum of bees. A jet airliner whined overhead.

In a sunless gallery in London's Science Museum, S.1595 – John Boothman and George Stainforth's record-breaking Supermarine S.6B – looks as dead as a dodo. While the aircraft is as it was in 1931, scratched paintwork and all, it is impossible not to wish it out of its South Kensington tomb and into the air. After Stainforth's 407.5 mph, the RAF High Speed Flight was stood down with immediate effect and S.1595 and a spare R engine were sent on tour. For a while the S.6B was displayed in the window of the Vickers showroom on Broadway, near Parliament Square, before moving to the lobby of the Science Museum in South Kensington and on to the British Industries Fair, Birmingham. Shipped across the Atlantic to the Vickers stand at the 1932 Canadian National Exhibition in Toronto, it returned home at the end of that year and was donated by Vickers-Supermarine to the Science Museum. In 1951, the S.6B was loaned to the Festival of Britain, where it was displayed imaginatively in the airy and extensively glazed gallery of the Transport Pavilion designed by Rodney Thomas of Arcon. In company with the DH.88 Comet *Grosvenor House*, S.1595 was hung from the roof in the attitude of a high-speed dive.

This legendary aircraft is exceedingly unlikely ever to fly again. It was only meant to fly long enough to win the Schneider Trophy and, when its sibling S.1596 crashed, to win the world airspeed record for Britain. What would be the point of restoring the aircraft at vast cost if it could only fly for a few hours before its engine had to be stripped down and rebuilt? In any case, S.1595 is pretty much exactly as it was when Boothman climbed out of the cockpit in September 1931, and should remain this way. If someone wanted to build a working replica, what would its engine be? Anything other than a full-blooded Rolls-Royce R in highly tuned form would be a disappointment.

For some years, S.6A N248 – one of the 1929 S.6s upgraded for the 1931 Schneider event as a substitute for one or other of the S.6Bs – was falsely on show as S.1596 in a building beside the Royal Pier, Southampton. Correctly restored from 1983, the reserve racer is housed today in Southampton's Solent Sky Museum. This is not far from what was once the South Western Hotel, where Mitchell and his Supermarine team, members of the RAF's High Speed Flight and guests celebrated after winning the Schneider Trophy for Britain. Today, the hotel is a block of flats.

Echoes of the Schneider Trophy can be found in buildings that have become world-famous – as well as those forgotten, buried under banal shopping malls and dismal new housing developments. Of the former, the Fiat factory at Lingotto, Turin, is a fount of Futurist wonder. Designed by the engineer Giacomo Mattè-Trucco, this is the building where Tranquillo Zerbi nurtured his powerful aero-engines and where new cars on test roared around the building's racetrack roof. Converted by the Genoese architect Renzo Piano into a cultural and commercial complex for the city in the 1980s, it is also home to the Automotive Engineering faculty of the Polytechnic University of Turin.

At the other extreme, the former Rex Cinema at Stonehouse, South Lanarkshire, is, to judge by its battered 1960s brick façade, nothing more than the warehouse it has been for many decades. On open days, its interior is a revelation. Here are parts of the first-class dining room, a grand stair and a chandelier that once graced the White Star liner RMS *Homeric*. Refitted by Harland and Wolff, the *Homeric* had begun life in Danzig in 1913 as the German liner *Columbus*. In her new guise, the liner served as a viewing platform for well-heeled spectators at the 1931 Schneider contest. It seems so strange that such people brushed against these walls, especially as during the Second World War – as Spitfires took on the Luftwaffe – the working-class music hall stars Harry Lauder and Will Fyffe took to the stage together here at the Rex singing 'I Love a Lassie' and 'I Belong to Glasgow'.

In Weymouth's Greenhill Gardens, I found – along with a giant floral clock, an 18-hole putting course, tennis courts and a wishing well – the Stainforth weather vane, a lithe and spirited thing featuring an accurate model of S.1595 facing the sea. Presented to Weymouth College in 1932, it adorned a building designed by George Rackstraw Crickmay in 1864 in what Nikolaus Pevsner described as 'the High Victorian style in a very debased form'. George Stainforth's old school was shut, for good, in 1940. It was too close for comfort to Royal Navy bases that might come under attack by German bombers.

In a shop window off Charing Cross Road, I peered at cigarette cards depicting famous British flyers including George Stainforth, and in one of my books, unopened for years, I found a Brooke Bond tea card showing the S.6B. On YouTube, you can watch snatches of Movietone newsreels of some of the Schneider contest aircrafts in action, and a little of those who flew them, too.

And yet, the legacy of these machines, many of them highly strung and temperamental, is best found away from memorabilia and even from the silent machines in museums in Britain, Europe and the United States. Ultimately, what mattered most about these racers was the effect they had on designers, engineers, the military, civil airlines and rescue launches. Designed, built and flown rapidly, they pushed the known boundaries of flight to new limits in the space of a very few years.

In an article entitled 'Racing Seaplanes and Their Influence on Design' published in the 1929 Christmas issue of *Aeronautical Engineering*, a supplement to *The Aeroplane*, Reginald Mitchell wrote:

> During the last ten years there has been an almost constant increase in speed in our racing types. To maintain this steady increase, very definite progress has been essential year by year. It has been necessary to increase the aerodynamic efficiency, and the power-to-weight ratios of our machines; to reduce the consumption, and the frontal areas of our engines; to devise new methods of construction; and to develop the use of new materials. The results obtained in the form of speed have been a direct and absolute indication of our progress in aeronautical development...
>
> It is quite safe to say that the engine used in this year's winning S.6 machine... would have taken at least three times as long to produce under normal processes of development had it not been for the spur of international competition. There is little doubt that this intensive engine development will have a very pronounced effect on our aircraft during the next few years.

As Arthur Sidgreaves, managing director of Rolls-Royce, commented at the time, 'From the development point of view the Schneider Trophy Contest is almost an economy because it saves so much time in arriving at certain technical improvements. It is not too much to say that research for the Schneider Trophy Contest over the past two years is what our aero-engine department would otherwise have taken six to ten years to learn.'

Sidgreaves, who had served with the RNAS and RAF, brought Rolls-Royce and Vickers-Armstrong together to produce the 1929 and 1931 supercharged Supermarine racers, and played a key role in the development of the Rolls-Royce Merlin that powered Mitchell's Supermarine Spitfire. And, of course, it was the very success of Mitchell's Schneider seaplanes that encouraged the British Air Ministry to include Supermarine in the select list of aircraft manufacturers asked to respond to its specification for a high-speed monoplane fighter.

The possibilities of supercharging witnessed in the Rolls-Royce–powered Supermarine racers led to Spitfires and Mustangs that could take on the most advanced fighters Nazi Germany could send hurtling into wartime skies, while Frank Whittle, a serving RAF officer and principal inventor of the jet engine, drew on Rolls-Royce superchargers in the design of his revolutionary gas turbines. The high-octane fuels concocted by Rod Banks and Jimmy Doolittle on both sides of the Atlantic meant engines of great and reliable power.

And while the Schneider Trophy contests did more to advance landplanes than seaplanes, it did make seaplanes glorious and deeply romantic things – whether racing along the Lido, taking off from and landing in exotic estuaries, coves, fjords and bays, or performing deeds that no landplane could possibly attempt.

Near midnight on 30 July 1945, the USS *Indianapolis*, a heavy cruiser and flagship of the Fifth Fleet, was heading to the Philippines from Guam, after delivering parts and nuclear material for the Hiroshima and Nagasaki bombs to the USAAF 509th Composite Group on the island of Tinian, in the Marianas Islands south-east of Japan. Torpedoes fired from a Japanese Type B submarine hit the American warship. She sank within 12 minutes, taking 300 men into the depths with her. The other 900 did their best to survive, but one in six of them was attacked and taken by swarming sharks.

On 2 August, the crew of a US Navy twin-engine Lockheed Vega PV-1 Ventura bomber spotted men in the sea but were unable to identify them. Lieutenant Adrian Marks was sent to investigate in a PBY-5A Catalina flying boat. He and his crew found hundreds of men bobbing on the ocean. Knowing that many would die before rescue ships were able to get to the scene, Marks made the decision to land in 12-foot swells. This was against regulations, yet his skilled landing saved the lives of 56 stragglers. They packed the fuselage and, secured to the Catalina's wings with parachute cords, waited until, many hours later, the destroyer USS *Cecil J. Doyle* came to the rescue. Although the Catalina was abandoned – it could never have taken off with so many on board, through 12-foot waves or with wings damaged by tightened parachute cords – it had proved to be a real boat as much as an aircraft.

Some of the same design details of the Consolidated Catalina, as well as its Pratt & Whitney Twin Wasp radial engines, could be found in the Consolidated B-24 Liberator four-engine bomber. No fewer than 18,188 of these tough machines were built between 1940 and 1945 – many in Ford's purpose-built Willow Run factory in Michigan, a mile-long building under a single roof designed by Albert Kahn. The Liberator could fly the Atlantic with some ease. It flew in flocks from the hastily constructed airbases of East Anglia to bomb German-occupied Europe.

Sergeant Charles A. Peck of the 446th Bomb Group was one of them. I mention him because I stopped with my Jack Russell to look inside the venerable church of St Michael and St Felix at Rumburgh, Suffolk. There, under a brass plaque commemorating the eight-strong crew of his last flight from RAF Bungay on 7 June 1944 on board a Liberator named *Nature's Nymph*, was a faded colour photograph of the young American airman framed by a pair of miniature Stars and Stripes. It struck me that the Schneider connection is never so very far away, despite the last contest having been held very nearly 90 years ago. Sergeant Peck's commander-in-chief was Lieutenant General James Doolittle, who had flown the Curtiss R3C-2 to victory at the 1925 Schneider contest in Baltimore, and who I had met at Duxford in 1990. As if on cue, and out of the grey, a Spitfire from Duxford flew overhead. How things bind and blend themselves together.

A part, though, of the joy of seaplanes and flying boats is that they can operate far, in every sense, from the landplane world of runways, control towers and crowded air routes; their pilots more or less as free as wheeling seagulls or, perhaps, flying fish. Sidelined in recent decades, no one races them today. And yet, any seaplane, flying boat or amphibian, even if unable to break the 100-mph barrier in level flight, offers something else and something very special: the spellbinding shadow, so close to the swell of the sea – and gone in a sun-flash – of wings over water.

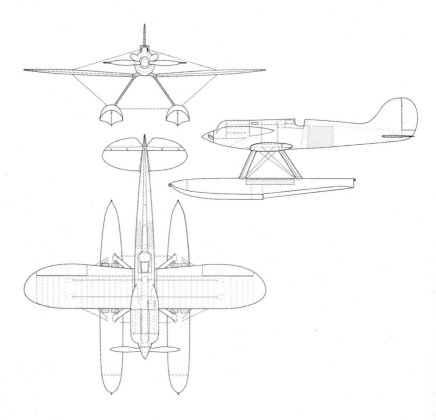

Schneider Trophy Contest Results

1913

Monaco

16 April

10-kilometre circuit, 28 laps – 173.98 miles

	Pilot	Country	Aircraft	Engine	Average Speed
1st	Maurice Prévost	France	Deperdussin	Gnome 160 hp	45.75 mph
2nd	Roland Garros	France	Morane-Saulnier	Gnome 80 hp	30.42 mph

Of seven entries, three failed to compete and two retired from the circuit

1914

Monaco

20 April

10-kilometre circuit, 28 laps – 173.98 miles

	Pilot	Country	Aircraft	Engine	Average Speed
1st	Howard Pixton	Great Britain	Sopwith Tabloid	Gnome Monosoupape 100 hp	86.78 mph
2nd	Ernest Burri	Switzerland	FBA Type A	Gnome Monosoupape 100 hp	51.00 mph

Of twelve entries, five failed to compete and five retired from the circuit

1919

Bournemouth

10 September

37.04-kilometre circuit, 10 laps – 230.16 miles

	Pilot	Country	Aircraft	Engine	Average Speed
	Sergeant Guido Janello	Italy	Savoia S.13	Isotta Fraschini V6 250 hp	n/a

Of seven entries, three failed to compete, three retired on the first lap and, after flying 11 incorrect laps, one entry – below – was disqualified

1920

Venice

21 September

37.04-kilometre circuit, 10 laps – 230.16 miles

	Pilot	Country	Aircraft	Engine	Average Speed
1st	Lieutenant Luigi Bologna	Italy	Savoia S.12 (3001)	Ansaldo-San Giorgio 4E 550 hp	107.22 mph

Of four entries, three failed to compete

1921

Venice

7 August

24.6-kilometre circuit, 16 laps – 244.57 miles

	Pilot	Country	Aircraft	Engine	Average Speed
1st	Giovanni de Briganti	Italy	Macchi M.7bis	Isotta Fraschini V6 250hp	117.90mph

Of four entries, one failed to compete and two retired from the circuit

1922

Naples

12 August

28.5-kilometre circuit, 13 laps – 230.22 miles

	Pilot	Country	Aircraft	Engine	Average Speed
1st	Captain Henri Biard	Great Britain	Supermarine Sea Lion II (G-EBAH)	Napier Lion II 450 hp	145.70 mph
2nd	Alessandro Passaleva	Italy	Savoia S.51 (I-BAIU)	Hispano-Suiza 8F 300 hp	143.20 mph
3rd	Arturo Zanetti	Italy	Macchi M.17 (I-BAHG)	Isotta-Fraschini V6 260 hp	139.75 mph
4th	Piero Corgnolino	Italy	Macchi M.7bis (I-BAFV)	Isotta-Fraschini V6 260 hp	123.70 mph

Of six entries, two failed to compete

1923

Cowes

28 September

37.2-nautical-mile (68.89-kilometre) circuit, 5 laps – 214.05 miles

	Pilot	Country	Aircraft	Engine	Average Speed
1st	Lieutenant David Rittenhouse	USA	Curtiss CR-3 (A6081)	Curtiss D-12 465 hp	177.38 mph
2nd	Lieutenant Rutledge Irvine	USA	Curtiss CR-3 (A6080)	Curtiss D-12 465 hp	173.46 mph
3rd	Captain Henri Biard	Great Britain	Supermarine Sea Lion III (G-EBAH)	Napier Lion III 525 hp	157.17 mph

Of nine entries, five failed to compete and one retired from the circuit

1925

Baltimore

26 October

50-kilometre circuit, 7 laps – 217.48 miles

	Pilot	Country	Aircraft	Engine	Average Speed
1st	Lieutenant James Doolittle	USA	Curtiss R3C-2 (A7054)	Curtiss V-1400 565 hp	232.57 mph
2nd	Hubert Broad	Great Britain	Gloster IIIA (N194)	Napier Lion VII 700 hp	199.17 mph

	Pilot	Country	Aircraft	Engine	Average Speed
3rd	Giovanni de Briganti	Italy	Macchi M.33 (MM49)	Curtiss D-12A 435 hp	168.44 mph

Of eight entries, three failed to compete and two retired from the circuit

1926

Hampton Roads

13 November

50-kilometre circuit, 7 laps – 217.48 miles

	Pilot	Country	Aircraft	Engine	Average Speed
1st	Major Mario de Bernardi	Italy	Macchi M.39 (MM76)	Fiat AS.2 800 hp	246.50 mph
2nd	Lieutenant Christian Schilt	USA	Curtiss R3C-2 (A7054)	Curtiss V-1400 565 hp	231.36 mph
3rd	Lieutenant Adriano Bacula	Italy	Macchi M.39 (MM74)	Fiat AS.2 800 hp	218.01 mph
4th	Lieutenant William Tomlinson	USA	Curtiss F6C-I Hawk* (A7128)	Curtiss D-12A 520 hp	136.95 mph

Of seven entries, one failed to compete and two retired from the circuit
*(*sometimes identified as F6C-3 Hawk)*

1927

Venice

26 September

50-kilometre circuit, 7 laps – 217.48 miles

	Pilot	Country	Aircraft	Engine	Average Speed
1st	Flight Lieutenant Sidney Webster	Great Britain	Supermarine S.5 (N220)	Napier Lion VIIB 875 hp	281.66 mph
2nd	Flight Lieutenant Oswald Worsley	Great Britain	Supermarine S.5 (N219)	Napier Lion VIIA 900 hp	273.07 mph

Of seven entries, one failed to compete and four retired from the circuit

1929

Calshot

7 September

50-kilometre circuit, 7 laps – 217.48 miles

	Pilot	Country	Aircraft	Engine	Average Speed
1st	Flying Officer Henry Waghorn	Great Britain	Supermarine S.6 (N247)	Rolls-Royce R 1,900 hp	328.63 mph
2nd	Warrant Officer Tomasso Dal Molin	Italy	Macchi M.52R	Fiat AS.3 1,000 hp	284.20 mph
3rd	Flight Lieutenant David D'Arcy Greig	Great Britain	Supermarine S.5 (N219)	Napier Lion VIIB 875 hp	282.11 mph

Of six entries, one was disqualified and two retired from the circuit

1931

Calshot

13 September

50-kilometre circuit, 7 laps – 217.48 miles

	Pilot	Country	Aircraft	Engine	Average Speed
1st	Flight Lieutenant John Boothman	Great Britain	Supermarine S.6B (S1595)	Rolls-Royce R 2,300 hp	340.08 mph

Of three entries, two were kept in reserve

Bibliography

Banks, Air Commodore F. R., 'Fifty Years of Engineering Learning' (*RAeSoc Journal*, March 1968)

Barker, Ralph, *The Schneider Trophy Races: The Extraordinary True Story of Aviation's Greatest Competition* (Chatto & Windus, 1971)

Biard, Henri Charles, *Wings* (Hurst & Blackett, 1934)

Brown, Captain Eric 'Winkle', *Wings on My Sleeve* (Weidenfeld & Nicolson, 2006)

Byttebier, Hugo T., *The Curtiss D-12 Aero-Engine* (Smithsonian Institution Press, 1972)

D'Arcy Greig, Air Commodore (David), *My Golden Flying Years*, ed. Franks, Norman with Muggleton, Simon (Grub Street Publishing, 2011)

Eves, Edward, *The Schneider Trophy Story* (The Crowood Press, 2001)

Harper, Harry, *The Aeroplane in War* (Blackie & Son, 1943)

James, Derek N., *Schneider Trophy Aircraft 1913–1931* (Fonthill Media, 2015)

Käsmann, Ferdinand C. W., *World Speed Record Aircraft: The Fastest Piston-Engined Landplanes since 1903* (Putnam Aeronautical Books, 1990)

Le Corbusier, *Aircraft* (The Studio, 1935)

Mondey, David, *The Schneider Trophy* (Robert Hale, 1975)

Orlebar, Wing Commander Augustus Henry, *Schneider Trophy* (Seeley, Service & Company, 1933)

Pegram, Ralph, *Schneider Trophy Seaplanes and Flying Boats: Victors, Vanquished and Visions* (Fonthill Media, 2012)

Pegram, Ralph, *Supermarine Rolls-Royce S6B: Owners' Workshop Manual* (J. H. Haynes & Co, 2018)

Roussel, Mike, *The Quest for Speed: Air Racing and the Influence of the Schneider Trophy Contests 1913–31* (The History Press, 2016)

Rubbra, A. A., *Rolls-Royce Piston Aero Engines: A Designer Remembers* (Rolls-Royce Heritage Trust, 1990)

Scott, Phil, *The Pioneers of Flight: A Documentary History* (Princeton University Press, 1999)

Stainforth, Flight Lieutenant G. H., et al., *The Book of Speed* (B. T. Batsford Ltd, 1934)

Acknowledgements

The author is indebted to Ralph Pegram for allowing him to reproduce a number of his excellent scale line drawings from his book *Schneider Trophy Seaplanes and Flying Boats*. He would like to thank Gordon Stainforth who is writing a long-awaited and revelatory biography of his great uncle, Wing Commander George Stainforth, Andrew Nahum, Keeper Emeritus The Science Museum, London, and those who have slipped the surly bonds of Earth for good, yet whose informative and sparkling conversations concerning early high-speed flight remain fresh in his mind: Christopher Orlebar, Captain Eric 'Winkle' Brown RN, General James Doolittle, Air Commodore David D'Arcy Greig and Professor Lucio Lazzarino, former director of the Department of Aerospace Engineering, University of Pisa. Thanks, too, to James Nightingale, my editor at Atlantic Books, Gemma Wain for copy-editing and, as always, my agent Sarah Chalfant.

Illustrations

Section One

1. Claude Grahame-White at the helm of his Farman III biplane. (*APIC/Getty Images*)

2. Maurice Prévost at Monaco in April 1913. (*Hulton Archive/ Getty Images*)

3. Howard Pixton in conversation with Jacques Schneider, 1914 contest. (*The Print Collector/Getty Images*)

4. Harry Hawker in his Sopwith Schneider at the 1919 contest held at Bournemouth. (*Topical Press Agency/Getty Images*)

5. Henri Biard and his Supermarine Sea Lion III. (*Topical Press Agency/Getty Images*)

6. James 'Jimmy' Doolittle with his Curtiss R3C-2 at Chesapeake Bay, 1925. (*George Rinhart/Corbis via Getty Images*)

7. Supermarine Napier S.4, 1926. (*National Physical Laboratory © Crown Copyright/Science Photo Library*)

8. The S.5 at Cowes. (*The Picture Art Collection/Alamy Stock Photo*)

9. Mario Castoldi with engineers and mechanics attending a M.67 at Calshot. (*Central Press/Hulton Archive/Getty Images*)

10. Remo Cadringher and Giovanni Monti observe a Gloster Napier VI. (*Puttnam /Topical Press Agency/Getty Images*)

11. Savoia Marchetti S.65. (*Aviation History Collection/Alamy Stock Photo*)

12. Raymond Lane in the cockpit of a Gloster Napier VI, 1929. (*Puttnam/Topical Press Agency/Getty Images*)

13. Supermarine S.6 N248 launched on the Solent at Cowes in August 1929. (*Mirrorpix via Getty Images*)

14. Reginald Mitchell with Flight Lieutenant Francis Long. (*Hulton Archive/Getty Images*)

15. Members of the RAF High Speed Flight line up for the camera at Calshot. (*A. Hudson/Topical Press Agency/Getty Images*)

16. Benito Mussolini, decorates Lieutenant Francesco Agello at a ceremony in Rome, 1935. (*Keystone-France/Gamma-Rapho via Getty Images*)

Section Two

1. The Schneider Trophy. (*SSPL/Getty Images*)

2. Jesse Harrison Mason's poster advertising the 1925 Schneider. (*Lordprice Collection/Alamy Stock Photo*)

3. April 1928 edition of *Illustrazione del Popolo*. (*Mary Evans Picture Library*)

4. Adrian Hill's advert for Amherst Villiers, 1931. (*SSPL/Getty Images*)

5. Aircraftman T. E. Shaw. (*Daily Herald Archive/SSPL/Getty Images*)

6. Mk IX Spitfire. (*Phil Chaplin/Imperial War Museums via Getty Images*)

7. Mk 1, Mk VB Spitfire. (*@ csp archive/Alamy Stock Photo*)

8. KLM Douglas DC-2. (© *Arjan Van De Logt/Dreamstime.com*)

9. Saunders-Roe SR.45 Princess. (*Fox Photos/Hulton Archive/Getty Images*)

10. Howard Hughes's H-4 Hercules, or *Spruce Goose*. (*Alun Reece/Alamy Stock Photo*)

11. Short Sunderland. (*Popperfoto via Getty Images*)

12. Boeing 707. (*Granger, NYC/Alamy Stock Photo*)

13. Saunders-Roe SR.N4 *Mountbatten* class hovercraft. (*Martin Carroll/Alamy Stock Photo*)

14. Beriev Be-200 *Altair. (aviation-images.com/Universal Images Group via Getty Images)*

15. A Supermarine S6A at the Transport Pavilion, Festival of Britain, 1951 *(Central Press/Getty Images)*

16. Progressive Aerodyne SeaRey. *(Edwin Remsburg/VW Pics via Getty Images)*

Line drawings (© Ralph Pegram, 2020)

p. viii Macchi M.39; p. 45 Blackburn Pellet; p. 47 FBA Type A; p. 85 Navy-Wright NW-2; p. 109 Dornier S.4 Greif; p. 125 Short-Bristow Crusader; p. 139 Fiat C.29; p. 157 Supermarine S.6A; p. 189 Bernard-Ferbois V.2; p. 191 Piaggio Pegna P.c.7; p. 203 Macchi Castoldi MC.72; p. 217 Supermarine S.4; p. 245 Dornier flying boat; p. 275 Savoia Marchetti S.65; p. 291 SIAI Savoia S.51; p. 316 Gloster Napier GVI

Index